The New Sourcebook for Teaching Reasoning and Problem Solving in Junior and Senior High School

Related Titles of Interest

Physics Begins with an M: Mysteries, Magic, and Myth
John W. Jewett, Jr.
Order No. H5133-7

Physics Begins with Another M: Mysteries, Magic, Myth, and Modern Physics
John W. Jewett, Jr.
Order No. H7406-5

150 Ways to Increase Intrinsic Motivation in the Classroom
James P. Raffini
Order No. H6567-5 (paperback)
Order No. H6566-7 (hardcover)

The New Sourcebook for Teaching Reasoning and Problem Solving in Junior and Senior High School

Stephen Krulik
Jesse A. Rudnick
Temple University

Allyn and Bacon
Boston   London   Toronto   Sydney   Tokyo   Singapore

Library of Congress Cataloging-in-Publication Data

Krulik, Stephen.
    The new sourcebook for teaching reasoning and problem solving in
junior and senior high school / Stephen Krulik, Jesse A. Rudnick.
      p. cm.
    ISBN 0-205-16520-6
    1. Problem solving—Study and teaching (Secondary) 2. Reasoning-
-Study and teaching (Secondary) I. Rudnick, Jesse A. II. Title.
QA63.K763 1996
370.15'24--dc20   95-48956
                                                       CIP

Printed in the United States of America
10 9 8 7 6 5 4 3 2 1   00 99 98 97 96

Contents

Preface   vii

About the Authors   ix

CHAPTER ONE   Introduction   1

What Is Reasoning?   2
What Is Problem Solving?   3
The Heuristics   5
The Subskills of Problem Solving   6
How to Use This Book   7
How to Evaluate Problem-Solving and Reasoning
    Activities   8

CHAPTER TWO   Read and Think   10

CHAPTER THREE   Explore and Plan   13

CHAPTER FOUR   Select a Strategy   15

Pattern Recognition   16
Reduction and Expansion   21
Working Backwards   25
Experimentation and Simulation   27
Guess and Test   30
Logical Deduction   32
Organized Listing/Exhaustive Listing   38
Divide and Conquer   41
Write an Equation   43

CHAPTER FIVE   Find an Answer   46

CHAPTER SIX   **Reflect and Extend**   48

Find Alternate Solutions   *50*
What If? and Extend   *54*

CHAPTER SEVEN   **A Collection of Nonroutine Problems**   60

CHAPTER EIGHT   **A Collection of Open-Ended Problems Requiring an Extended Response**   **110**

SECTION A   **Reproduction Pages for the Heuristics**   119

SECTION B   **Masters for Selected Problems (Problem Cards)**   273

SECTION C   **Masters for Open-Ended Problems**   325

Preface

Approximately 15 years have elapsed since the National Council of Supervisors of Mathematics and the National Council of Teachers of Mathematics issued a challenge to the mathematics community to make problem solving the major thrust of mathematics teaching. Historically, such challenges have had little impact; indeed, most vanish within a short period of time. Not only has the focus on problem solving not abated but it has even expanded to include reasoning. The vitality of this movement is due, in part, to the *Curriculum and Evaluation Standards for School Mathematics*, published by the National Council of Teachers of Mathematics in 1989, and the inclusion of this material in almost all basal K–8 text series. But mainly, what happened has taken place because teachers and administrators alike have recognized that problem solving and reasoning represent one of the primary goals in the education of our children.

However, if teachers are to be successful in achieving this goal, they must have appropriate materials available to them. Teachers have said that textbooks do not provide sufficient materials and that additional problems and activities are needed. This, along with the success of our earlier volumes, *Problem Solving: A Handbook for Senior High School Teachers* (1989), *Reasoning and Problem Solving: A Handbook for Elementary School Teachers* (1993), and *A Sourcebook for Teaching Problem Solving* (1984), has given us the impetus to write this new sourcebook.

This book includes materials to help teachers both teach and assess problem solving and reasoning. *Reasoning* and *thinking* are terms that have come to the fore in the last few years. But how does one teach a child to think? To reason? We are convinced that reasoning and thinking can best be taught through the problem-solving process!

The text is divided into three parts. The first part consists of suggestions for teaching and testing problem solving and reasoning. This is done by examining each of the heuristic components in detail and supporting each with a series of problems, activities, and black-line masters. In addition, a discussion focuses on comprehensive assessment, including such items as observations, metacognitive journals, summary paragraphs, tests, and portfolios. The second part of the book contains more than 100 problems, designed to intrigue children and to provide them with practice in problem solving and reasoning. Each problem is carefully discussed in the text portion of the book and is then reproduced on a black-line master. These masters, in card form, can be reproduced, cut, and mounted on cards to form a Problem Deck, something we consider to be a valuable resource. The third part of the book contains problems that can be used for both evaluation and diagnostic assessment of problem solving and reasoning. Again, these are reproduced on black-line masters for your use.

We are confident that the materials in this book will provide teachers with an excellent resource in helping students become better problem solvers and reasoners, and thus improve their thinking and reasoning.

We wish to thank the following reviewers for their helpful suggestions: Michele A. Nahas, Kramer Middle School, Windham, Connecticut; Irwin Ozer, Math Sense Mathematics Consulting, Aberdeen, New Jersey; and John Welch, Winter Hill Community School, Somerville, Massachusetts.

About the Authors

Dr. Stephen Krulik's professional background includes 15 years of classroom teaching in the Brooklyn, New York, public schools, as well as more than 25 years at Temple University as professor of mathematics education.

Together with Jesse Rudnick, he has authored more than a dozen professional books for teachers, as well as numerous articles on problem solving and reasoning in major journals. They are the senior problem-solving authors for the Silver Burdett Ginn K–8 basal series in mathematics, as well as contributing authors to the Prentice Hall Algebra series.

Dr. Krulik has been active in regional, state, and national mathematics education organizations. He was the editor of the NCTM's 1980 Yearbook, *Problem Solving in School Mathematics,* as well as a member of the team that wrote the *Professional Standards for Teaching Mathematics.* He is former president of the Association of Mathematics Teachers of New Jersey. He also has spoken at literally hundreds of conferences and has conducted numerous workshops for school districts throughout the country.

Dr. Jesse A. Rudnick's professional background includes 15 years of classroom teaching in the Philadelphia public schools, as well as more than 25 years as professor of mathematics education at Temple University.

Together with Stephen Krulik, he has authored more than a dozen professional books for teachers, as well as numerous articles on problem solving and reasoning in major journals. They are the senior problem-solving authors for the Silver Burdett Ginn K–8 basal series in mathematics, as well as contributing authors to the Prentice Hall Algebra series.

Dr. Rudnick has been very active with national, regional, and local mathematics education organizations. He was a director of the NCTM, a regional director of the NCSM, and the president of the Association of Teachers of Mathematics of Philadelphia and Vicinity. He has led many workshops and has spoken at countless conferences throughout the United States.

CHAPTER ONE

Introduction

Significant changes are taking place in school mathematics, in both content and pedagogy. The direction being taken is a direct result of three major publications of the National Council of Teachers of Mathematics: the *Curriculum and Evaluation Standards for School Mathematics* (1989), the *Professional Standards for Teaching Mathematics* (1991), and the *Assessment Standards for School Mathematics* (1995). These visions of the teaching and learning of mathematics in the nation's schools have met with virtually unanimous acceptance by the mathematics education community. Highlighted in these documents are problem solving and reasoning; indeed, these two areas are the nucleus of the changes now taking place across the grades. These changes are not only affecting the course content but also the actual way in which mathematics is being taught.

Problem solving and reasoning have gained this important status partly because calculators and computers have relieved us of the necessity for learning and practicing many long, complicated algorithms such as long division, extracting square roots, logarithmic computation, and so on. Regardless of the time or the available technology, people will always have to resolve problems and make decisions. Whether they face them at work or at play, face them they must!! Even the computer must be programmed and the proper buttons on the calculator pressed if these tools are to provide correct answers. Technology can compute, but only the human mind can reason. Problem solving and reasoning are the primary skills that students must take with them when they leave the classrooms and enter the "real world."

As already stated, not only is the content of what educators teach changing but also the ways in which educators teach it. No longer will the teacher be in front of the class demonstrating "how to...." Rather, the teacher will be the choreographer who designs activities by which the students gain those experiences necessary for the development of mathematical power.

This book is designed to assist junior and senior high school teachers in creating classroom experiences that will help their students achieve competency in reasoning and problem solving. It contains a variety of problems that require the mastery of specific skills, as well as provides applications of these skills. Mainly, however, the problems provide the experiences necessary for developing critical and creative thinking skills. Not only will the problems serve the traditional college preparatory student population but they will also benefit those students for whom college preparatory mathematics is not their major interest. For these students, the problems will generate reasoning and problem-solving skills that are essential for *all* students.

WHAT IS REASONING?

Currently, a great deal of effort is being expended by theorists attempting to distinguish between reasoning and thinking. However, to the practitioner, such a distinction is hardly important. For the purposes of this book, we shall consider *reasoning* to be the part of thinking that goes beyond the recall level. Reasoning will include basic thinking, critical thinking, and creative thinking, as shown in Figure 1–1. It must be noted that the categories shown are not discrete. In fact, there is always a great deal of moving back and forth between them. It is difficult to define each of these categories precisely; however, the following are some descriptors that can be associated with each.

Basic

Understanding of concepts

Recognizing a concept when it appears in a setting

Critical

Examining, relating, and evaluating all aspects of a situation or problem

Focusing on parts of a situation or problem

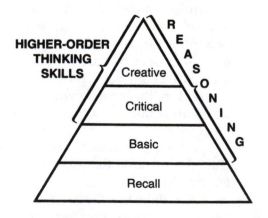

Figure 1–1

Gathering and organizing information

Validating and analyzing information

Remembering and associating previously learned information

Determining reasonableness of an answer

Drawing valid conclusions

Analytical and reflexive in nature

Creative

Original, effective, and produces a complex product

Inventive

Synthesizing ideas

Generating ideas

Applying ideas

WHAT IS PROBLEM SOLVING?

The formal definition of a *problem*, which we shall use throughout this book, is the following:

> A *problem* is a situation, quantitative or otherwise, that confronts an individual or group of individuals, that requires resolution, and for which the individual sees no apparent or obvious means or path to obtaining a solution.[1]

Using this idea of a problem, *problem solving* emerges as a process. In fact,

> It [problem solving] is the means by which an individual uses previously acquired knowledge, skills, and understanding to satisfy the demands of an unfamiliar situation.[2]

It begins with the initial confrontation and ends when an answer has been obtained and checked against the conditions of the problems.

Problem solving can and should be taught! The process has been analyzed and can be represented as a series of steps, referred to as a *heuristic plan*, or, simply, *heuristics*. One such plan is shown in Figure 1–2. It shows the mental and physical activities that a person engages in when resolving a problem. Note that the major headings are expanded upon by a set of subskills that constitute the individual tasks one performs to facilitate the solution.

The heuristics we use in problem solving differ markedly from the algorithms we teach in our mathematics classrooms. An *algorithm* guarantees success if applied correctly and if the proper algorithm has been selected. Algorithms are task specific, whereas problem solving requires a

---

[1]Stephen Krulik and Jesse A. Rudnick, *Problem Solving: A Handbook For Teachers, 2nd Edition* (Boston: Allyn and Bacon, 1987), p. 3.
[2]Ibid.

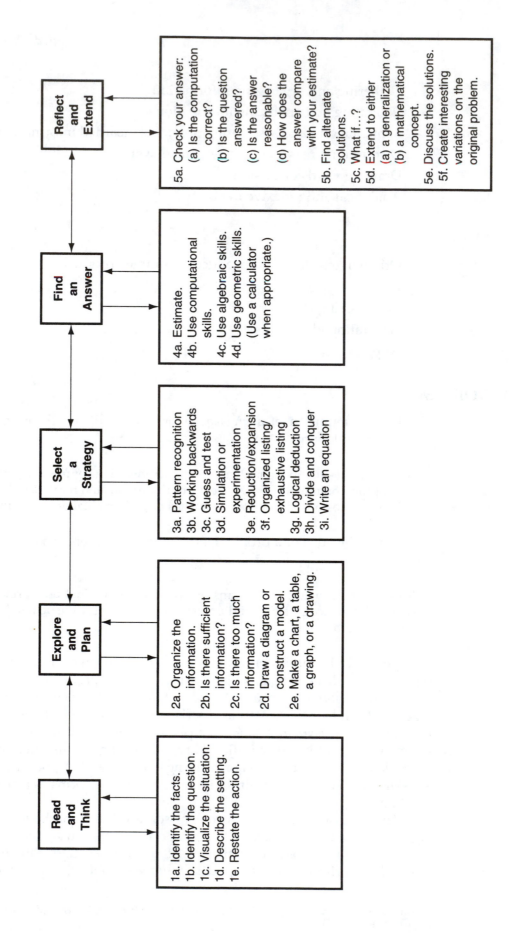

Read and Think

1a. Identify the facts.
1b. Identify the question.
1c. Visualize the situation.
1d. Describe the setting.
1e. Restate the action.

Explore and Plan

2a. Organize the information.
2b. Is there sufficient information?
2c. Is there too much information?
2d. Draw a diagram or construct a model.
2e. Make a chart, a table, a graph, or a drawing.

Select a Strategy

3a. Pattern recognition
3b. Working backwards
3c. Guess and test
3d. Simulation or experimentation
3e. Reduction/expansion
3f. Organized listing/ exhaustive listing
3g. Logical deduction
3h. Divide and conquer
3i. Write an equation

Find an Answer

4a. Estimate.
4b. Use computational skills.
4c. Use algebraic skills.
4d. Use geometric skills. (Use a calculator when appropriate.)

Reflect and Extend

5a. Check your answer:
(a) Is the computation correct?
(b) Is the question answered?
(c) Is the answer reasonable?
(d) How does the answer compare with your estimate?
5b. Find alternate solutions.
5c. What if...?
5d. Extend to either
(a) a generalization or
(b) a mathematical concept.
5e. Discuss the solutions.
5f. Create interesting variations on the original problem.

Figure 1–2   Flowchart of the Problem-Solving Process

more general approach. Heuristics provide a "road map"; they are a blueprint that directs one's path toward a solution and resolution of a problem situation. Unlike an algorithm, they cannot guarantee success! However, if students are taught to follow these heuristics in *every* problem situation they face, then they will be in a good position to resolve successfully the problems they will face in the classroom and in life. Again, let us emphasize that although we do want students to successfully complete the solution of a problem and find the required answer, it is the problem-solving *process* that we emphasize in this book.

THE HEURISTICS

The five stages of the heuristics that constitute the heuristic process are:

> Read and Think
> Explore and Plan
> Select a Strategy
> Find an Answer
> Reflect and Extend

These stages are neither independent nor consecutive. Indeed, a person engaged in the process moves back and forth, sometimes unconsciously. However, each of the individual steps has a distinct goal that can be achieved by means of the associated subskills.

Read and Think

In this heuristic, the problem is analyzed; critical thinking begins. The facts are examined and evaluated. The question is determined. The physical setting is visualized, described, and understood. The problem is translated into the language of the reader. Connections are made between the parts of the problem.

Explore and Plan

At this stage, the problem solver analyzes the data and determines whether there is sufficient information. Distractors are eliminated. The data are organized in a table, a drawing, a model, and so on. From this, a plan for finding the answer is developed.

Select a Strategy

The third heuristic is considered by many people to be the most difficult heuristic of all. A *strategy* is that part of the problem-solving process that provides the direction the problem solver should take in finding the answer. Its selection is suggested by the previous two phases that precede it in the heuristic plan. Strategies are not as problem specific as are algorithms, and strategies are often used in combinations. The difficult question in problem solving is how to select the appropriate strategy. What tells the student which strategy to select? As with any skill. success in problem solving comes with practice. If students are to succeed in problem solving, they must continuously practice the art of problem solving by actually solving problems. They must also attempt to solve problems using as wide a variety of strategies as possible.

By examining the strategies of problem solving that are most frequently and most widely used by problem solvers of all ages, nine strategies can be isolated and identified:

Strategies for Problem Solving

1. Pattern recognition
2. Working backwards
3. Guess and test
4. Experimentation or simulation
5. Reduction Expansion
6. Organized listing/Exhaustive listing
7. Logical deduction
8. Divide and conquer
9. Write an equation

For those students who have achieved a degree of competence in algebra, algebraic power can be used to solve many problems more directly and more efficiently. However, the use of algebra might eliminate some of the creative thinking skills that solving the problem without algebra provides. Thus, even though an algebraic solution has been found, alternate solutions should be attempted and discussed.

Find an Answer

Here, the appropriate mathematical skills are employed to find an answer. Estimation, where appropriate, should be encouraged. Full use should be made of a calculator and other technology.

Reflect and Extend

First of all, the answer or answers must be checked for accuracy to see if the initial conditions of the problem have been met and if the question has been answered correctly. However, much more should be done at this stage. This is the place where creative thinking can be maximized. Alternate solutions should be found and discussed. The problem can be altered ("What if…?") by changing some of the initial conditions or interpretations. If possible, the process should be extended to discover a generalization or the mathematical concepts that underlie the situation. Interesting variations of the original problem should be fashioned and discussed by the students.

THE SUBSKILLS OF PROBLEM SOLVING

Successful problem solving depends on the possession and utilization of a set of subskills associated with each of the heuristic steps. Much of the research in problem solving indicates that mastery of these subskills will increase overall performance in problem solving and reasoning. Subskills are a combination of verbal and mathematical skills that enable a student to achieve the objectives of that stage of the heuristics.

A successful procedure will involve combinations of these subskills to generate the information needed to attack the problem. Then, too, using the subskills as the building blocks of problem solving will often result in combinations that become more meaningful and more effective as the student "sharpens" these subskills. Students need many opportunities to practice the subskills. This book will provide materials to do just that.

HOW TO USE THIS BOOK

The teaching of problem solving and reasoning, which has now become a major focus in school mathematics, necessitates a different classroom environment. This environment must be nonthreatening; the free discourse and interaction between students and students as well as between students and teacher is paramount.

Since it is the thought processes that are so important in problem solving and reasoning (and not merely the answers), and since thinking takes time, careful planning must be undertaken.

You should plan on integrating problem solving and reasoning into every mathematics class. Problem solving is not a process that can be taught in one week or one month and then ignored. Rather, it must permeate the entire classroom atmosphere—the very essence of how educators teach. It should be actively pursued throughout the student's career in mathematics, with an ever-increasing degree of skill and expertise. Above all, *your students must practice thinking and problem solving in order to succeed at them.*

This book is organized according to the heuristics. The subskills have been grouped along with the appropriate heuristics. Each chapter of the book is independent of the others. That is, the chapters may be undertaken in any order. As you examine each of the chapters, you will find a series of activities, games, and references to Reproduction Pages. These Reproduction Pages provide materials that you can use immediately with your students to develop their abilities within each subskill. Each subskill is important by itself; together they all contribute to the problem-solving process.

To use this book, decide on which subskills of problem solving you wish to help your students master at any particular time. You may or may not decide to follow the suggested order by chapters. As you read through each chapter, you will find some activities that involve the Reproduction Pages and others that do not. The text material will suggest some ways to approach the materials and discuss what you can expect to achieve as a result of using them. In addition, directions for using each activity are included. If the activity you wish to use has associated Reproduction Pages, select the one you wish to use. Remove the page, duplicate copies for all students, and have them work through as a group or individual activity.

Many of the activities are designed for use with small groups. You will have to decide what constitutes a "small group" (usually from two to five students). In some cases, the entire class will serve as "the group." Your role will vary from activity to activity. Many of them are self-directed and can be used with individual students on their own, with minimal input from you. Others require extensive teacher direction and/or participation. Some will require repetition throughout the school year to be most effective. In some cases, the activity will suggest others, which you can develop on your own for further exploration with the students.

In preparing a book such as this one, it is often difficult to discriminate exactly between what is suitable for students in the junior high or the senior high levels. Fortunately, in problem solving, many of these arbitrary divisions are unnecessary. As a result, we have not designated any grade level for much of the material. You will have to examine each Reproduction Page within a specific subskill and see if it is suitable for your own personal situation. What we *have* done is to make the activities span as wide an ability level as possible. We cannot stress enough the role *you* must play in selecting activities best suited for your own classes. No one knows your classes as well as you do! Select those materials that you feel are best suited for your students and use them! Then, if you want still more practice, create more of them in a similar manner for your own use.

HOW TO EVALUATE PROBLEM-SOLVING AND REASONING ACTIVITIES

Evaluation techniques for measuring problem solving and reasoning will have to be more flexible and more varied than for many other kinds of instructional tasks. Since you will be assessing a *process*, traditional instruments such as teacher-made tests and those in objective format are not sufficient. In addition to these instruments, you will have to use subjective data to evaluate students' growth. You should maintain a file for each of the students in your class. In this file you should keep observation notes, samples from students' metacognitive journals, summary paragraphs, project reports, test results, and so on. Anecdotal comments should also be placed in this file.

Observations

While the students are working on a problem in small groups, you walk around the room simply observing them in action. As they work in their groups, you move about the room focusing your observations on some aspects of the situation that you deem to be important. You should make some mental notes of the students' behaviors as you move about the room. These will be written down right after class. Are the students willing to try to solve the problem? Do they work cooperatively in groups? Do they keep on trying, even after they have experienced some trouble solving the problem? Do they demonstrate self-confidence? These notes will become a part of each student's file.

Metacognitive Journals

Helping students to think about their own thinking and to make changes in how they think is the essence of metacognition. You want your students to become better and better in this process as they engage in reasoning and problem solving. Many of these metacognitive ideas should be built right into your lessons. Encourage your students to think about their own thinking as they work. This is important for many reasons, but especially to help students rethink their own process, to make ongoing changes in their thinking patterns.

In a metacognitive journal, the students work a problem on the right-hand page of a two-page spread. On the left-side page, the students record their own thinking as they proceed through the solution, concurrent with their actions.

Summary Paragraphs

In a summary paragraph, the same considerations are included as in a metacognitive journal. However, this is a single paragraph, written after the solution has been completed, and not concurrent with every step. This procedure does not disturb the natural flow of thinking during the actual solution process.

Tests

We will consider three types of questions that might appear on an assessment test for problem solving and reasoning. These are multiple-choice questions, open-ended questions, and performance questions.

Most teachers are very familiar with the *multiple-choice question*. Each question contains a stem, followed by several options. The student must select the correct answer. This may involve only recall or recognition, and thus does not reveal to the reader the thought processes undertaken by the student.

An *open-ended question* is a problem that usually requires the student to make a decision. That is, the student is given a set of facts and is asked: What would you do? In these cases, the problem is divergent—that is, it has multiple solutions and multiple answers. In other cases, the problem may be somewhat convergent in the sense that it still has multiple solutions but they all lead to the same answer.

The *performance question* requires that the student solve a given problem completely and correctly. The ultimate goal in problem solving is to develop the skills necessary to solve problems and get the correct answer. This type of question should be traditionally scored, with partial credit being given when a student demonstrates the proper direction, and full credit given only when the solution and the answer are both correct. As part of the solution, the student should include a summary paragraph explaining the thought processes used in arriving at the solution. Reproduction Pages 1 through 6 will provide some illustrations of appropriate multiple-choice and open-ended questions.

You must also realize that problem solving involves "risk taking" on the part of your students. For some students, merely taking such a risk represents tremendous growth—a major jump forward. At the same time, the frustration, perseverance, and tenacity that are all a part of problem solving should be considered. As a result, you will have to place more emphasis on nonnumerical measures of growth.

CHAPTER TWO

Read and Think

Problem solving and reasoning are now more prominent in school mathematics than ever before. As we have stated previously, we believe that reasoning skills will be developed through a continuous emphasis on problem solving. Thus, a major goal of mathematics instruction is to develop in students the ability to solve problems. Students are confronted by problems both in school and in their daily activities. These problems usually appear in verbalized form (oral or written) or in a visual form (as in a store window). For example, in the classroom, problems are presented by the teacher or from the textbook. These are usually part of the mathematics curriculum and are intended to improve computational, algorithmic and problem-solving skills. Outside of school, students must make decisions regarding purchases and activities, which require careful analysis and reasoning.

Successful problem solvers are those who can visualize the setting and gather important data from the problem as it is written or appears. With most students, full comprehension of a problem does not take place all at once; rather, it takes place in stages. That is, the first reading results in only a general familiarity with the setting of the problem. The second reading will begin to allow students to think about the specifics—the relevant data and important facts in the problem. Further readings may lead to a strategy selection based on previous experiences in problem solving.

In this chapter, we will focus on activities that will help students increase their ability to read, to think, to understand, and to interpret a problem. It is rare that teachers can err by giving too much practice to their students in reading mastery within subject matter areas; the error is usually the other way around.

ACTIVITY 2.1   Fundamental to solving problems is an understanding of the setting and situation. The problem setting must be familiar to the students. For example, a problem requiring knowledge of farming procedures, such as planting a field, would require background information not necessarily known by an inner-city youngster. Thus, for that youngster, this problem could contain innuendos and inferences that would make it impossible to understand, and thus resolve.

Have students restate problems in their own words. Sometimes this will not only help the problem solver begin his or her deliberations but the restatement of the problem will also help the student visualize what is taking place. The class should serve as a reviewing team to make certain the reader has understandably described the situation. Questions directed to the reader by the class will help in this effort. Use problems similar to those on Reproduction Pages 7 through 9. Have one student describe the problem in his or her own words.

ACTIVITY 2.2   Research has shown that the ability to recognize words is fundamental to reading. Since reading is a vital part of problem solving, any expansion of the ability to read will assist in the development of problem-solving skills. Reproduction Pages 10 and 11 contain paragraphs in which number names are embedded. The student is directed to identify each of the numbers and to write them in both literal and numeric forms.

ACTIVITY 2.3   This activity provides a desirable extension to word and number recognition that moves from basic recognition to understanding—a critical thought process. Reproduction Pages 12 through 14 describe real situations in which students may find themselves, where numbers are involved. The actual numbers have been removed from the paragraph and are listed in ascending order of magnitude. The student is to insert the missing numbers in the appropriate spaces. Each number must be used once and only once. The final selection must be arithmetically correct and consistent with the text.

ACTIVITY 2.4   When problems are presented in written form, many students experience trouble because they misinterpret some words that have multiple meanings depending on context. There are many words that have different meanings when they are used in nonmathematical situations and when they are used in mathematics. For example, the word *prime*, when used in mathematics, refers to a number that has only itself and 1 as factors. In the nonmathematical sense, *prime* can refer to special or choice, as in a "prime cut of meat" or "prime-time television programming." In still another context, *prime* may be used as a verb as in to "prime a pump" to get it started.

It may be that some of your students will recognize a word they have encountered in their everyday reading. Teachers often assume that, because students recognize a word, they are using its mathematical meaning in a problem, This may not be true at all. In fact, students may impose the nonmathematical meaning and thus completely lose the sense of the problem. Reproduction Pages 15 and 16 provide students with practice in identifying words with multiple meanings.

Reproduction Page 15 shows a list of words that have more than one meaning. This list is followed by pairs of sentences that illustrate both the mathematical and the nonmathematical meanings. The student should look through the list and select the one word that fits into both blanks in each pair.

In Reproduction Page 16, the procedure is the same except that the list of words has not been provided for the students. These must be drawn on from memory.

One valuable extension of this activity is to have students keep a mathematics dictionary. Whenever a new word is discovered that has a double meaning, have the students write the word and both meanings in their dictionaries and then write a sentence to illustrate each.

ACTIVITY 2.5   Understanding the anatomy of a problem is fundamental to its solution. Problems usually contain four components: facts, questions, a setting, and distractors. In some simple problems, these latter two are minimally present. In order to begin the solution process, the student must be able to see beyond the distractors and determine the important facts and the question.

Reproduction Pages 17 and 18 are designed to help your students discover the question being asked by recognizing the correct question from a given set.

Reproduction Pages 19 through 21 require the students to underline the question within a given problem.

Reproduction Pages 22 through 24 require the students to complete the problem by supplying an appropriate question.

ACTIVITY 2.6   The facts of a problem can be presented in a variety of ways. They can appear in picture form, written text, or a combination of these. They may also be presented in tabular or graphic format.

Reproduction Pages 25 and 26 provide pictures, followed by a series of questions. The information needed for students to answer the questions can be found in the pictures.

Reproduction Pages 27 through 29 contain paragraphs of text material, with the necessary facts embedded in the text. Students should read the paragraphs and answer the questions that follow.

Reproduction Pages 30 through 35 show different types of graphs that can be used to provide practice in obtaining data from graphs.

Reproduction Pages 36 through 38 provide different kinds of tables and charts.

ACTIVITY 2.7   This activity is designed to sharpen the students' ability to read a problem quickly and accurately. At the same time, the student must decide which facts are relevant. It also provides the students with an opportunity to develop their communication skills.

Pair the students in your class. Designate one of each pair as the "Problem Reader" and the other as the "Problem Solver." The Problem Readers are then presented a problem via an overhead projector for a limited time period (15–30 seconds). During this time, the Problem Solvers are not permitted to view the screen. The Problem Readers can make any notes—written or mental—that they wish during this time. At the end of the visual period, the overhead projector is turned off. The Problem Readers then eliminate the distractors and relate what they consider to be the relevant facts and the question to their individual partners, who then attempt to solve the problem. Reverse the students' roles and repeat the procedure.

CHAPTER THREE

Explore and Plan

Explore and Plan is the second heuristic in the problem-solving process. After the students comprehend the nature of the problem and understand what they are being asked to do, they should be given additional experiences in analysis and organization. A careful analysis might reveal a hidden question indicating a two-stage problem, whereas organizing the data in a table or in a graph could easily lead the students to successful strategy selection. This heuristic also provides students with an excellent opportunity to further develop their critical and creative thinking skills.

In this chapter, we present a group of activities that will provide the students with experiences in organizing and analyzing data, finding the hidden question in a two-stage problem, and determining extra or insufficient data.

For the expansion of creative thinking skills, there are activities in which students are required to create problems from stories and graphs, as well as some that require the students to supply and answer as many questions as they can from a given problem situation. Students will be given the opportunity to determine whether or not data are consistent or contradictory.

ACTIVITY 3.1   In this activity, the students are presented a series of two-stage problems. To solve a two-stage problem, the hidden question must first be identified and answered. Reproduction Pages 39 and 40 require the students to identify the hidden question for a set of given problems.

Reproduction Pages 41 through 43 require the students to write the hidden questions on their own. After completing the given activity, have students solve each problem in small groups.

ACTIVITY 3.2   Here is an activity in which students must differentiate between necessary and unnecessary information. Successful problem solving and reasoning depend on this ability, since distractors can often mask important data. Reproduction Pages 44 through 46 require students to identify extra information.

ACTIVITY 3.3   One major objective is to have students develop critical thinking skills. One way of contributing to this development is to provide problems from which necessary pieces of data have been omitted. This presents the students with two vital tasks: first, to detect that an important piece of data is indeed missing; and second, to supply appropriate data that are reasonable within the problem's context, and thus make the resolution of the problem possible. Reproduction Pages 47 through 49 present problems with missing data. Have the students identify what is missing, then supply a reasonable fact or facts. Finally, have them solve each problem.

ACTIVITY 3.4   Some problems, as well as true-life situations, contain contradictions. Critical thinking reveals these inconsistencies and allows students to analyze problem situations. Reproduction Pages 50 through 52 contain several kinds of activities to sharpen critical thinking skills. Reproduction Pages 50 and 51 contain two kinds of activities. The first presents sets of statements. Students should examine each set to decide whether or not they are consistent—that is, determine if both items can be true at the same time. The second presents situations in paragraph form, which may or may not contain inconsistencies. Students are asked to discover the inconsistencies and to correct them. Reproduction Page 52 contains a set of statements followed by a conclusion. Students must decide whether or not the conclusion follows from the given statements.

ACTIVITY 3.5   Students' understanding of problems can be greatly enhanced by encouraging them to create their own problems. When students write problems of their own, they include all the necessary features (i.e., the setting, the facts, the question, and usually some distractors as well). In addition, creative thinking skills are brought into play. The stimulus for problems can come from presenting the answer, some data, and graphs. Reproduction Pages 53 and 54 give the students the answers. The students must then create a problem whose solution results in the given answer.

Reproduction Pages 55 and 56 provide data and ask the students to create a problem using some or all of the given facts.

Reproduction Pages 57 and 58 present graphs for which an appropriate problem should be developed. Students may provide additional data if they wish.

CHAPTER FOUR

Select a Strategy

The next phase of the problem-solving heuristic is Selecting a Strategy. In Chapter One, nine commonly used strategies were identified. This is far from an exhaustive list, nor are the nine strategies necessarily used independently. In many cases, two or more strategies are combined to obtain the answer.

Care must be exercised not to classify problems according to strategy. Applications of each strategy should be discussed and illustrated, thus enabling the students to select an appropriate strategy from their collection when confronted by a problem.

Strategy selection is difficult! For a few students, knowing what strategy to use in a specific problem comes about intuitively. (In fact, many times these fortunate few are unaware of why or how they chose the strategy they did.) For most people, however, selecting an appropriate strategy is the result of repeated exposure to lots and lots of problems.

The activities that follow are intended to provide practice for your students. We have divided these activities by strategies along with associated subskills. Remember, there is a great divergence among students in their ability to analyze problems and to select appropriate strategies. This ability does not necessarily correlate with computational skill. Thus, class time must be devoted to the discussion of the problem and the consequences of the implementation of a variety of strategies. Each child's contribution should be considered, even though it might not result in the expected answer. Remember, it is the experience gained by exploring a path that is important. Keeping careful records of these experiences—in other words, a metacognitive journal—will greatly assist children in developing their thinking skills.

The Reproduction Pages referred to in this chapter contain various kinds of problems. The pages can be distributed to students for practice. Note, however, that each problem is discussed in the text. It is important that you spend sufficient time discussing the solutions as well as the answer to each problem, emphasizing the choice(s) of strategy.

PATTERN RECOGNITION

Patterns are all around us! They appear in nature, design, architecture, and science, as well as mathematics. In fact, a major part of all mathematics is the search for patterns and pattern rules that determine them. These are patterns of number, patterns of form, patterns of letters, and patterns of words. Recognizing patterns is a critical thinking skill, and critical thinking enables children to recognize patterns.

Because most patterns are obvious to adults, many of us take for granted that children just naturally see patterns too. In fact, many children see nothing at all! Pattern recognition requires a careful observation of common characteristics, variations, and differences, as well as repetitive properties and shapes.

In order to teach children to recognize patterns, they must constantly be exposed to as wide a variety of patterns as possible. The pedagogical procedure should include observing the situation, describing what has been seen, communicating what has been seen, and, eventually, formalizing this description into a pattern rule.

Pattern recognition is a powerful strategy that usually occurs in conjunction with other strategies. Activities 4.1 through 4.3 are designed to help students use their critical thinking skills to recognize patterns and state the pattern rule.

ACTIVITY 4.1   This activity, Reproduction Pages 59 through 61, gives students experience with a variety of patterns. Each of the pages contains, at differing levels of sophistication, patterns determined by affinity groups, literal patterns, and number patterns. At first glance, some of the sequences appear rather simple. However, a careful analysis can reveal more subtle relationships. For example, refer to Reproduction Page 59, item 2: baseball, football, soccer, tennis, _____. Some students may say "hockey" (a team sport, but not played with a ball). Others may say "golf" (a sport played with a ball, but not a team sport). Still others may say "polo" (played with a ball *and* is a team sport). Still others may say "volleyball" (a team sport, played with a ball, *and* spelled with a double letter). In fact, some students might respond "rubber," reasoning that the given words all have a double letter, and so does "rubber." The student is looking at the words themselves, and not at their meaning. An in-depth discussion of each of these sequences provides the students with practice in analysis and critical thinking. It would be to everyone's advantage if students would be encouraged to create their own sequences.

In Reproduction Page 59, item 5 contains all 3-lettered words with the letter *a* in the middle. Item 6 contains girls' names, each of which contains exactly five letters, including an *a*. Item 8 consists of word palindromes (i.e., spelled the same backwards and forwards). Item 12 simply shows proper fractions.

In Reproduction Page 60, item 1 contains things that have wheels. Item 6 contains words with the letter *p*. Every word in item 7 ends with *er*. Item 8 contains only 5-lettered words. Item 10 contains prime numbers.

Item 11 shows multiples of 6, and item 12 contains trigonometric functions that have a value of 1.

In Reproduction Page 61, item 6 contains 5-lettered words with *m* as the middle letter. In item 7, the words begin and end with the same letter. In item 8, all the words begin with two consecutive letters of the alphabet. Item 10 contains two-digit prime numbers. Item 11 shows powers of 3, and item 12 contains numbers that differ from the nearest multiple of 100 by 2.

ACTIVITY 4.2   In this activity, Reproduction Pages 62 through 64 deal with sequential patterns. Each sheet contains literal, numerical, and geometric sequences. Students are asked to write the next term in each sequence and to state the pattern rule. More than one answer is possible, depending on the pattern rule observed by the student. To extend this activity, ask other students for additional terms.

In Reproduction Page 62, item 4 can be answered in more than one way. For example, if the pattern rule is the Fibonacci sequence, then $1 + 2 = 3, 2 + 3 = 5, 3 + 5 = 8$. However, some students may notice that the sequential differences between pairs of terms form a sequence:

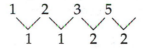

thus the next term could be 7. Item 7 contains words with an increasing number of letters. Item 8 contains 5-lettered names, alternating in gender, and the first letter in alphabetic sequence (starting with the letter *F*).

In Reproduction Page 63, item 3 gives the first two terms, 3 and 4. After that, subsequent terms can be found by adding all the previous terms in the sequence. In item 9, the answer can be any shaded, closed figure. In item 10, the 1 could be rewritten as x^0. Thus, the next term would be x^{-1}, or $1/x$. In Reproduction Page 64, item 3 contains consecutive sets of so-called twin primes—the next would be 41–43, 59–61, and so on. In item 7, the letters are the first letters of the sequence "one, two, three, four." In item 8, students should recognize that, similar to item 7, these are the first two letters in the words "triangle" (three-sides), "quadrilateral" (four-sides), "pentagon" (five-sides), and "hexagon" (six-sides). The next would be *se* for "septagon" (seven-sides) then *oc* for "octagon" (eight-sides). Item 10 alternates a "flip" followed by a rotation of the figure.

ACTIVITY 4.3   Reproduction Pages 65 through 67 provide an opportunity for students to build their observational skills. They must discover what characteristic is common to all of the elements except for one. Different sets of items might display different common characteristics, and thus the answers need not be uniform. For example, in Reproduction Page 65, item 4 could be viewed as a set of odd numbers, thus making 6 the different element. However, the series might also be viewed as a set of multiples of 3, thus excluding 11. In item 9, several different observations can easily be made. For example, 4 is a perfect square, but not a perfect cube. The only odd number in the set is 81. The number 8 could be considered the oddball characteristic, since it is the only one that is not a perfect square.

In Reproduction Page 66, item 2 contains two-digit numbers whose digits are consecutive, except for 41. Item 3 contains two-digit numbers whose digit-sum is 10, except for 56. Item 4 could be viewed as a set of multiples of 3 (eliminating 25), or a set of odd numbers (eliminating 18), or a set of two-digit numbers (eliminating 9).

In item 8, Halloween is not a legal holiday. In item 9, (14, 8) is the only ordered pair not on the line $y = 1/2x$. In item 10, $x^2 + 1$ is the only expression not factorable in the domain of the real numbers.

In Reproduction Page 67, item 2, some students may select the number 2 as the only even number. Others may select 39 as the only composite number. Item 3 contains Pythagorean triples, except for 7–9–11. Item 4 contains all odd numbers except for 84. Or, the series can be viewed as all two-digit numbers except for 147. Or, the digit sum is always 12, except for 47. Item 5 contains the names of baseball teams except for the Packers, a football team. In item 6, the pine is the only conifer. In item 8, Nixon is the only president of the United States in the set who does not appear on a U.S. coin. In item 9, cos 180° –1; the rest are all equal to +1. In item 10, only vertical angles must be equal (although the others may be).

ACTIVITY 4.4   Activities 4.1, 4.2, and 4.3 were intended to develop student facility in recognizing patterns. This activity is designed to have the students use their ability to recognize patterns in the solution of problems. Note that most problems are not resolved by merely recognizing patterns, but utilize other strategies as well. We will present a few problems here that *are* nicely solved by the use of pattern recognition, but in the sections that follow, pattern recognition will be combined with other strategies.

PROBLEM   (Reproduction Page 68)

How many beads are on the chain shown?

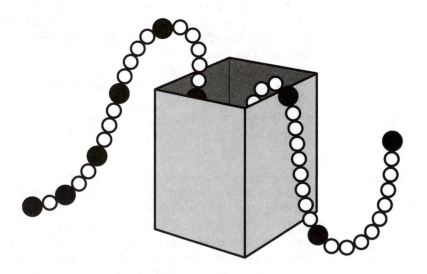

Discussion   A determination of the actual number of beads depends on whether or not the pattern continues inside the box. If it does, then there will be

$$1 + 2 + 3 + 4 + \ldots + 8 + 9 = 45 \text{ white} + 10 \text{ black}$$

for a total of 55 beads.

However, a great deal of discussion is possible. For example, how many beads *must* there be? (Those we can actually see and count, at least 44.)

PROBLEM   (Reproduction Page 69)

How many beads are on the chain shown?

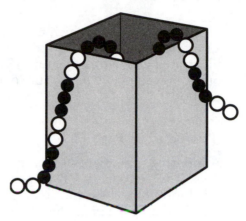

Discussion   Here is a situation in which students can determine the pattern rule (i.e., 2 light, 3 dark, 2 light, 3 dark,...) yet cannot obtain the exact number of beads on the string. Again, a great deal of discussion can take place, such as, there are *at least* 26 beads, since these are visible and may be counted. Also, students should conclude that, if the pattern continues, the number of beads will be 2 more than a multiple of 5 (i.e., $5n + 2$ in algebraic form).

PROBLEM   (Reproduction Page 70)

Jose is arranging grapefruits in the produce department of the supermarket, in the form of a triangle. When he has finished, the first (or top) row had 1 grapefruit, the second row had 3 grapefruits, the third row had 6 grapefruits, the fourth row had 10 grapefruits, and so on for a total of seven rows. How many grapefruits did Jose use in the display?

Discussion   Have the students make a table to organize the data and help them discover the pattern:

Row number	1	2	3	4	5	6	7
Grapefruits	1	3	6	10			

The pattern rule shows that the terms of the sequence differ by 2, by 3, by 4, and so on. Thus, continue to carry out the table through seven rows:

Row number	1	2	3	4	5	6	7
Grapefruits	1	3	6	10	15	21	28

There will be 28 + 21 + 15 + 10 + 6 + 3 + 1 = 84 grapefruits.

PROBLEM   (Reproduction Page 71)

The local Public Broadcasting System is having a five-day fundraiser. On the first day, Monday, the host called three people. He asked each of them to call 3 of their friends on Tuesday and to ask each of them to call 3 friends on Wednesday. Everyone who is called will call 3 different friends on the next day. After the Friday calls had been made, how many people will have been called?

Discussion   This is a problem in which the pattern is based on powers of 3. The host is $1 (3^0)$; he calls 3 (3^1); each of these calls 3 (3^2), and so on. (This can be nicely illustrated with a tree diagram.) The sequence is 1, 3, 9, 27, 81. The number of people called will be the sum of these last four terms, or 120. (Don't count the host!)

PROBLEM   (Reproduction Page 72)

A mooring rope that is 1 inch thick and 63 feet long is being coiled on the dock. The first coil took 12 inches of rope, the second coil took 24 inches, the third took 48 inches, and so on. How many coils are needed for the entire rope? What is the diameter of the circle formed by the coiled rope?

Discussion   The coils form a geometric sequence. Each term is twice the term preceding it (i.e., 1, 2, 4, 8, 16,...). Sum the sequence as you add terms until the sum of the sequence reaches 63 feet.

Coil	1	2	3	4	5	6
Length	1	2	4	8	16	32
Total length	1	3	7	15	31	63

Notice that the sum of any given number of terms can be represented by the expression $2^n - 1$. There will be 6 coils. Since the rope was 1 inch thick, the radius will be 6 inches, and the diameter of the circle of coiled rope will be 12 inches. (This could lead to a discussion of approximate answers.)

PROBLEM   (Reproduction Page 73)

The seventh grade is going on a field trip to the local aquarium. The teacher told the children to remember which of the three buses they had been assigned to—Bus Two, Bus Three, or Bus Eight. She assigned Amy, Nancy, and David to Bus Two. She put Jeff, Danny, Charlotte, and Clarissa on Bus Three. Mabel, Justin, Nora, Lars, and Denise were assigned to Bus Eight. To which bus did the teacher assign each of these children: Booker, Steve, Barbara, Michael, Susanne, Claire, Alex, Helen, Amanda, Matthew, Stanley, Murray, Jimmy, and Hope? To which bus should she assign Dennis? Why?

Discussion   The key to the solution lies within the letter arrangements of each bus. All children whose names contain a *double-letter* were assigned to Bus Three. Those with a pair of *alphabetically consecutive letters* in their name were assigned to Bus Ei*gh*t. All others were assigned to Bus Two. Of course Dennis could be assigned to either Bus Three (double *n* in his name) or to Bus Eight (consecutive letters *De* in his name).

The answers are:

Bus Two	Bus Three	Bus Eight
Amy	Jeff	Mabel
Nancy	Danny	Justin
David	Charlotte	Nora
Barbara	Clarissa	Denise
Michael	Susanne	Hope
Claire	Matthew	Lars
Alex	Murray	Steve
Helen	Jimmy	Stanley
Amanda	Booker	

REDUCTION AND EXPANSION

Patterns are often the key to the solution to a problem, even though no pattern is apparent at first sight. The pattern may be obscured by the complexity of the problem or the large numbers contained in the problem. By reducing the complexity to a simpler case and gradually expanding the numbers, one can often observe a pattern developing. Along with the Reduction and Expansion process, some kind of organized table should be made to keep track of each expansion. Careful observation of this table will most likely reveal the pattern.

PROBLEM   (Reproduction Page 74)

For Gilda's party, the Hoagie House prepared a huge sub sandwich on a 7-foot long hoagie roll. Gilda wants to feed 16 people. How many cuts must she make?

Discussion   It should be apparent that 16 is an arbitrary number. Try reducing the complexity of the problem to 2 people and expand, making a table to record the results:

Number of People	Number of Cuts
2	1
3	2
4	3
.	.
.	.
.	.
n	$(n-1)$

The number of cuts is always one less than the number of people. Thus, for 16 people, Gilda must make 15 cuts. Notice that the 7-foot length of the roll is extraneous data.

PROBLEM   (Reproduction Page 75)

Eric is arranging the dining room in his restaurant to accommodate a party of 34 people. He is taking small, square tables that seat one person on each side, and is placing them end-to-end to make one long table. How many tables will Eric need?

Discussion   Reduce the complexity of the problem by starting with one table and then adding tables, one at a time, to see what happens. Make a chart and look for a pattern

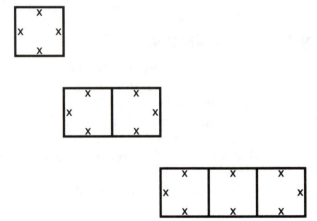

Number of diners	4	6	8	. . .	34
Number of tables	1	2	3	. . .	?

To find the number of tables, decrease the number of diners by 2 and then divide by 2. Thus,

$$T = \frac{D-2}{2}$$

For 34 diners, Eric will need $(34 - 2) \div 2 = 16$ tables.

PROBLEM   (Reproduction Page 76)

Joanne and her friends are seated around a large, circular table at a banquet. Twenty-five dishes are passed around the table, with each person taking one dish in turn, until there are no dishes left. Joanne takes the first dish and also gets the last one. She may have more than just the first and last dishes, however. How many people are at the banquet?

Discussion   Again, begin by reducing the complexity of the problem, gradually expanding, and looking for a pattern. Remember to include Joanne in the number of people at the table, and that she must get the first and last dishes. Thus, begin the table with 2 people, noting that Joanne is number 1.

Number of People at the Table	Number of Person Who Receives Number 25
2	1
3	1
4	1
5	5
6	1
7	4
8	1
9	7
10	5
.	.
.	.
.	.

A careful examination of the table reveals that Joanne (person number 1) gets the first and last plate when there are 2, 3, 4, 6, 8,... people at the table. Critical analysis shows that these are the factors of 24.

PROBLEM   (Reproduction Page 77)

Laura is training her pet white rabbit, Ghost, to climb up a flight of 10 steps. Ghost can only hop up 1 or 2 steps each time he hops. He never hops down, only up. How many different ways can Ghost hop up the flight of 10 steps?

Discussion   During the Read and Think stage of the heuristics when the anatomy of a problem is discussed, student should learn that all of the numbers that appear in a problem are arbitrary decisions, made by the person creating the problem. In some cases, one or more of these numbers can be modified without affecting the underlying problem, in order to simplify the solution. Students should develop a feeling for which numbers can be modified and which must be kept as they are. In this problem, the number of steps can easily be changed, but the pattern of 1 or 2 steps at a time cannot. Specifically, begin by reducing the number of steps (originally given as 10) to 1, then expand to 2 steps, 3 steps, 4 steps, and so on, see if a pattern emerges. The sequence 1, 2, 3, 5, 8,... is a familiar one (a Fibonacci sequence). Thus, continuing the sequence, we obtain the answer:

1, 2, 3, 5, 8, 13, 21, 34, 55, 89

Number of Ways Steps	Ways	Number of Ways
1	1	1
2	1-1,2	2
3	1-1-1 1-2 2-1	3

(Is this the sequence of the counting numbers? Don't be a conclusion jumper.)

| 4 | 1-1-1-1
1-1-2
1-2-1
2-1-1
2-2 | 5 |
| 5 | 1-1-1-1-1   2-2-1
2-1-1-1   2-1-2
1-2-1-1   1-2-2
1-1-2-1
1-1-1-2 | 8 |

There are 89 different ways for Ghost to hop up the flight of 10 steps.

Some students may recognize that this problem can be approached as a problem in combinatorials. Indeed, it is closely related to the traditional problem, "How many arrangements can be made from the letters in the word MISSISSIPPI?" For these students, an an alternate solution might be as follows:

Jumps of 2 Steps	Jumps of 1 Step	Ways	Number of Ways
5	0		1
4	2	$\dfrac{(4+2)!}{4!+2!}$	15
3	4	$\dfrac{(3+4)!}{3!+4!}$	35
2	6	$\dfrac{(2+6)!}{2!+6!}$	26
1	8	$\dfrac{(1+8)!}{8!}$	9
0	10		1
			89

Once again, the solution provides the same answer—namely, 89 ways.

PROBLEM   (Reproduction Page 78)

The circus is setting up its tent. There are 12 poles holding the tent upright. Between every two poles, there will be a rope full of banners. How many ropes will there be?

Discussion   Once again, reduction appears to be a viable approach. The number 12 is arbitrary. What happens if there were 1, 2, 3, 4,… poles? A drawing/table helps:

Number of Poles	Drawing	Number of Ropes
1	●	0
2	●———●	1
3	△	3
4		6
5		10

etc.

The number of ropes is given by the formula $n(n-1)/2$. That is, for 5 poles, there will be $\dfrac{5 \times 4}{2} = 10$ ropes. For 6 poles, there will be $\dfrac{6 \times 5}{2} = 15$ ropes. Thus, for 12 poles, there will be $\dfrac{12 \times 11}{2} = 66$ ropes.

WORKING BACKWARDS

Working backwards is a strategy that is successfully used when the outcome of a situation is known and the initial conditions are required. A direct approach can sometimes be used as well, especially with an algebraic solution, but the working backwards strategy is often more efficient. When working backwards, the operations required by the original action will be replaced by their inverses. Addition and subtraction are inverse operations, as are multiplication and division.

PROBLEM   (Reproduction Page 79)

Mr. Rafaelo runs a bicycle store. He sells a bike for $165, including the tax. To determine his selling price, he added $10 to the cost of the bike for a child's seat on the back. Then he doubled the total for his own markup. Last, he added $15 for sales tax. How much did the bike cost Mr. Rafaelo?

Discussion   Begin with the total selling price, $165. Since Mr. Rafaelo added $15 for sales tax, you will subtract $15 (the inverse) to get $150. He doubled the price for his markup—you divide by 2 and get $75. He added $10 for the child's seat—you subtract $10. The cost for the bike was originally $65. Note that this problem could also be solved by constructing an algebraic equation. If you let X = the original cost of the bike, then

$$2(X + 10) + 15 = 165$$

PROBLEM   (Reproduction Page 80)

The local library fine schedule for overdue books is as follows:

> 25¢ per day for each of the first three days
> 10¢ per day thereafter

Sandra paid a fine of $1.35. How many days overdue was her book?

Discussion   The students know the final outcome was a $1.35 fine. Sandra paid 25¢ for each of the first three days, or 75¢, which leaves 60¢. At 10¢ per day, this represents six days. Her book was nine days overdue.

PROBLEM   (Reproduction Page 81)

Mr. Davis wants to encourage his son Jimmy to save money. Each time Jimmy puts $3 into his savings account (once a month), Mr. Davis doubles the amount of money in the account. Jimmy now has exactly $90 in the account. How many months ago did he start?

Discussion   Jimmy now has $90 in the bank. His dad doubled the amount, so there must have been $45. Jimmy put in $3; there had been $42 (month A). Previously, there was $21; Jimmy's $3 left $18 (month B). Prior to that, there was $9; Jimmy's $3 left $6 (month C). Prior to that, there was $3 that Jimmy used to start the account. The account was four months old. Notice that an excellent extension might be to ask how much money each of them actually put into the account (Jimmy put $12; his father put $78).

PROBLEM   (Reproduction Page 82)

Loretta owns a pet shop that specializes in exotic tropical fish. In April, Loretta doubled the number of fish she had on hand, and then sold 30 of them. In May, she tripled the number of fish she had on hand, and then sold 54 of them. In June, she quadrupled the number of fish she had, and then sold 72 of them. She now had 48 fish left. How many fish did she start with?

Discussion   Work backwards from 48 fish. Since Loretta had sold 72 fish in June, she must have had 120. But this was after quadrupling the number she had. Thus, she ended May with 30 fish. But she had sold 54, thus she must have had 84. This was after tripling, so she had 28 at the end of April. She sold 30, so she must have had 58. This was after doubling, so she started with 29 fish in April.

Again, an algebraic solution is possible.

EXPERIMENTATION AND SIMULATION

Some problems lend themselves to *experimentation*—to acting it out. That is, the student can best solve the problem by DOING IT! Indeed, acting out a problem forces an understanding of the nature of the problem. If someone is capable of acting out a problem, you can almost be certain that he or she understands it. For example, if a student is asked to determine how many board erasers can be placed end to end on the chalk tray of a blackboard in the front of the room, the answer can be obtained by actually lining up a series of board erasers and counting them. If a student performs this experiment, he or she not only will find the answer but will also indicate a complete understanding of the problem.

A more sophisticated solution might be to measure the length of one board eraser and the length of the tray. The problem is then solved by division. This is a paper and pencil solution that demonstrates the power of mathematics. It is dependent on the student's understanding of the division concept.

Some problem situations are difficult to actually carry out because of the numbers and/or the situation. For these, a *simulation* is more practical. For instance, bottle caps can be used in place of snowballs, chips can represent people, and so on. Better yet, at the junior and senior high school levels, simulation should take place with pencil and paper, by making a drawing or a table. As students mature mathematically, they should become less dependent on acting it out and on physical simulations, and more inclined toward a paper and pencil solution. Mathematics power permits people to represent action symbolically! This is what mathematics is all about!

ACTIVITY 4.5   Here are some problems for which performing an experiment is the solution strategy. Students must act them out either completely or in part.

1. How long does it take you to walk to school?
2. How many "heads" will you get if you toss a coin 50 times?
3. How many nickels stacked on top of each other will make a stack an inch high?
4. How many checkers will fill a coffee can?
5. How many teachers are there in your school?
6. How many people in your mathematics class were born in the month of November?
7. Which has more pages: your dictionary or your local telephone book?
8. Which is the favorite movie of the students in your class?

9. How many pretzels are in a box of pretzels?
10. (Reproduction Page 83) Place 20 pennies on the table in a row. Now replace every fourth coin with a nickel. Now replace every third coin with a dime. Now replace every sixth coin with a quarter. What is the value of the 20 coins now on the table?
11. How many words are on a typical page in your mathematics text-book?
12. Can you run a 100-yard dash faster than a car can drive one-half mile at 30 miles per hour?

PROBLEM   (Reproduction Page 84)

There are four boys and five girls standing outside the new record shop. The sign in the window offers a prize to every couple (one boy and one girl) that enters the store. How many prizes can the nine people get?

Discussion   This problem lends itself to actually carrying out the action. Get four boys and five girls. See how many different couples can be formed. Have the rest of the class keep track of the action to be certain that there are no repetitions and that every possible combination is actually used. However, you can also simulate the action with a pencil and paper, by assigning letters to each of the children and preparing a table:

b1 g1	b2 g1	b3 g1	b4 g1
b1 g2	b2 g2	b3 g2	b4 g2
b1 g3	b2 g3	b3 g3	b4 g3
b1 g4	b2 g4	b3 g4	b4 g4
b1 g5	b2 g5	b3 g5	b4 g5

If the mathematical maturity level is such that the student recognizes this as an example of the fundamental counting principle, then the answer is obtained by multiplying 5×4.

PROBLEM   (Reproduction Page 85)

The Art Club at the Carroll School decided to exchange gifts at the end-of-school party. Each of the eight members brought a gift for each of the other members. How many gifts were exchanged?

Discussion   This problem can be acted out, replacing the gifts with chips or some other appropriate objects. It can be simulated with paper and pencil by drawing eight points (to represent the members) and then connecting each point to every one of the other points with two lines (gifts exchanged). It can also be done by reduction and expansion. That is, begin by drawing two dots (club members) and connecting them with 2 lines each (gifts). Now draw three dots and connect them with 2 lines each, or 6 lines (gifts). Continue until a pattern is discovered. Some students may notice that the problem can be simplified even further by using *one* line between each pair of points and then doubling the final answer.

PROBLEM   (Reproduction Page 86)

The new school has exactly 1,000 lockers and exactly 1,000 students. On the first day of school, the students meet outside the building and agree on the following plan: The first student will enter the school and open all the lockers. The second student will then enter the school and close every locker with an even number (2, 4, 6, 8,...). The third student will then "reverse" every third locker (3, 6, 9, 12,...). That is, if the locker is closed, the student will open it; if the locker is open, he or she will close it. The fourth student will then reverse every fourth locker, and so on until all 1,000 students, in turn have entered the building and reversed the proper lockers. Which lockers finally remain open?

Discussion   This well-known problem is a beautiful example of a situation that can be resolved through a variety of strategies. First of all, it can actually be performed with 1,000 students and 1,000 lockers. However, this is obviously unreasonable, and, in fact, unnecessary. It can be acted out with 100 students and 100 lockers, a reduction. It can further be reduced to 20 of each. This is a size that is ample enough to observe an existing pattern.

A more sophisticated approach utilizing reduction would be to *simulate* the action by using coins or bottle caps to represent the lockers, and "flipping" them to represent opening and closing them. Or perhaps students could represent the lockers by holding cards with numbers, and turning forwards and backwards as the lockers are reversed.

However, a paper and pencil simulation would be the most efficient procedure, using a chart as shown:

Locker #	1	2	3	4	5	6	7	8	9	10	11	12	13	14	15	16	17	18	19	20
Student 1	o	o	o	o	o	o	o	o	o	o	o	o	o	o	o	o	o	o	o	o
2	↑	c	o	c	o	c	o	c	o	c	o	c	o	c	o	c	o	c	o	c
3			c	c	o	o	o	c	c	c	o	o	o	c	c	c	o	o	o	c
4				o	o	o	o	o	c	c	o	c	o	c	c	o	o	o	o	o
5				↑	c	o	o	o	c	o	o	c	o	c	o	o	o	o	c	o
6						c	o	o	c	o	o	o	o	c	o	o	o	c	o	c
7							c	o	c	o	o	o	o	o	o	o	o	c	o	c
8								c	c	o	o	o	o	o	o	c	o	c	o	c
9									o	o	o	o	o	o	o	c	o	o	o	c
10									↑	c	o	o	o	o	o	c	o	o	o	o
11											c	o	o	o	o	c	o	o	o	o
12												c	o	o	o	c	o	o	o	o
13													c	o	o	c	o	o	o	o
14														c	o	c	o	o	o	o
15															c	c	o	o	o	o
16																o	o	o	o	o
17																↑	c	o	o	o
18																		c	o	o
19																			c	o
20																				c

All this now requires is pattern recognition to complete the solution.

This problem is particularly valuable in that it includes some very interesting mathematical concepts. The key to the solution is the well-known theoretic property that all numbers have an even number of factors except the perfect squares. The problem also lends itself to a variety of extensions:

1. For a particular locker, how many times was it touched? (The number of factors)
2. How many lockers, and which ones, were touched exactly twice? (The lockers with prime numbers)
3. Which locker was touched the most times? (The one with the most factors)
4. What is the sum of the numbers on all the lockers left open?

$$(\frac{N^3}{3} + \frac{N^2}{2} + \frac{N}{6} \text{ , where } N \text{ is the number of open lockers}).$$

PROBLEM   (Reproduction Page 87)

The Continental Hockey League consists of two conferences, each with six teams. Every team plays the teams within its own conference twice and plays each team in the other conference once. How many games are played during the season?

Discussion   This problem can be nicely simulated by assigning letters and subscripts to each team, and pairing them for each game. Let A_1, B_1, C_1,... represent the teams in the first conference; and A_2, B_2, C_2...represent the teams in the other conference. Then,

$$
\begin{array}{lllll}
A_1 B_1 & & & & \\
A_1 C_1 & B_1 C_1 & & & \\
A_1 D_1 & B_1 D_1 & C_1 D_1 & & \\
A_1 E_1 & B_1 E_1 & C_1 E_1 & D_1 E_1 & \\
A_1 F_1 & B_1 F_1 & C_1 F_1 & D_1 F_1 & E_1 F_1
\end{array}
$$

Thus, there will be 15 games for each round, within the conference, or 30 games. But there are two conferences. There will be a total of 60 games within

$$
\begin{array}{l}
A_1 A_2 \\
A_1 B_2 \\
A_1 C_2 \\
A_1 D_2 \\
A_1 E_2 \\
A_1 F_2
\end{array}
$$

Each team plays 6 games, for a total of 36 games played between teams in the conferences. Thus, the total number of games played is $60 + 36 = 96$. For those students who have experience with permutations and combinations, the following approach is appropriate. Within each conference, the total number of games is $2 \times 6C2$, or 30 games. This means 60 games within the two conferences. The same 6×6, or 36, games are to be played between the conferences, for a total of 96 games.

GUESS AND TEST

Probably the most commonly used strategy outside of school is guess and test. In this strategy, one guesses at an answer, then tests the guess to see if it works. By repeating this procedure and refining each guess on the basis of the results of previous trials, the answer—or at least a close approximation—can often be found. This is contrary to traditional teaching, when guessing is discouraged. Often heard in the classroom is a comment such as, "Do you know or are you just guessing?" Of course, blind guessing should be discouraged. Guess and test is a viable method in most fields of science and mathematics, where hypotheses are generated (the guess) and then verified by testing them (the test). Well-known mathematicians—such as Newton, Horner, Goldbach, and Euler, among others—utilized this method extensively in their work.

Guesses and results should be carefully recorded in an appropriately labeled table or list. The table or list will often reveal the direction in which subsequent guesses should be made. It might also reveal a pattern.

ACTIVITY 4.7   Here are some problems that should be done using the Guess and Test strategy.

PROBLEM   (Reproduction Page 88)

Matt is selling baseball cards at a local flea market. Rookie cards sell for $5 each, Champion cards sell for $6 each, Old-Timer cards sell for $7 each, and Hall-of-Famer cards sell for $9 each. Renee bought 3 cards and spent $18. What cards did she buy?

Discussion   Use guess and test. The problem has two possible ways to reach $18 with three cards. They are either $6–$6–$6 or $5–$6–$7. Thus, Renee bought either three Champion cards—or one Rookie card, one Champion card, and one Old-Timer card.

PROBLEM   (Reproduction Page 89)

Nancy sells rings and bracelets at the local crafts fair. She receives $6 for a bracelet and $4 for a ring. She started the day with the same number of bracelets as rings, and, at the end of the day, she found that she had twice as many rings left as bracelets. She had taken in $96 altogether. How many of each did she sell?

Discussion   Since Nancy had twice as many rings left as bracelets, she must have sold twice as many bracelets as rings (since she started with the same number of each). Make a table and use guess and test.

Rings ($4 each)	Bracelets ($6 each)	Total
10 ($40)	20 ($120)	$160
8 ($32)	16 ($ 96)	$128
6 ($24)	12 ($ 72)	$ 96

Nancy sold 12 bracelets and 6 rings.

PROBLEM   (Reproduction Page 90)

In a game at the County Fair, each color marker has a different point value: black = 2, green = 3, and red = 5. Howard has a score of 55 points. He has 12 green markers. How many red markers does he have?

Discussion   Howard has 12 green markers for a total of 36 points. This leaves 19 points to be divided between the red and the black markers. Guess and test! There are two possible answers:

> 1 red   7 black   1 2 green
> 3 red   2 black   12 green

PROBLEM   (Reproduction Page 91)

Ruth took a multiple-choice test with 20 questions. The test is scored +5 for each correct answer, –2 for each incorrect one, and 0 if the question is not answered. She scored 48 on the test. How did she do this?

Discussion   This is a perfect illustration of a problem to be solved with the guess and test strategy. Ruth must have had at least 10 correct questions—otherwise, her score would be 45 or less. Thus, 10 correct = 50, 1 incorrect = –2, for a total of 48. (This means that 9 questions were left unanswered).
A student should realize that $5C - 2I$ cannot yield an even answer when C is odd (C = number correct, I = number incorrect). Thus, guesses are limited to even numbers:

> 10 correct = 50   1 incorrect = –2   9 unanswered
> 12 correct = 60   6 incorrect = –12   2 unanswered
> 14 correct = 70   6 incorrect = –12   impossible!

There are no other possible answers.

LOGICAL DEDUCTION

In all walks of life, everyone must be able to analyze given facts and draw appropriate, correct, logical conclusions. The *Curriculum and Evaluation Standards for School Mathematics* of the National Council of Teachers of Mathematics has indeed identified reasoning as one of the four goals common to all grade levels. Critical thinking is the foundation of reasoning. Traditionally, this kind of thinking was emphasized in formal geometry courses. Today, however, it is included in *all* school mathematics courses.

In Activities 4.8 through 4.10, we present a series of exercises designed to assist your students in developing their critical thinking skills by drawing valid conclusions from sets of data. In addition, we present some problems whose solutions depend on logical deduction.

ACTIVITY 4.8   This activity presents some simple syllogisms. The students are presented with two hypotheses, along with a conclusion. They must determine if the conclusion can be validly drawn from the given hypotheses. Remember that a conclusion is valid if it follows from the given statements. This may not necessarily reflect real-life experiences. Reproduction Pages 92 and 93 provide practice in syllogisms. Notice that item 8 on Reproduction Page 92 is logically correct as it stands, although experience indicates the conclusion is false. It is the original hypothesis that was incorrect. Similarly, in item 8 on Reproduction Page 93, the original hypothesis is incorrect, but the conclusion follows from the given hypotheses. Thus, the conclusion is valid, even though it is really incorrect.

ACTIVITY 4.9   Problem solving and reasoning require drawing proper conclusions from given data. Reproduction Pages 94 and 95 present the students with a collection of facts from which conclusions have been drawn. Have the students decide whether each conclusion is true, false, or cannot be determined from the given data.

ACTIVITY 4.10   Reproduction Pages 96 through 98 contain activities that require more sophisticated thought by the students than in the previous ones. They serve as the transition from the simple syllogisms in Activity 4.8 to the problems that follow in Activity 4.11. Students must select proper conclusions from a set of conclusions, based on a set of given statements.

ACTIVITY 4.11   Use the subskills from the previous activities to solve the following problems.

PROBLEM   (Reproduction Page 99)

There were three prizes given at the Arithmetic Contest: a calculator, a book, and a ruler. The winners were Roger, Sally, and Tom.

1. Tom did not win the calculator.
2. Sally won the book.

Who won each prize?

Discussion   Set up a 3 × 3 array, commonly called a *matrix*.

	Calculator	Book	Ruler
Roger			
Sally			
Tom			

Placing an X in a cell (box) indicates that this event could not take place. Thus, clue number 1 reveals that "Tom did not win the calculator." Place an X in the appropriate cell:

	Calculator	Book	Ruler
Roger			
Sally			
Tom	X		

Placing a check in a cell indicates that this event did occur. Clue number 2, "Sally won the book" is shown by placing a check in the cell:

	Calculator	Book	Ruler
Roger			
Sally		✔	
Tom	X		

Since only one person could win each item, no one else can win the book. Thus, place an X in each of the cells in the book column and in Sally's row. Now, only one cell is left for Tom. He won the ruler. By using similar reasoning, you will find that Roger won the calculator, Sally won the book, and Tom won the ruler.

PROBLEM   (Reproduction Page 100)

The electrician, plumber, and grocer in a small town are Ruiz, Johnson, and Lee. Lee lives next door to the plumber. The electrician is Lee's daughter. Ruiz and the plumber were on the school debating team back in high school. Which job does each person have?

Discussion   Use the clues to complete a matrix:

	Electrician	Plumber	Grocer
Ruiz	✔	X	X
Johnson	X	✔	X
Lee	X	X	✔

Thus, Ruiz is the electrican, Johnson is the plumber, and Lee is the grocer.

PROBLEM   (Reproduction Page 101)

Today is really your busiest day! You have to meet Mark for lunch at the neighborhood deli, visit the Art Museum, and go to the dentist. In addition, you promised to visit your sick buddy. The deli is closed on Monday and the Art Museum is open only on Monday, Wednesday, and Friday. Your dentist has office hours on Thursday, Friday, and Saturday. Your sick buddy can have visitors only on Friday and Saturday. What is your busiest day?

DISCUSSION   Again, use the clues to fill out the matrix:

	Monday	Wednesday	Friday
Deli		X	X
Art Museum	X	X	X
Dentist			X
Sick buddy			X

Your busiest day is Friday.

PROBLEM   (Reproduction Page 102)

Marv, Stan, Ralph, and Anita (in that order) came to pick up the last four uniforms at the athletic office. There was one of each shirt left on the shelf: a baseball sweatshirt, a football jersey, a basketball shirt , and a hockey jersey. These were orange, green, black, and yellow, but not in that order. Use the following clues to match the person with the sport and color shirt:

1. Anita did not want the football jersey, but she was required to take it.
2. After Marv picked up his shirt, he wished he had gotten the green one or the baseball sweatshirt.
3. When Stan left, the basketball shirt was still on the shelf.
4. Stan received either the black shirt or the football jersey.
5. Ralph received the yellow shirt.

Discussion   Careful examination of this problem reveals three 4 × 4 matrices are needed:

	Baseball	Football	Basketball	Hockey
Marv				
Stan				
Ralph				
Anita				

MATRIX #1

	Orange	Green	Black	Yellow
Marv				
Stan				
Ralph				
Anita				

MATRIX #2

	Baseball	Football	Basketball	Hockey
Orange				
Green				
Black				
Yellow				

MATRIX #3

The first clue reveals that Anita received the football jersey. Place a check in the appropriate column and cross out the others:

	Baseball	Football	Basketball	Hockey
Marv		X		
Stan		X		
Ralph		X		
Anita	X	✔	X	X

Clues 2 and 3 enable you to determine that Marv took the hockey jersey.

	Baseball	Football	Basketball	Hockey
Marv	X	X	X	✔
Stan		X		X
Ralph		X		X
Anita	X	✔	X	X

Clue 4 reveals that Stan received either the football jersey or the black shirt. But Anita already has the football jersey, so Stan did not receive it; rather, he received the black shirt. Complete the problem using shirt ownership to help determine color.

Marv: Orange hockey jersey
Stan: Black baseball sweatshirt

Ralph: Yellow basketball shirt

Anita: Green football jersey

PROBLEM   (Reproduction Page 103)

The following figure shows one side of a diving submarine that takes people down under the water to look at a coral reef. Everyone wears a colored hat. A green hat is just below a yellow hat. A yellow hat is just above a red hat. A blue hat is in front of two yellow hats. Which seat is empty?

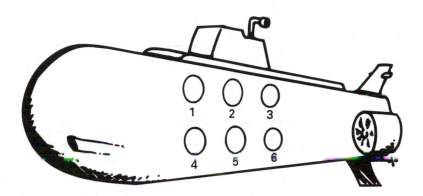

Discussion   Many logic problems can be solved by simulation, using either manipulatives or a drawing. This problem illustrates this form of solution. Draw a picture and use colored chips to represent the hats. Seat 4 is the vacant one.

PROBLEM   (Reproduction Page 104)

Laurie, Allan, Scott, and Adam all entered their pet frogs in a distance-jumping contest. Laurie's frog finished ahead of Allan's, but was not first. Scott's frog finished behind Laurie's, but was not last. In what order did the frogs finish?

Discussion   Again, this problem can be solved by using manipulatives (chips) or by making a drawing. In this case, we opt for a drawing. The first clue states that Laurie's frog finished ahead of Allan's, but not first.

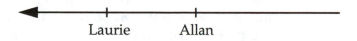

Scott's frog was behind Laurie's, but was not last. Thus, the order of finish is:

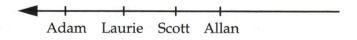

PROBLEM   (Reproduction Page 105)

The main event at the auto races had seven entries. In what order did the cars finish?

1. The driver of car #1 was the only one wearing green.
2. Car #6 blew a tire and finished last.
3. Car #2 and car #3 crossed the finish line together.
4. Car #4 beat car #7 by two lengths.
5. Only one car finished ahead of car #5.
6. The winning car had an even number.
7. The driver of car #2 saw green on the driver of the car ahead of him.
8. Car #7 finished two lengths ahead of car #1.

Discussion   Draw a time line. Use the clues to establish the order in which the cars finished.

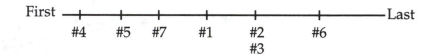

First ——+———+———+———+———+———+————Last
      #4   #5   #7   #1   #2   #6
                              #3

PROBLEM   (Reproduction Page 106)

Four married couples went to the theater last week. The wives' names were Carol, Sue, Jeanette, and Arlene. The husbands' names were Dan, Bob, Gary and Frank. Bob and Jeanette are brother and sister. Jeanette and Frank were once engaged, but they broke up when Jeanette met her husband. Arlene has a brother and a sister, but her husband is an only child. Carol is married to Gary. Who is married to whom?

Discussion   Prepare a 4 × 4 matrix and use the clues to eliminate the incorrect choices.

	Carol	Sue	Jeanette	Arlene
Frank	X	X	X	Yes
Gary	Yes	X	X	X
Bob	X	Yes	X	X
Dan	X	X	Yes	X

This section included primarily problems that might be considered "formal logic." However, the main thrust of this entire book is to provide materials to help students develop their critical thinking skills and reasoning power. Keep in mind that, as your students analyze and solve each problem in the book, they are adding to their thinking and reasoning skills.

ORGANIZED LISTING/EXHAUSTIVE LISTING

Making a list is a widely used technique in problem solving, either as a strategy itself or in conjunction with another strategy. For example, one rarely uses the Guess and Test strategy without an organized list to keep track of the guesses and the test results. Also, when one uses the Simulation strategy, a list is again a part of the solution. Sometimes the problem can be resolved by listing *all* of the possible answers and, by elimination, identifying the correct one. This is referred to as an *exhaustive list*. In some cases, an exhaustive list is too long, or it may not be necessary, since a pattern can be seen developing or an answer appears.

PROBLEM   (Reproduction Page 107)

The citizens of Surreytown have decided to put license plates on every bicycle. Each license plate will consist of a letter followed by a numeral. The possible letters are the vowels A, E, I, O, and U. The possible numerals are 1, 2, 3, 4, 5, and 6. How many different license plates are possible?

Discussion   Make an organized list for each vowel followed by each numeral. Notice that this will be an exhaustive list, since all possible pairs appear.

A1	E1	I1	O1	U1
A2	E2	I2	O2	U2
A3	E3	I3	O3	U3
A4	E4	I4	O4	U4
A5	E5	I5	O5	U5
A6	E6	I6	O6	U6

There are 30 possible license plates. Some students will not have to complete the entire list. They may recognize that the answer can be found by multiplying the number of letters (5) by the number of numerals (6).

PROBLEM   (Reproduction Page 108)

In an elevator bank of two elevators, the following schedule is installed: Elevator #1 takes two minutes between floors, whereas elevator #2 takes only one minute between floors. The elevator that arrives at a given floor first must wait three minutes before leaving. No waiting time is required of the elevator that arrives second at a given floor. Both elevators leave the sixth floor on a downward trip at exactly 1:00. Which elevator arrives at the ground floor first, and at what time?

Discussion   Make an organized list of the floors and the arrival and departure times for each elevator. (*Note*: Some people may consider this to be a table; we will make no distinction between the two.)

Floor		Elevator #1	Elevator #2
6	Leaves	1:00	1:00
5	Arrives	1:02	1:01
	Leaves	1:02	1:04
4	Arrives	1:04	1:05
	Leaves	1:07	1:05
3	Arrives	1:09	1:06
	Leaves	1:09	1:09
2	Arrives	1:11	1:10
	Leaves	1:11	1:13

Floor		Elevator #1	Elevator #2
1	Arrives	1:13	1:14
	Leaves	1:16	1:14
G	Arrives	1:18	1:15
	(Leaves	1:18	1:18)

The first question to be resolved is: What constitutes the "ground" floor? In many areas, the ground floor is the level below the first floor. In others, the first floor *is* the ground floor. This discussion is important, since it involves the critical analysis of the problem. If the first floor is considered to be the ground floor, then Elevator #1 arrives first at 1:13. If not, then Elevator #2 arrives first at 1:15.

Discuss with the class the pattern that develops as the elevators leave floors 6, 3, and 0.

PROBLEM   (Reproduction Page 109)

Mr. Homeowner wants to put fresh grass seed down on his front lawn. Grass seed is available in three-pound boxes and in five-pound boxes. A three-pound box costs $4.50, and a five-pound box costs $6.58. Mr. Homeowner needs 17 pounds of the grass seed. How many of each size box should he purchase to get the best buy?

Discussion   In order to determine the best buy, make an organized list:

Number of 5-lb. Boxes	Cost at $6.58	Number of 3-lb. Boxes	Cost at $4.50	Total Amount	Total Cost
4	$26.32	0	0	20	$26.32
3	19.74	1	$ 4.50	18	24.24
2	13.16	3	13.50	19	26.66
1	6.58	4	18.00	17	24.58
0	0	6	27.00	18	27.00

Notice that, in this case, the best buy is to purchase three five-pound boxes and one three-pound box, a total of 18 pounds at $24.24 to get the 17 pounds he needs.

PROBLEM   (Reproduction Page 110)

During the recent census, a man told the census taker that he had three children. When asked their ages, the man replied, "The product of their ages is 72. The sum of their ages is the same as my house number." The census taker ran to the door and looked at the house number. "I still can't tell," she complained. The man replied, "Oh, that's right. I forgot to tell you that the oldest one likes chocolate pudding." The census taker promptly wrote down the ages of the three children. How old are they? (Consider only integral ages.)

Discussion   Begin by preparing an exhaustive list of all the number triples whose product is 72, together with the sum of each triple:

$$1\text{--}1\text{--}72 = 74 \qquad 2\text{--}2\text{--}18 = 22 \qquad 3\text{--}3\text{--}8 = 14$$
$$1\text{--}2\text{--}36 = 39 \qquad 2\text{--}3\text{--}12 = 17 \qquad 3\text{--}4\text{--}6 = 13$$
$$1\text{--}3\text{--}24 = 28 \qquad 2\text{--}4\text{--}9 \ = 15$$
$$1\text{--}4\text{--}18 = 23 \qquad 2\text{--}6\text{--}6 \ = 14$$
$$1\text{--}6\text{--}12 = 19$$
$$1\text{--}8\text{--}9 \ = 18$$

Since there was still a question after seeing the sum of the ages (the house number), there had to be more than one set of factors whose sum equaled this number (3-3-8 and 2-6-6). Since 2-6-6 does not yield an "oldest child" but 3-3-8 does, the ages of the children must have been 3, 3, and 8.

PROBLEM   (Reproduction Page 111)

There is a game at the County Fair in which five balls are placed into a basket. Each ball has a number printed on it: 0, 2, 4, 6, 7. A person picks three of the balls from the basket at one time and adds the numbers.

1. How many different sums are possible?
2. What is the probability of scoring higher than 12?

Discussion   Make an organized list of the triples and their sums:

$$0 + 2 + 4 = 6 \qquad 2 + 4 + 6 = 12$$
$$0 + 2 + 6 = 8 \qquad 2 + 4 + 7 = 13$$
$$0 + 2 + 7 = 9 \qquad 2 + 6 + 7 = 15$$
$$0 + 4 + 6 = 10 \qquad 4 + 6 + 7 = 17$$
$$0 + 4 + 7 = 11$$
$$0 + 6 + 7 = 13$$

1. There are only 9 different scores. Note that a score of 13 occurs twice.
2. The list shows 10 possibilities, of which 4 are greater than 12. The probability is 4/10.

DIVIDE AND CONQUER

There are really two forms of this strategy. In one case, the problem consists of several parts, each of which is independent of the others. The final answer is obtained by combining the results of the individual parts, which can be done in any order. In the second case, the order in which the individual parts are answered is important. The second and following parts are each dependent on those that precede them. We have previously referred to this as a *hidden question*.

PROBLEM   (Reproduction Page 112)

Billy and Maria ordered flyers to advertise the school dance. Flyers cost $8.75 for the first 50, and $1.50 for each additional 10. The bill was $19.25. How many flyers did they order?

Discussion   The total bill was $19.25. First, subtract the cost for 50:

$$\begin{array}{r} \$\ 19.2\,5 \\ -\ \ \ 8.7\,5 \\ \hline \$\ 10.5\,0 \end{array}$$

Now divide this total ($10.50) by $1.50 and get 7. They bought 7 groups of 10, or 70 flyers. Adding 70 + 50 gives the total number of flyers Billy and Maria ordered.

PROBLEM   (Reproduction Page 113)

This chart shows the cost of birthday cards in Mrs. Henry's Card Shop:

Number of cards	1–3	4–6	7–9	10–12	13 or more
Cost per card	$2.50	$2.25	$2.00	$1.65	$1.50

Mrs. Ross went into the store in the morning and bought 5 cards. That same afternoon, Mr. Ross bought 8 cards. How much could Mr. and Mrs. Ross have saved if they made their purchases together?

Discussion
Part 1:   Mrs. Ross bought 5 cards at $2.25 each, for a total of $11.25.
Part 2:   Mr. Ross bought 8 cards at $2.00 each, for a total of $16.00.
Part 3:   They spent $27.25 together.
Part 4:   If they had bought the 13 cards together, they would have spent 13 × $1.50, or $19.50.
Part 5:   Subtract
$$\begin{array}{r} \$27.25 \\ -\ 19.50 \\ \hline 7.75 \end{array}$$

They would have saved $7.75.

PROBLEM   (Reproduction Page 114)

Andy went to the local supermarket to shop for his family. He bought 3 loaves of bread at $1.59 a loaf, 5 pounds of bananas at 59¢ a pound, and 2 boxes of cereal at $2.59 a box. He had a 45¢ coupon for 1 box of the cereal, which the store doubled. How much change did he receive from a $20 bill?

Discussion

Part 1:   3 loaves of bread at $1.59 = $4.77
5 pounds of bananas at 59¢ =$2.95
2 boxes of cereal at $2.59 = $5.18
Part 2:   Total spent is 4.77 + 2.95 + 5.18 = $12.90
Part 3:   One 45¢ coupon doubled = 90¢
Part 4: $12.90 – .90 = $12.00
Part 5: $20.00 – $12.00 = $8.00

Andy received $8.00 in change.

PROBLEM

(Reproduction Page 115)

Mr. Ryan's total income was $53,750. His deductions were as follows:

Contributions	$ 856
Mortgage Interest	$1250
Deductible Taxes	$2630
Casualty Losses	$1550

Mr. Ryan can either take the standard deduction of 10 percent, or he can itemize his deductions. Which method gives the larger deduction and by how much?

Discussion

The first step is to add the itemized deductions, which amount to $6,286. The second step is to take 10 percent of his income, which is $5,375. Mr. Ryan should itemize his deductions in order to save $911.

WRITE AN EQUATION

Writing an equation (i.e., using the skills of algebra) is a very powerful strategy. In order to write an equation that correctly represents the problem situation, students must have a good understanding of the problem. Knowledge of algebra provides students with the mathematics power necessary to solve many of the problems they face. Indeed, strategies such as Guess and Test as well as Working Backwards, for example, can often be replaced by an algebraic solution. A person with strong algebra skills is in an enviable position when it comes to problem solving. Some students may even use algebraic solutions to the total exclusion of all others. In this case, we suggest that you require alternate solutions wherever possible.

PROBLEM

(Reproduction Page 116)

A firefighter is standing on the middle rung of a ladder. She moved up 9 rungs. The smoke got worse, so she moved back down 13 rungs. When the smoke cleared, she went up 19 rungs to the top. How many rungs does the ladder have?

Discussion   Let n = the number of rungs on the ladder. Then $n/2$ is the place where the firefighter is standing at the start.

$$\frac{n}{2} + 9 - 13 + 19 = n$$

$$\frac{n}{2} + 15 = n$$

$$30 = n$$

There are 30 rungs on the ladder.

PROBLEM   (Reproduction Page 117)

Renee collects baseball cards. She has 240 cards in her collection. For every outfielder card, she has 5 cards of players from other positions. How many cards with outfielders does she have?

Discussion   Let b represent the number of outfielder cards in Renee's collection. Then $5b$ represents the number of cards with players in other positions.

$$b + 5b = 240$$

$$6b = 240$$

$$b = 40$$

Renee has 40 outfielder cards.

PROBLEM   (Reproduction Page 118)

Mike puts 104 feet of plastic edging around the perimeter of Mrs. Flores's garden in order to make it easy to trim. If her garden is in the shape of a rectangle with a length of 25 feet, how wide is it?

Discussion   Use the formula $P = 2L + 2W$. Then,

$$104 = 2(35) + 2W$$

$$104 = 70 + 2W$$

$$34 = 2W$$

$$17 = W$$

The width is 17 feet.

PROBLEM   (Reproduction Page 119)

The new movie, *Return to Monkey Island*, opened on Monday, March 1st. On the first day, 50 people attended the show. On the second day, there were 78 people in attendance. On the third day, 106 people were there. If the pattern continues, what is the first day on which there will be at least 200 people in the audience?

Discussion   Each day there are 28 more people than the day before. That is, on Day 1 there were 50 people. On Day 2 there were 50 + 28 people. On Day 3 there were $50 + 2 \cdot 28$ people. Thus, on any day, there will be $50 + (n - 1)28$ people.

$$200 = 50 + (n - 1)\,28$$
$$150 = (n - 1)28$$
$$150 = 28n - 28$$
$$178 = 28n$$
$$6.36 = n$$

Therefore, on the 7th day there will be at least 200 people. This is one case in which the answer requires the problem solver to "round up."

An alternate solution might be to make a table.

PROBLEM   (Reproduction Page 120)

At the zoo, Michelle paid $7.00 for two sandwiches and a container of milk. Her brother, Ralph, paid $5.00 for one sandwich and two containers of milk. How much would one sandwich and one container of milk cost?

Discussion   Let s = the cost for one sandwich and let m = the cost of one container of milk. Then,

$$2s + m = 700$$
$$s + 2m = 500$$
$$4s + 2m = 1400$$
$$\underline{s + 2m = 500}$$
$$3s \qquad = 900$$
$$s \qquad = 300$$
$$m \qquad = 100$$

A sandwich costs $3.00; a container of milk costs $1.00. A sandwich and a container of milk together cost $4.00.

Some students might notice that they can add the two original equations:

$$2s + m = 700$$
$$\underline{s + 2m = 500}$$
$$3s + 3m = 1200$$

Dividing both sides by 3,

$$s + m = 400$$

Thus, one sandwich and a container of milk cost $4.00, without even finding the individual costs for each. An alternate solution would be to use the Guess and Test strategy.

CHAPTER FIVE

Find an Answer

Once students have decided on a strategy with which they hope to solve the problem, they reach the next step—actually solving the problem and finding the answer. This step usually consists of applying arithmetic, algebraic, or geometric skills to the facts assembled and organized in previous steps. This is a fairly routine procedure and its success depends on the skills possessed by the students. *These skills are imperative and must not be overlooked!* If necessary, drill and practice in these manipulative operations should be provided from other sources. Of course, the problems in this book also provide such practice.

At this stage of the heuristics, most of the computation will be done either mentally or with the help of a calculator. The use of a calculator requires that students be proficient in placing the decimal point and in estimating the order of the answer. By having an idea of a "ballpark" answer to a problem, the students are less likely to make errors of great magnitude.

In this stage of the heuristic process, teachers should help students become more proficient in their ability to estimate. Estimation is an extremely important skill that is used virtually every day. In this section, we will present some activities to provide practice for your students in this often neglected area.

Reproduction Page 121 provides practice in the placing of decimal points in a computational setting. In each of numbers 6 through 10, an error has been made while finding the answer with a calculator. Both an incorrect answer as well as the correct answer have been given. Students are to decide which is correct (without using a calculator) and where the error was made in using the calculator. In some cases, the decimal point has been improperly placed; in others, an incorrect key has been hit.

In Reproduction Page 122, the studens are asked to provide an estimate for each of the shopping lists given. They must then find the actual cost (with or without their calculators) and see how close they were able to come.

In Reproduction Pages 123 and 124, students are asked to estimate the answer and then solve the problem. In problems 1 and 4 on Reproduction Page 123, students are required to "round up," as opposed to the traditional "if it's 5 or more" rounding procedure. If the students use their calculators to solve these problems, be certain that they give their answers to a reasonable number of decimal places. For example, if the problem involves money (i.e., problems 2, 3, 6, 7, and 8 on Reproduction Page 123 and problems 1, 3, and 4 in Reproduction Page 124), students should not use more than two decimal places.

CHAPTER SIX

Reflect and Extend

The problem does not end when an answer has been found. To many people, the final step of the heuristics simply means examining the answer to determine if it is mathematically correct, to see if it is reasonable, and to assure that the original question has been answered. These very important tasks, however, do not go far enough. In other words, they are necessary but not sufficient. Much more must be done. Additional tasks will allow students to further develop their thinking skills, to improve their problem-solving skills, and to discover how mathematics can explain many events that occur in the problems that surround us all—the *real* power of mathematics.

This heuristic should be used to expand the critical and creative thinking of the students, to allow metacognition to take place, and for further self-assessment. It is an opportunity for the teacher and students to create a series of new problems—some more or less difficult than the original and others at the same difficulty level. The word *reflect* indicates the students' actions that should occur at this point in the problem-solving process.

After the answer has been found, the following actions should take place:

1. *Check your answer.*
   a. Is the computation correct?
   b. Has the question been answered?
   c. Is the answer reasonable?
2. *Find alternate solutions.*
3. *Ask "What if?" questions.*
   a. Change the conditions of the problem.
   b. See what effect this change has on the answer.
4. *Extend.*
   a. Generalize the answer (try to find a formula).
   b. Look for the mathematical underpinnings of the problem.

ACTIVITY 6.1   Obviously, the answer to a problem must be correct! The algorithmic skills must be performed accurately, without error. They can be performed or checked with a calculator, as appropriate. Students must know how to check their work. Reproduction Pages 125 through 127 provide problems and answers. In Reproduction Page 125, the answer to each problem is incorrect; an error has been made. Students must identify and correct the error. The error may have been computational, operational, conceptual, or misinterpreted. For example, in problem 2, the computation gives 14.285 buses. The student rounds to 14 instead of 15. In item 3, the addition of the four scores is incorrect. In item 4, there is a division error. Problem 5 contains an operational error, and problem 7 involves a misinterpretation. Item 8 *does* yield 8⅓, but the student has failed to realize that fencing cannot be purchased in ⅓ of a length.

In Reproduction Pages 126 and 127, answers are provided. However, the student must determine if each answer is correct or incorrect. If the answer is incorrect, the student should determine the error and give the correct answer. In Reproduction Page 126, problem 1 contains a misinterpretation of the problem (omitting the $50 already in the treasury). Problem 3 involves an error in concept (the wrong number has been used as the base). Number four has been misinterpreted (forgetting to count Reggie himself). In problem 5, the student has averaged averages, and in problem 7, the student has not answered the required question.

In Reproduction Page 127, problem 1, the student appears to have missed the charge of 25¢ for *each* of the first three minutes, and used 25¢ for the entire three minutes. In item 3, the student added 6 to 30 instead of subtracting. In problem 5, the student "rounded down" from 57.14 instead of "rounding up" to 58 games. In problem 6, the student added 15 + 8 instead of using the Pythagorean Theorem. And in problem 7, the student seems to have assumed that "up 50 percent" and "down 50 percent" yield no change. Actually, the store made a profit:

$$1.5x = \text{the original selling price}$$
$$\tfrac{1}{2}(1.5x) = \text{the sale price}$$
$$1.5x - \tfrac{1}{2}(1.5x) = .75x, \text{ which is a profit}$$

ACTIVITY 6.2   Students should develop a sense of magnitude for an answer.(This ties in with the discussion of estimation in the previous chapter.) After all, a desk that is 40 feet long, or a bus that holds 532 people hardly makes any sense. Reproduction Pages 128 and 129 each provide a series of problems followed by several choices. The student should not solve the problem, but should simply decide which of the three choices is most reasonable. Notice that in question 6 in Reproduction Page 128, students must realize that there will always be 90 percent of what is then remaining left in the pile of mulch. Thus, the correct answer is (c) never. However, this is an excellent opportunity to discuss the concept of approaching a limit. In question 7, areas of similar figures are related as the square of the change, thus the new picture has an area of 108 square inches.

In Reproduction Page 129, number 4, the correct answer is probably 400 miles (choice c). However, under some conditions, it might be 200 miles. Students must defend their choices. In number 5, probability must occur in the interval from 0 to 1 inclusive. However, some students may confuse 100 with 100 percent. In number 7, the answer must be negative.

Reproduction Page 130 provides a set of problems together with answers. Students must decide whether the question has been answered correctly. If it has not, students should describe in words what was wrong and find the correct answer. In some cases, the error is due to not answering the proper question. In other cases, a conceptual or computational error may have been made. In number 4, students should allow some area for the fin's thickness. Thus, the answer is correct. In number 5, the answer is incorrect since the student failed to indicate that this was a *profit* of $2,500. In problem 8, the answer is given in digits, not in dollars and cents. The correct answer is $128.40, arrived at as follows:

Pages	Number of Pages	Number of Digits
1–9	9	9
10–99	90	180
100–250	151	453
		642

$$642 \times .20 = \$128.40$$

FIND ALTERNATE SOLUTIONS

Once an answer has been found and checked for computational accuracy and reasonableness, it is time to "play it again." Finding additional solutions to a problem provides students with an opportunity to develop and improve their creative thinking skills. Most problems can be solved in more than one way. Thus, students should be encouraged to solve a problem in as many ways as they can. Since they are already familiar with the problem, they need not spend time on organizing the facts, identifying what is to be found, and so on. All their creative energies can be put into finding different approaches, different models, different solutions. These can involve using manipulatives, acting the problem out, using algebraic solutions, or employing any other combination of techniques and strategies.

Keep in mind that when students look for an alternate solution, the problem itself is not changed in any way—they are only searching for different solutions! Hopefully, the answer in all cases will be the same.

PROBLEM   (Reproduction Page 131)

A landscape architectural firm is constructing a fence by cementing granite blocks together in a row. Each block is a cube, four feet on each edge, and having a sculptured design on each face. If 10 blocks are used in constructing the fence, how many sculptured designs are visible?

Discussion   *Solution #1.* It is impossible to solve this problem by doing it! However, a simulation seems plausible. It can be simulated by placing 10 cubes in a row and counting the visible faces. There will be 32 sculptured designs visible.

Solution #2. The problem situation may also be simulated with a drawing rather than by actually using blocks. This will help students develop the skill of making three-dimensional drawings and visualizing three-dimensional space.

Solution #3. Another solution is to use the Reduction/Expansion strategy. Begin with one block; five faces can be seen. Make a table to keep track of results. Now expand to two blocks; there are eight visible faces. Continue adding blocks and counting faces:

Number of Blocks	Visible Faces
1	5
2	8
3	11
4	14
.	.
.	.
.	.

Some students may wish to carry the table all the way through until they reach 10 blocks. Others may recognize the pattern rule as 3 × the number of blocks + 2, and stop earlier. The answer, however, is still 32 visible designs. Notice that the four-foot dimension is simply a distractor (extraneous information).

PROBLEM

(Reproduction Page 132)

A bicycle dealer just put together a shipment of two-wheel bicycles and three-wheel tricycles. He used 50 seats and 130 wheels. How many bikes and how many trikes did he put together?

Discussion

Solution #1. The problem can be solved algebraically by setting up a system of two equations in two variables and solving them simultaneously:

$$b + t = 50$$
$$2b + 3t = 130$$
$$\vdots$$
$$b = 20$$
$$t = 30$$

There were 20 bikes (40 wheels) and 30 trikes (90 wheels).

Solution #2. Use guess and test with a table:

	Bikes		Trikes		
Seats	*Wheels*	*Seats*	*Wheels*	**Total Wheels**	
30	60	20	60	120 (too few)	
25	50	25	75	125 (too few)	
22	44	28	84	128 (better)	
20	40	30	90	130 (correct!)	

Solution #3.   Reduce the complexity and make a drawing. Reduce the number of seats to 5 and the number of wheels to 13. Now draw 5 cycles:

Every cycle has at least two wheels:

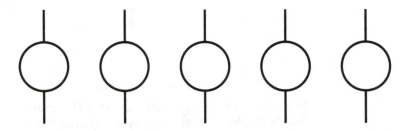

You've used 10 wheels—there are 3 wheels left. Put them on one at a time: Thus, there are 2 (20) bikes and 3 (30) trikes.

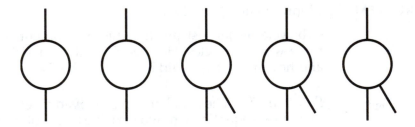

Solution #4.   Stack the bikes and trikes against the side of a truck so that each has one wheel against the wall of the truck and the other wheel(s) on the floor of the truck. There will be 50 wheels against the side of the truck, since there are a total of 50 cycles. If all the cycles had been bikes, there would be exactly 50 wheels on the floor of the truck. This would account for 100 wheels (50 on the floor and 50 resting against the side). But there are actually 130 wheels. Thus, there are 30 extra wheels—they must belong to the trikes!

PROBLEM   (Reproduction Page 133)

Find the dimensions of all rectangles such that their perimeter and area are numerically equal. (Consider only integral answers.)

Discussion   Although this does not contain all of the ingredients of a problem (i.e., there is no real-world setting nor any distractors), we feel that it is a problem of interest to the students who study mathematics.

Solution #1.   The first solution that occurs to many students is an algebraic one:

$$L \times W = 2L + 2W$$
$$LW - 2L = 2W$$
$$L(W - 2) = 2W$$
$$L = \frac{2W}{W - 2}$$

Now carry through the indicated division:

$$L \times W = \frac{2W}{W - 2} = 2 + \frac{4}{W - 2}$$

(*Note*: $W \neq 2$)

If the dimensions of the rectangle are to be integral, an examination of $\frac{4}{W-2}$ reveals that $7 > W > 2$. This leads to $W = 3$, 4, 5, or 6. The solutions are $W = 3$, $W = 4$, and $W = 6$. Thus the dimensions of the rectangle are 3×6 or 4×4.

Solution #2.   A table containing an exhaustive list of all the possibilities can be constructed:

L	W	A	P
1	1	1	4
1	2	2	6
1	3	3	8
1	4	4	10

The perimeter (P) is increasing faster than the area(A). Thus, there will be no rectangles with a dimension of 1.

L	W	A	P
2	2	4	8
2	3	6	10
2	4	8	12
2	5	10	14

The perimeter is increasing faster than the area. Thus, there will be no rectangles with a dimension of 2.

L	W	A	P
3	3	9	12
3	4	12	14
3	5	15	16
3	6	18	18

You have found an answer! Since the area is increasing by 3 and the perimeter by only 2, there will be no additional rectangles with a dimension of 3.

L	W	A	P
4	4	16	16

You have found a second answer! Noting the pattern of increases reveals that there will be no more rectangles satisfying the given conditions.

Solution #3.   It is possible to actually graph the situation described in Solution #2. Keeping L constant, one can graph perimeter and area on the same set of axes. Figure 6–1 shows graphs constructed for $L = 1, L = 2, L = 3, L = 4$, and $L = 5$.

WHAT IF? AND EXTEND

In the previous section, Finding Alternate Solutions, we discussed how students were given the opportunity to sharpen their creative thinking skills by searching for different ways to solve the same problem. Nothing in the problem was changed—students merely looked for different solutions. Now, in this section, the conditions of the problem will be altered and the students should direct their attention to the impact of the changed conditions on the previously obtained answer; in other words, the cause and effect relationship between data and outcomes. Some of the solution strategies that were used when the original problem had been solved may be used in this new situation. Naturally, one would expect the answer to change as well. What is important, however, is for students to discover how the new answer reflects the changed conditions. This cause and effect relationship should be carefully discussed.

Very often, the change in the conditions of the problem reveal the generic nature of the problem. This permits one to make a generalization about the problem, and sometimes to discover the mathematical concepts that underly the problem. This is the real power of mathematics. The goal of all mathematics instruction should be to provide students with mathematics power! That is, students should understand why a particular answer occurs, what mathematical concepts are involved, how mathematics can be used to describe what has taken place, and, finally, if and how the answer can be generalized.

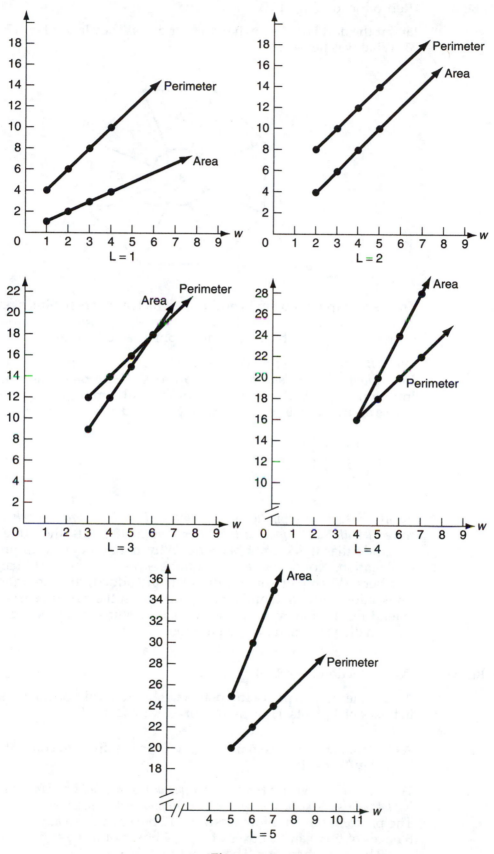

Figure 6–1

PROBLEM   (Reproduction Page 134)

Jan hit the dart board shown with four darts. They landed on 17, 3, 10, and 31. What was her score?

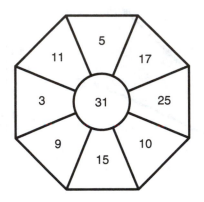

Discussion   This is a simple problem in addition, which appears in almost every basal text series. As such, it is not much of a challenge for your students. However, this can easily be made more sophisticated by playing "What if ?"

What if? #1.   Jan hit the dartboard with four darts. What if she had scored 61? How might she have done this? The nature of the problem has now changed. Intuition suggests that there will probably be multiple answers. In fact, Guess and Test reveals some. Have your students find others:

31–10–10–10

15– 5–31–10

9–10–11–31

What if? #2.   What if the "10" is removed from the board? Now how might Jan score 61 with exactly four darts? After several attempts, the students should conclude that this cannot be done. Why not? Mathematics provides the explanation. Notice that all the numbers now on the dart board are odd numbers. When pairs of odd numbers are added, the sum must be even. Thus, adding four odd numbers can never result in an odd answer. You can extend this notion even further to include sums and products of various combinations of odd and even numbers.

PROBLEM   (Reproduction Page 135)

A gardener has 36 poinsettia plants to ship to local florists. He ships them in boxes of 4 plants. How many boxes does he need?

Discussion   As it stands, this problem merely involves the division concept. However, let's play "What if ?"

What if? #1.   What if the gardener has boxes that hold 3 plants and boxes that hold 4 plants? Now how might he ship 36 plants if all boxes shipped must be full? The problem now has four answers: 12 boxes of three and 0 boxes of four; 8 boxes of three and 3 boxes of four; 4 boxes of three and 6 boxes of four; and 0 boxes of three and 9 boxes of four.

What if? #2.   What if he also had boxes in which he could ship 5 plants; now how might he ship 36 plants if all boxes shipped must be full?

What if? #3.   A slight variation of the "What if?" procedure would be to change the question. For example, *if the gardener has boxes that hold 3 plants and boxes that hold 4 plants, what numbers of plants could he not ship if each box must be full?* Make a table to see what is taking place:

Number of Plants	How to Ship
1	Cannot be shipped
2	Cannot be shipped
3	1(3) + 0(4)
4	0(3) + 1(4)
5	Cannot be shipped
6	2(3) + 0(4)
7	1(3) + 1(4)
8	0(3) + 2(4)
9	3(3) + 0(4)
10	2(3) + 1(4)
11	1(3) + 2(4)
12	4(3) + 0(4)
13	3(3) + 1(4)
14	2(3) + 2(4)
.	.
.	.
.	.

Thus, the table shows that 5 is the largest number of plants that cannot be shipped with the given conditions. However, an analysis of the table reveals some interesting mathematics. Notice that, after 5, each set of three numbers contains 0(4), 1(4), and 2(4). At the same time, the sets of three are each increased by one. Take any number, say 85. Remove 0(4). Is 85 divisible by 3 ? No. Remove 1(4). Is 81 divisible by 3? Yes. Thus, you can express 85 as 27(3) + 1(4). Any number can be expressed in this way:

$$0 = 0 \bmod 3$$
$$4 = 1 \bmod 3$$
$$8 = 2 \bmod 3$$

A different table can be constructed, beginning at 12 and focusing on the 4s instead of the 3s. Some teachers may recognize that this is an application of a theorem from number theory:

If a and b are relatively prime, then the largest number that cannot be represented as a sum of multiples of a and b is $a \cdot b - (a + b)$

PROBLEM   (Reproduction Page 136)

Edward had grades of 68, 70, 78, 76, and 88 on five mathematics tests. What was his average?

Discussion   This routine problem gives an answer of 76.

What if? #1.   What if Edward needs an 80 average to receive a grade of B and qualify for the honor roll? What must he store on the next test? To have an average of 80 for six tests, Edward must have a total of 480 points (6 × 80 = 480). He already has a total of 380. He must score 100 on the next test.

What if? #2.   Edward has grades of 68, 70, 78, 76, and 88 on five math tests. There is one more exam—the final, which will count as two tests. What must he score to have an average of 90? This turns out to be impossible, since 7 × 90 = 630 and the maximum Edward can achieve is a total of 380 + 100 + 100 = 580. This problem can be explained by examining the formula for averages, $\overline{X} = t/n$, where t is the sum of all the scores and n is the number of scores. Probably a more revealing formula is $t = n \cdot \overline{X}$.

PROBLEM   (Reproduction Page 137)

In the state aquarium, there is a reserve tank that is used to store and age water. Through leakage and evaporation, the tank loses two gallons each day. At the end of every fourth day, an automatic timer opens a valve and allows five gallons of water to flow into the tank. If the tank contained 1,000 gallons at the start, how many gallons are in the tank at the end of the 21st day?

Discussion   Make a table to show what's happening:

End of Day	Out	In	Amount in the Tank
- - -	- - -	- - -	1, 000
1	2	0	998
2	2	0	996
3	2	0	994
4	2	5	997
5	2	0	995
6	2	0	993
7	2	0	991
8	2	5	994
.	.	.	.
.	.	.	.
.	.	.	.
21	2	0	983

There are 983 gallons of water in the tank at the end of the 21st day.

What if? #1.   How many gallons of water are in the tank at the end of the 42nd day? (The correct answer is 966 gallons.)

What if? #2.   How many gallons of water are in the tank at the end of the nth day?

$$A = 1,000 - 2n + \left[\frac{n}{4}\right] \cdot 5$$

where A is the amount of water in the tank, n is the number of days, and

[   ] is the greatest integer function; that is, $\left[\frac{1}{4}\right] = 0$, $\left[\frac{4}{4}\right] = 1$, $\left[\frac{5}{4}\right] = 1$,

$\left[\frac{9}{4}\right] = 2$, etc.

What if? #3.   On what day will the tank become empty, in order to move it? Every 4 days, the tank nets a loss of 3 gallons. Thus, it will take 1,334 days to be completely emptied. Another interesting project would be to have the class graph the water level in the tank. The results yield a "sawtooth" graph.

PROBLEM   (Reproduction Page 138)

At the end of the eighth inning of the baseball game, the score was tied at 8–8. How many different scores were possible at the end of the seventh inning?

Discussion   Some students may recognize this problem as an example of the fundamental counting principle—that is, there are 9 possible scores for team A (0–8) and 9 possible scores for team B. Thus, there are $9 \times 9 = 81$ possible scores. For those students who are not familiar with the principle, make a list. Reduce the complexity, expand, and look for a pattern:

Score	Possible Previous Scores			Number of Scores	
0–0	0–0			1	(1^2)
1–1	0–0	1–0		4	(2^2)
	0–1	1–1			
2–2	0–0	1–1	2–2	9	(3^2)
	0–1	1–2	1–0		
	0–2	2–1	2–0		
.	.			.	
.	.			.	
.	.			.	
8–8				81	(9^2)

There were 81 possible scores.

What if? #1.   What if the score had been b–b? A careful examination of the solutions to the original problem reveals that there could have been $(b + 1)(b + 1)$ possible scores, or $(b + 1)^2$.

What if? #2.   What if the score had been b–c? Again, from the previous solutions, team A could have had $(b + 1)$ different scores, and team B could have had $(c + 1)$ different scores. Therefore, the answer would be $(b + 1)(c + 1)$ possible scores.

CHAPTER SEVEN

A Collection of Nonroutine Problems

Problems are the vehicles by which problem solving and reasoning skills are developed. This section contains problems for you to use with your students. Let the students work alone or in collaborative groups to develop as many solutions as possible for each. You should encourage extensions whenever possible.

Each problem is discussed in the text for your convenience, with one or more solutions presented. For each problem, there is a Reproduction Page in card format. These can easily be duplicated and placed on cards to create a problem deck.

The problem are arranged in order of mathematical sophistication. The beginning ones can be done with arithmetic skills only (although many can also be done algebraically). The problems then proceed through algebra, geometry, probability, and so on. Regardless of the mathematics required, all the problems require logical thought and reasoning.

PROBLEM 1   (Reproduction Page 139)

Georgette earned $500 a week for the first 20 weeks of the year. She then received a 10 percent raise. How much did she earn for the entire year?

Discussion   Divide and conquer. Divide the problem into two parts. Remember that a year has 52 weeks. Georgette worked 20 weeks at $500 per week and 32 weeks at $550 (a 10 percent raise) for the remaining part of the year. Use a calculator.

> 20 weeks @ $500 = $ 10,000
> 32 weeks @ $550 = $ 17,600

Georgette earned a total of $27,600 during the year.

PROBLEM 2   (Reproduction Page 139)

Here are the current rates for the Metro Taxi Company:

> *TAXI RATES*
> $2.00 for the first half-mile
> 45¢ for each additional quarter-mile
> 25¢ for each minute of waiting time
> $1.00 additional after 6:00 P.M.
> $1.00 for each additional passenger

Mr. Robbins took a taxi from the airport to his downtown hotel at 8:00 P.M. An accident blocked the highway for 10 minutes, but otherwise the trip went smoothly. Mr. Robbins gave the driver $23.50, which included a $3.60 tip. How far was the hotel from the airport?

Discussion   Work backwards. This is a multistep problem.

Total fare:	$ 23.50
Tip:	− 3.60
	19.90
Night Charge:	− 1.00
	18.90
1st half mile	− 2.00
	16.90
Waiting time	− 2.50
	14.40
Divide by .45	32 quarter miles

Mr. Robbins's trip was 32 quarter-miles (8 miles) plus the initial half-mile, or 8½ miles.

PROBLEM 3   (Reproduction Page 140)

Miguel and Charles started their new jobs on the same day. Miguel's schedule provides for 3 workdays, followed by 1 day off. Charles's schedule provides for 7 workdays, followed by 3 days off. On how many of their first 500 days will they both have a day off on the same day?

Discussion   Miguel works on a 4-day cycle, whereas Charles works on a 10-day cycle. The least common multiple of 4 and 10 is 20. Thus, they are following a 20-day cycle together, and there are 25 such cycles in the first 500 days. Miguel is off on days 4, 8, 12, 16, and 20. Charles is off on days 8, 9, 10, 18, 19, and 20. They will both be off on days 8 and 20, or 2 days in each 20-day cycle.

Thus, Miguel and Charles will have $25 \times 2 = 50$ days off in the first 500 days.

PROBLEM 4   (Reproduction Page 140)

Raymond and Boris went to, the ball game last evening. They spent exactly $20.00 on hot dogs and soft drinks. They bought at least 5 hot dogs at $2.00 each and at least 5 soft drinks at $1.00 each. What exactly did they buy?

Discussion   Raymond and Boris spent at least $10.00 on hot dogs and at least $5.00 on soft drinks. This leaves $5.00 to spend. They could have spent the $5.00 on 2 hot dogs and 1 soft drink, 1 hot dog and 3 soft drinks, or 0 hot dogs and 5 soft drinks. There are three possible answers:

> 7 hot dogs and 6 soft drinks
> 6 hot dogs and 8 soft drinks
> 5 hot dogs and 10 soft drinks

PROBLEM 5   (Reproduction Page 141)

There is a big special at the local pizza shop! You can buy either a square pizza, 12 inches on a side, or a round pizza with a 12-inch diameter for the same price. Which is the better buy? Explain your answer.

Discussion   The area of a square pizza with a 12-inch side is 12×12, or 144 square inches. The area of a round pizza with a 12-inch diameter (a 6-inch radius) is 113 square inches. The square pizza is the better buy.

A drawing will reveal that the circle can be inscribed inside the square. The square is larger by the "corners."

PROBLEM 6   (Reproduction Page 141)

Farmer McDonald rotates his herd of cattle weekly, by allowing them to graze in each of three pastures, as shown in the diagram. In order to be most economical, he uses his knowledge of mathematics to design three gates, such that when two of them are swung together, they completely close the entrance to one of the pastures with no overlap. How long is each gate if Farmer McDonald used whole number lengths?

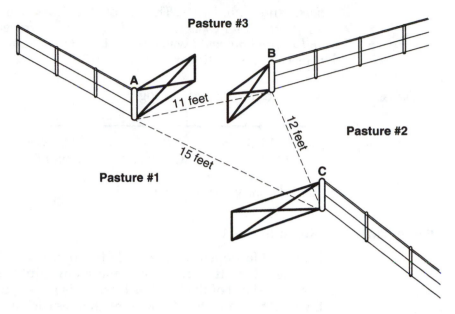

Discussion   The guess and test technique can be used. You know that Gate A + Gate B = 11, Gate B + Gate C = 12, and Gate C + Gate A = 15.

Guess Gate A = 5:
$$A = 5 \Rightarrow B = 6 \Rightarrow C = 6. \quad \text{But } A + C \neq 11$$
Guess Gate A = 6:
$$A = 6 \Rightarrow B = 5 \Rightarrow C = 7. \quad \text{But } A + C \neq 13$$
Guess Gate A = 7:
$$A = 7 \Rightarrow B = 4 \Rightarrow C = 8. \quad A + C = 15.$$

Thus, Gate A is 7 feet long, Gate B is 4 feet long, and Gate C is 8 feet long.

An alternate method uses the simultaneous solution of three equations in three unknowns:

$$A + B = 11$$
$$B + C = 12$$
$$C + A = 15$$

Using the first two equations,

$$C - A = 1$$
$$C + A = 15$$
$$2C = 16$$
$$C = 8$$
$$B = 4$$
$$A = 7$$

PROBLEM 7   (Reproduction Page 142)

Richard Rodgers and Oscar Hammerstein wrote four smash musical hits in a short period of time. The four musicals were *Carousel, The King and I, Okla-*

homa, and *South Pacific.* They wrote the first one in 1943. *Carousel* was written 2 years after *Oklahoma. South Pacific* was written 2 years before *The King and I.* The *King and I* was written last, 8 years after *Oklahoma.* Which of the musicals was written in the year 1949?

Discussion   Make a time line and use logic.

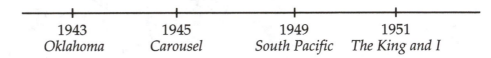

1943	1945	1949	1951
Oklahoma	*Carousel*	*South Pacific*	*The King and I*

South Pacific was written in 1949.

PROBLEM 8   (Reproduction Page 142)

Ruth and Jeanette are taking Gladys to lunch for her birthday. At the last minute, Harriett decides to come along. Ruth and Jeanette are paying Gladys's share of the bill, but Harriett is paying only for her own share. If the total bill came to $72, how much does each girl pay?

Discussion   The total bill was $72. Therefore, each individual share was $18.00 (72 ÷ 4). Ruth and Jeanette are paying three of the shares, or $54.00. Or, Ruth and Jeanette are paying for ³/₄ of the bill, or $54.00. Ruth will pay $27.00, Jeanette will pay $27.00, and Harriett will pay $18.00.

PROBLEM 9   (Reproduction Page 143)

A couple wanted to buy a piece of land on which to build their home. They saw an ad in a local newspaper offering a plot of land with an excellent location. The asking price was $50 per square foot. The couple requested a drawing of the plot of land and were given the following sketch:

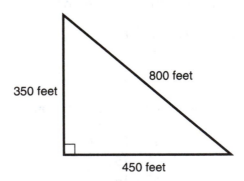

How much should they pay for the land?

Discussion   Since 350' + 450' = 800', this plot of land cannot exist. There is no area and therefore no cost!

PROBLEM 10   (Reproduction Page 143)

A square mile of land has become contaminated. The Environmental Protection Agency has regulated that no one can live within one mile of any point in the contaminated area. Find the area of the uninhabitable land.

Discussion   Draw a diagram and calculate the required area.

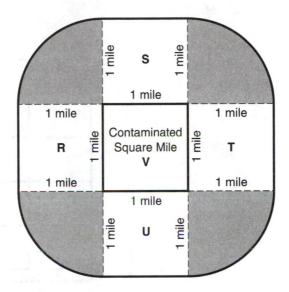

The area under restriction consists of the original square, (square V), four unit squares (squares R, S, T, and U)., plus four shaded quarter-circles with $r = 1$. Thus, the required area = $5 + \pi$ square feet.

PROBLEM 11   (Reproduction Page 144)

The students in the Douglass School have left for their annual school trip. One-third of the students went to Washington, D.C. One-third of them went to Annapolis. One-fourth of them went to Williamsburg, and the remaining 100 students went to Monticello. How many students are in the class? How many went to each place?

Discussion   Adding the given fractions ($1/3 + 1/3 + 1/4$) yields $11/12$. Thus, the 100 students who went to Monticello represent the remaining $1/12$. There were 1,200 students in all; 400 of them went to Washington, D.C.; 400 went to Annapolis; 300 went to Williamsburg; 100 went to Monticello.

PROBLEM 12   (Reproduction Page 144)

On the quiz show "How Much Do You Really Know?" each question is worth four times as much as the previous question. The fourth question is worth $1,600. How much was the first question worth?

Discussion   Work backwards. If the fourth question was worth $1,600, the third was worth $400, the second was worth $100, and the first was worth $25.

PROBLEM 13   (Reproduction Page 145)

Lucille makes copper bracelets to sell at the local crafts show. Each bracelet requires a rectangular strip of hammered copper that is 5" × 7". She buys copper in rectangular sheets that measure 21" × 24". What is the maximum number of bracelets she can get from a single sheet of copper?

Discussion   Use manipulatives or make a drawing. She can cut 14 bracelets from each sheet.

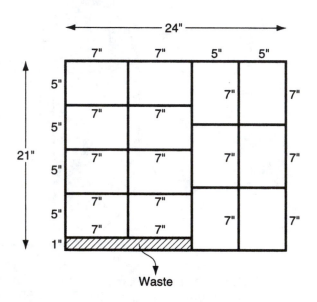

PROBLEM 14   (Reproduction Page 145)

Maxine paid her restaurant check of $3.00 by using the same number of half-dollars and quarters. How many of each did she use?

Discussion   Use guess and test. Maxine paid with four quarters and four half-dollars. Notice that an algebraic equation yields the same results:

$$.25x + .50x = 3.00$$

PROBLEM 15   (Reproduction Page 146)

Jenny has a nickel-box with 40 nickels in it, and a penny-box with 50 pennies in it. Her younger brother took 10 coins from the nickel-box, put them into the pennybox, and mixed them all up. Then he took 10 coins from the penny-box, put them into the nickel-box, and mixed them all up. Are there more pennies in the nickelbox, or more nickels in the penny-box?

Discussion   Have the students actually perform the experiment. Have them work in pairs and follow the action as described in the problem. Use different colored tokens or chips to represent the pennies and the nickels. Perform the experiment several times until the students realize that the same number of "wrong" coins is in each box. Logically, since each box ends up with the same number of coins as in the beginning, each nickel in the penny-box must have been replaced by a penny in the nickel-box.

PROBLEM 16   (Reproduction Page 146)

Laura and Bernadette each bought the same number of computer disks at a closeout sale. The drawing shown below shows how many each bought. Each box contains the same number of disks. How many disks are in each box?

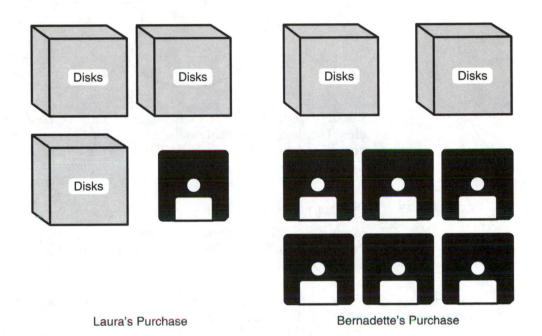

Laura's Purchase   Bernadette's Purchase

Discussion   Use manipulatives or guess and test. The problem can also be solved with an elementary algebraic equation:

$$3B + 1 = 2B + 6$$
$$B = 5$$

There are 5 disks in each box.

PROBLEM 17   (Reproduction Page 147)

There are 23 students in the school orchestra. There are 25 students in the school band. Seven of these students are in both. How many students are there altogether?

Discussion   Use Euler circles (a Venn diagram) to solve this problem.

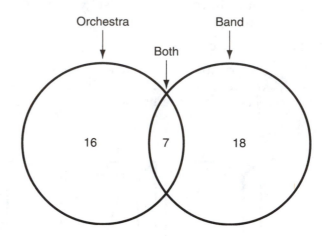

Begin by putting the 7 students in the "Both" or common region of the circles. This leaves 16 additional students for the region marked "Orchestra" and 18 for the region marked "Band." Thus, there are 16 + 7 + 18 = 41 students altogether.

PROBLEM 18   (Reproduction Page 147)

Jaime opened his mathematics textbook and multiplied the two page numbers that were facing him. Their product was 1,806. To what pages was the book opened?

Discussion   Use a calculator and take the square root of 1,806, which is 42.497. Try 42 and 43 as the page numbers. Another way to reason the problem is to note that $40^2 = 1,600$ and $50^2 = 2,500$. The answer lies between 40 and 50. Since 1,806 ends in a "6," the page numbers must be 42 and 43, or 47 and 48. But the even-numbered page is on the left side. Thus, 47 and 48 cannot be facing pages. The answer must be 42 and 43.

PROBLEM 19   (Reproduction Page 148)

The arithmetic mean of George's 10 tests was 87. His teacher decided to discard the best and worst grades, a 95 and a 55. What was George's new arithmetic mean?

Discussion   If the arithmetic mean for 10 tests is 87, then the sum of the 10 grades would be 10 × 87 = 870. If you discard 95 and 55, the remaining sum for 8 tests would be 720. George's new average is 90.

PROBLEM 20   (Reproduction Page 148)

A dartboard has sections labeled 2, 3, 5, 11, and 13. Patti scored exactly 150. What is the minimum number of darts she might have thrown?

Discussion Since you want to use a minimum number of darts, you must examine the higher numbers first. Use guess and test with a table.

13	11	5	3	2	No. Darts	Total Score	
12					12	156	(too large)
11		1		1	13	150	
10		4			14	150	
9	3				12	150	
8	4			1	13	150	

The answer is 12 darts.

PROBLEM 21 (Reproduction Page 149)

Jones High School is constructing a circular ice-skating rink. It wants to design the rink so that 15 trips around the outside rail will equal 1 mile. To the nearest foot, what should be the radius of the rink?

Discussion There are 15 trips around the outside rail in one mile, or $5,280 \div 15 = 352$ feet for the circumference of the rink (around the outside rail once). Thus,

$$2\pi r = 352$$
$$\pi r = 176$$
$$r = 56 \text{ feet}$$

PROBLEM 22 (Reproduction Page 149)

An automobile driveway is 54 feet long by 8 feet wide. It is to be covered with blacktop. If 3 loads of blacktop are available for the job, how deep a layer of blacktop is possible? (One load = 2 cubic yards.)

Discussion The area of the driveway is 54 feet × 8 feet, or 432 square feet. Six cubic yards (3 × 3 × 3) equals 162 cubic feet.

$$432h = 162$$
$$h = .375, \text{ or } 4\tfrac{1}{2} \text{ inches}$$

PROBLEM 23 (Reproduction Page 150)

A man spent $\frac{1}{3}$ of his money and then lost $\frac{2}{3}$ of the remainder. He was left with $12.00. How much did he start with?

Discussion Work backwards. Since the man spent $\frac{1}{3}$, he had $\frac{2}{3}$ left. He lost $\frac{2}{3}$ of that $\frac{2}{3}$, or $\frac{4}{9}$. Therefore, the $\frac{2}{9}$ left ($\frac{1}{3} + \frac{4}{9} = \frac{7}{9}$) equals $12.00. He started with $54.00.

PROBLEM 24   (Reproduction Page 150)

Kevin can mow a square lawn that is 30 yards on each side in 45 minutes. At the same rate, how long will it take him to mow a square lawn that is 60 yards on a side?

Discussion   Calculate the area of each of the lawns. Then use ratio and proportion. The areas are 30 × 30, or 900 square yards, and 60 × 60, or 3,600 square yards. The proportion is

$$\frac{900}{45} = \frac{3600}{x}$$

$$x = 180$$

It will take Kevin 3 hours.

PROBLEM 25   (Reproduction Page 151)

Find all triangles with integral lengths for sides and whose perimeter is 12 inches.

Discussion   Prepare an organized list of all number triples whose sum is 12 and which consists of only whole numbers.

A	1	1	1	1	1	2	2	2	2	3	3	4
B	1	2	3	4	5	2	3	4	5	3	4	4
C	10	9	8	7	6	8	7	6	5	6	5	4

Remember that in a triangle, the sum of two sides must be greater than the third side. Thus, there are only two such triangles—namely, 3-4-5 and 4-4-4.

PROBLEM 26   (Reproduction Page 151)

About how many feet of audiotape are there in a 90-minute cassette, if the tape moves at a rate of $1\frac{7}{8}$ inches per second?

Discussion   A 90-minute cassette is really 45 minutes on a side. Since it moves at $1\frac{7}{8}$ inches per second, 45 minutes = 45 × 60 = 2700 seconds. Then, 2700 × 1.875 = 5,062.5 inches, or approximately 421.875 feet of tape. (You should discuss the idea of the tape "leaders" at each end of the tape as well.)

PROBLEM 27   (Reproduction Page 152)

The floor of a storage shed is a rectangle with an area of 99 square feet. The volume of the shed is advertised as 627 cubic feet. Lawrence is six feet, three inches tall. Can Lawrence stand upright in the storage shed?

Discussion The area of the floor is found by multiplying the length times the width ($l \times w$). The volume of the shed is found by multiplying the area times the height ($l \times w \times h$). Thus, divide 627 cubic feet by 99 square feet to find the height of the shed. A calculator shows the height to be 6.3333 feet, which is 6 feet 4 inches tall. Lawrence *can* stand upright in the shed, but just barely.

PROBLEM 28 (Reproduction Page 152)

The new playing field behind the school is in the shape of a rectangle that is 80 yards long and 50 yards wide. On each of the shorter sides, there is a semi-circle whose diameter is the shorter side. Approximately how much will it cost to sod the new field if sod costs $1 per square yard?

Discussion The area under consideration consists of two parts. The rectangle is $50 \times 80 = 4,000$ square yards. The two semi-circles are equivalent to a circle whose area is πr^2 or 625π (approximately 1,963.5 square yards). The total area is 5,963.5, or about 6,000 square yards. The cost will be approximately $6,000.

PROBLEM 29 (Reproduction Page 153)

Janice has an average of 74 on the first three tests in her algebra class. On the final four tests, she scored 92, 90, 94, and 76. What was her average for the entire year?

Discussion Students must remember that the final average must be her *total* score divided by the number of tests taken. The *total* score for the first three tests is 222, (74×3). The total score for all seven tests is 574. Dividing by 7 yields an average of 82.

PROBLEM 30 (Reproduction Page 153)

A bowling ball and a bag together cost $88. The ball costs three times as much as the bag. How much does each cost?

Discussion Use guess and test with a systematic list.

Bag	10	15	20	30	22
Ball	70	55	60	50	66
Ratio	7:1	11:3	3:1	5:3	3:1

An alternate solution would be to use the equation

$$C + 3C = 88$$

PROBLEM 31 (Reproduction Page 154)

A manufacturer of novelty buttons uses square sheets of metal that are 24 inches on each side. The press punches out 144 circular buttons, each with a diameter of 2 inches from a sheet. How much metal is wasted from each sheet?

Discussion   The area of the sheet of metal is 576 square inches (24" × 24"). The total area of the buttons is 144π (144 × πr^2, where $r = 1$), or 452.4 square inches. There are 123.6 square inches of wasted metal.

PROBLEM 32   (Reproduction Page 154)

In the old west, Eric and his gang stole a wagon full of gunpowder from Fort Laramie at 9:00 P.M. one night. They drove off at the rate of 16 miles per hour, across the plains, and stopped after 2 hours to rest the horses. Unfortunately for them, one of the powder kegs had a hole and left a trail of gunpowder all the way back to the fort along their path. An hour after they stole the wagon, a soldier discovered the trail and set it on fire. If the fire travels at the same rate of 16 miles per hour, at what time was Eric jolted?

Discussion   Eric and his gang traveled for 2 hours, or 32 miles when they stopped at 11:00 P.M. The soldier lit the gunpowder trail at 10:00 P.M. It also took 2 hours to reach the wagon 32 miles away. Thus, Eric was jolted at midnight.

PROBLEM 33   (Reproduction Page 155)

A recycling plant was packaging aluminum cans in containers. They packed five containers and weighed them in pairs. The weights were 110, 112, 113, 114, 115, 116, 117, 118, 120, and 121 pounds. What were the weights of the individual containers?

Discussion   First, find the average weight of a single container. There are 10 weighings of 2 containers each; thus, you divide the sum of all the weights by 20 (1156 ÷ 20 = 58). Use the guess and test technique.

> (a) 54 and 56   yields 110
> (b) Add 58
>
> $\quad\quad$ 54 + 58 = 112
> $\quad\quad$ 56 + 58 = 114
>
> (c) Add 59   54 + 59 = 113
> $\quad\quad$ 56 + 59 = 115
> $\quad\quad$ 58 + 59 = 117

(Notice that 57 is omitted, since 54 + 57 = 111, which is a duplicate.)

> (d) Add 62   54 + 62 = 116
> $\quad\quad$ 56 + 62 = 118
> $\quad\quad$ 58 + 62 = 120
> $\quad\quad$ 59 + 62 = 121

Thus, the five containers weighed 54, 56, 58, 59, and 62 pounds. Notice that again several choices (i.e., 60 and 61) are omitted, since these yield duplicate weights.

PROBLEM 34   (Reproduction Page 155)

After the first 57 games of the basketball season, the Supersonics have a winning percent of .561 and the Jazz have a winning percent of .491. How many games behind the Supersonics are the Jazz?

Discussion   The Supersonics have a winning percent of .561. Thus, they won 32 games. The Jazz won 28 games. The Jazz are 4 games behind the Supersonics.

PROBLEM 35   (Reproduction Page 156)

Ann is the weakest foul shooter on the girls' basketball team. Out of her first 30 foul shots, she made only 50 percent. Her coach had her go through several practice sessions. She raised her season's average to 60 percent after 20 more foul shots in the next three games. How many of these 20 foul shots did she make?

Discussion   Of the first 30 shots, Ann made 50 percent, or 15 shots. Since her percent moves up to 60 percent out of 50 shots (30 + 20), she must have made a total of 30 foul shots altogether. Thus, she scored 15 of that next 20. Note that the "next three games" is excess information.

PROBLEM 36   (Reproduction Page 156)

Bikeport uses license plates for its motorcycles. Each license plate consists of one vowel followed by one digit. There are 5 possible vowels and 10 possible digits. Since the zero and capital O look the same, they cannot be used together. How many different license plates are possible?

Discussion   Five vowels followed by 10 digits yields 50 possible license plates. However, O0 must be excluded. Thus, there are 49 possible license plates.

PROBLEM 37   (Reproduction Page 157)

Michelle has 72 baseball cards. She gave 2-for-1 in five trades, and received 3-for-1 in three trades. How many cards does she now have?

Discussion   She begins with 72. Giving 2-for-1 in five trades yields a –5, or 67 cards. Receiving 3-for-1 in three trades yields a +6. Her total is now 73 cards.

PROBLEM 38   (Reproduction Page 157)

The Stewarts are buying cups and plates for the annual family picnic. Cups come in packages of 54, whereas plates come in packages of 42. How many packages of each must the Stewarts buy to have the same number of cups and plates?

Discussion   Make a table.
The Stewarts must buy 7 packs of cups (7 × 54 = 378) and 9 packs of plates (9 × 42 = 378). Notice that you may approach 54 as 9 × 6 and 42 as 7 × 6. Thus, 9 packages of plates and 7 packages of cups are needed.

Number of Packs	1	2	3	4	5	6	7	8	9
Cups	54	108	162	216	270	324	(378)	432	
Plates	42	84	126	168	210	252	294	336	(378)

PROBLEM 39

(Reproduction Page 158)

In order to win a prize in the state lottery, a person must select the correct three-digit number. Jane chose 345. What is the probability that she will win? Someone told her to "box" the number to have a better chance of winning. ("Box" the number means the digits can occur in any order, such as 354, 534, 453, etc.) What would be the probability of Jane winning if she did "box" her numbers?

Discussion

There are 10 possible choices for each number (0–9). Thus, the probability of Jane winning with 345 is $1/10 \times 1/10 \times 1/10$, or 1 out of 1,000. If Jane boxes the numbers, there would be 6 possible arrangements. Her probability of winning is 6 out of 1,000.

PROBLEM 40

(Reproduction Page 158)

The players on the Hawks hockey team wear the numbers from 1 through 18 on the backs of their jerseys. On opening night, as the players were being introduced, Maura noticed that the players were standing in nine pairs. She also noticed that the sum of the numbers on the jerseys of each pair was a perfect square. The goalie wore number 1. With what numbered player was he paired?

Discussion

Use Guess and Test with reasoning. Since the goalie wore number 1, his partner must wear number 3, number 8, or number 15. However, the player who wears number 18 has only a single option: His partner must be wearing number 7. Similarly, number 17 is paired with number 8, and number 16 is paired with number 9. Through guess and test, you arrive at the following pairings:

    18 is paired with 7   13 is paired with 3
    17 is paired with 8   12 is paired with 4
    16 is paired with 9   11 is paired with 5
    15 is paired with 1   10 is paired with 6
    14 is paired with 2

The goalie, wearing number 1, must be paired with the player wearing number 15.

PROBLEM 41

(Reproduction Page 159)

The coach of the tennis team was having problems selecting his team. He had to choose four players, two men and two women, from the six who had tried out. Personal feelings were making it difficult for him.

1. Paul said, "I'll play only if Sarah plays."
2. Sarah said, "I won't play if Eric is on the team."
3. Eric said, "I won't play if David or Linda is chosen."
4. David said, "I'll play only if Amy plays."
5. Amy had no likes nor dislikes.

Who will the coach select?

Discussion   Clue (1) says that Paul and Sarah must be together. Clue (4) says David and Amy must be together. If Eric is chosen (clues 2 and 3), three people must be eliminated: David, Linda, and Sarah. Thus, Eric cannot play. The team is Paul, Sarah, David and Amy.

PROBLEM 42   (Reproduction Page 159)

In the Appalachian Hockey League, a team gets 2 points for a win, 1 point for a tie, and 0 points for a loss. In the five-team Northern Division, each team played each of the other teams twice. The computer failed to print part of the league standings. Complete the table.

Teams	Games				Points			Standings
	Played	*Won*	*Lost*	*Tied*	*Win*	*Tie*	*Total*	
Suns	8	4	3	1	8	1	9	
Devils	8		2	1				
Mountaineers	8	4			8			2
Sharks	8	2					6	
Panthers	8	2						

Discussion   There are a total of 20 games, yielding 40 points. This, along with the fact that the number of wins and losses must be equal, enables a logical completion of the table.

Teams	Games				Points			Standings
	Played	*Won*	*Lost*	*Tied*	*Win*	*Tie*	*Total*	
Suns	8	4	3	1	8	1	9	3rd
Devils	8	5	2	1	10	1	11	1st
Mountaineers	8	4	2	2	8	2	10	2nd
Sharks	8	2	3	2	4	2	6	4th
Panthers	8	2	6	0	4	0	4	5th

PROBLEM 43   (Reproduction Page 160)

There are 55 containers of milk in the school refrigerator. Some are chocolate milk and some are white milk. If you select any 2 containers without looking at them, at least 1 of them will be chocolate milk. How many of each kind of milk are there in the refrigerator?

Discussion   Since one of the containers *must* be chocolate, there cannot be two containers of white milk. Thus, there are 54 containers of chocolate milk and 1 container of white milk.

PROBLEM 44   (Reproduction Page 160)

The Acme Tinplate Corporation has been asked to manufacture one million cans for a new product about to go to market. Each can is to be cylindrical, with a radius of 3 inches and a height of 6 inches. How many square feet of tinplate are used in making the cans?

Discussion   Make a drawing. The top and bottom of the cans are each circles with a radius of 3 inches. Thus, the area of the top and bottom of each can is $A = 2 \cdot \pi \cdot 9$, or 18π square inches. The body of the can is really a rectangle, whose base is the circumference of the bottom and whose height is 6 inches. The area of this part is $A = 2 \cdot \pi \cdot r \cdot h = 2 \cdot \pi \cdot 9 \cdot 6$, or 108π square inches. Each can has a surface area of 126π square inches. For 1,000,000 cans, the company needs $1,000,000 \times 26\pi = 26,000,000\pi$ square inches, or 395,840,674.4 square inches of tinplate.

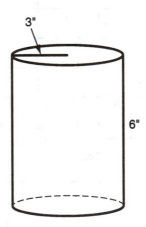

PROBLEM 45   (Reproduction Page 161)

The bow and arrow target shown here has a 4-foot radius. Each ring is 6 inches wide, and the bull's eye is 1 foot across. Johanna fired an arrow that stuck in the target. What is the probability that it landed in the "200" region?

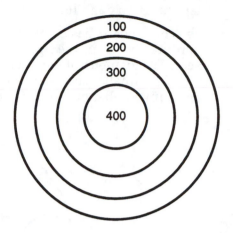

Discussion   The total area of the target is 4π feet. To find the area of the 200-ring, take the complete area through the 200-circle and subtract the area through the 300 circle:

$$\pi(1.5)^2 - \pi(1)^2$$
$$= 2.25\pi - \pi$$
$$= 1.25\pi$$

Thus, the probability would be $\dfrac{1.25\pi}{4\pi}$, or 1.25/4 which equals .3125.

PROBLEM 46   (Reproduction Page 161)

Mike, Ray, and Lucy went into the record store for the big "Dollars Only Sale." Mike bought 2 CDs and 1 cassette for $16. Ray bought 1 CD and 2 cassettes for $11. Lucy bought 1 CD and 1 cassette. How much did she pay?

Discussion   This problem may be represented in a pair of "equations":

2 CD + 1 cassette   = $16
1 CD + 2 cassettes   = $11

Adding:

3 CDs + 3 cassettes   = $27

Dividing by 3:

1 CD + 1 cassette   = $9

Lucy paid $9 for her purchase. Notice that you have *not* found the individual price for 1 CD or 1 cassette. An alternate solution would be to use guess and test to find the price of 1 CD ($7) and 1 cassette ($2).

PROBLEM 47   (Reproduction Page 162)

The school board has commissioned a local artist to create the five-circle sculpture shown in the figure. The centers of the five circles are all collinear. The diameter of the larger circle is 12 feet, and the diameters of each of the four smaller circles are equal. Tubing is sold by the foot. What is the minimum number of feet of tubing required to make the sculpture?

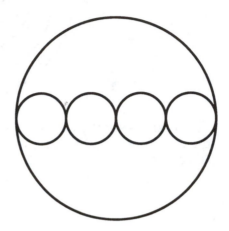

Discussion   The large outer circle will require 12π feet of the aluminum tubing. Each of the smaller circles will require ¼ as much, or 3π feet. The total needed will be 24π feet, or 75.36 feet. The sculpture will require 76 feet of tubing. (It is interesting to note that regardless of the number of small circles or the size of their diameters, the total circumference of the small circles will always equal the circumference of the larger circle.)

PROBLEM 48   (Reproduction Page 162)

Jennifer's mother is in Paris; Jennifer lives in Los Angeles. When it is 11:00 A.M. in New York, it is 5:00 P.M. in Paris. Jennifer wants to call her mother from Los Angeles at 1:00 P.M., Paris time. At what time in Los Angeles should she place her call?

Discussion   When it is 11:00 A.M. in New York, it is 8:00 A.M. in Los Angeles. Thus, there is a 9-hour time difference between Los Angeles and Paris. Jennifer should place her call at 4:00 A.M., Los Angeles time.

PROBLEM 49   (Reproduction Page 163)

The distance between Exit 1 and Exit 20 on the turnpike is 130 miles. If any two exits must be at least 6 miles apart, what is the largest number of miles between any two consecutive exits?

Discussion   The minimum distance between any two exits is 6 miles. There are 19 such "distances" between exits 1 and 20. If 18 exits were exactly 6 miles apart, that would be 18 × 6 = 108 miles. This would leave 130 − 108 = 22 miles as the maximum distance between two consecutive exits.

PROBLEM 50   (Reproduction Page 163)

Sarah, Amanda, and Ian took a true-false test last week. The test had three questions. Only one of their test papers had all three questions answered correctly; the other two papers each had two correct answers and one incorrect answer. Who had all three questions answered correctly?

Sarah	Amanda	Ian
1. True	1. False	1. False
2. True	2. False	2. True
3. False	3. False	3. False

Discussion   Ian had the perfect paper. If it had been Sarah who had the answers all correct, Amanda would have both numbers 1 and 2 wrong. If it had been Amanda who had all three correct, then Sarah would have had numbers 1 and 2 incorrect. If Ian's paper has all three correct, then Sarah has only number 1 incorrect and Amanda has only number 2 incorrect.

PROBLEM 51   (Reproduction Page 164)

The Great Western Limited express train is exactly one kilometer long and is traveling at 80 kilometers per hour. It passes through a tunnel that is 7 kilometers long. How long will it take the train to pass completely through the tunnel?

Discussion   Since the train itself is 1 kilometer long, the engine will travel 8 kilometers (7 + 1) before the entire train passes through the tunnel. This will take $^8/_{80}$ or $^1/_{10}$ of an hour, which is 6 minutes. (A drawing might be helpful in the analysis.)

PROBLEM 52   (Reproduction Page 164)

A garden is laid out in the shape as shown in the drawing here. Only the shaded isosceles, right triangles are to be used for planting vegetables. The unshaded portion is to be filled in with stones to make paths. What is the total area that is to be used for planting? What is the total area of the paths?

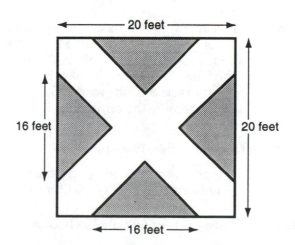

Discussion   The four shaded, right, isosceles triangles can be put together to form a smaller square with sides 16 feet, and whose area is 256 square feet. Thus, the area for the paths will be the area of the larger square minus the area of the smaller one, or $400 - 256 = 144$ square feet of path.

PROBLEM 53   (Reproduction Page 165)

A new airline is beginning flights next week. In the preliminary instructions, all flight attendants are told that they must wear a different outfit every day. Maria is one of the new flight attendants. She has three times as many blouses as pairs of slacks, and twice as many colorful scarves as blouses. How many blouses, scarves, and pairs of slacks must Maria own in order to be able to wear a different outfit every day for at least three years?

Discussion   Write an equation/inequality. Let the number of pairs of slacks $= N$, the number of blouses $= 3N$, and the number of scarves $= 6N$. Then,

$$(6N)(3N)(n) \geq 365 \times 3$$
$$18N^3 \geq 1095$$
$$N^3 \geq 60.8$$
$$N \geq 4$$
$$3N \geq 12$$
$$6N \geq 24$$

Maria must have four pairs of slacks, 12 blouses and 24 scarves.

PROBLEM 54   (Reproduction Page 165)

Amy and Nancy bought three sets of golf clubs at the Golfland going-out-of-business sale. All three sets of clubs are of equal value. They paid $1,680 in all. Nancy paid $900 and Amy paid $780. They took the clubs to an auction for resale. One set was sold for $1,680. At the end of the auction, Amy decided to take the remaining two sets for herself. How should they divide the cash equitably?

Discussion   Each set of golf clubs cost Amy and Nancy $560. Thus, they have two sets of clubs worth $1,120 and $1,680 in cash, for a total value of $2,800. Amy should take 780/1680, or 13/28, and Nancy should take 900/1680, or 15/28, of the $2,800. Amy's share is $1,300; Nancy's share is $1,500. Since Amy took two sets of clubs worth $1,120, she should only get $180 in cash. Nancy should receive the remaining $1,500.

PROBLEM 55   (Reproduction Page 166)

Two people were sitting on a blanket on the beach. One of the two is male. What is the probability that they are both male?

Discussion   There are four equally likely combinations:

M-M   M-F   F-M   F-F

(This last case is impossible, since we already know that one is a male.) There is a probability of ⅓ that both are male.

PROBLEM 56 (Reproduction Page 166)

A rectangular barn measures 50 feet by 100 feet. At one corner, a horse is tethered with a 28-foot rope, as shown in the figure. On how many square feet of grass is the horse able to graze? What if the dimensions of the barn were 60 feet by 150 feet?

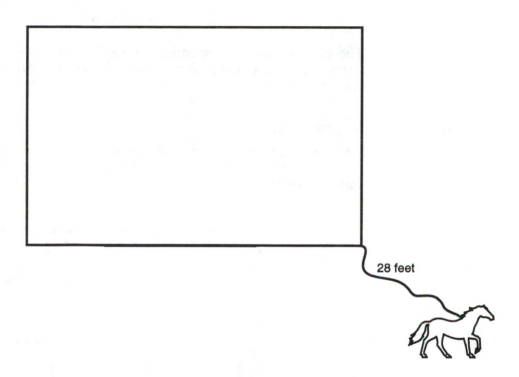

28 feet

Discussion The figure reveals that the area over which the horse can graze is ¾ of a circle with a radius of 28 feet.

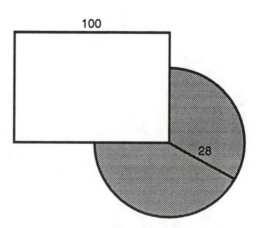

$$A = \frac{3}{4}\pi\,r^2$$

$$A = \frac{3}{4}\pi\,28^2$$

$$A = \frac{3}{4}\pi\,784$$

$$A = 1848 \text{ feet}$$

The grazing area is independent of the dimensions of the barn as long as the barn is rectangular in shape and its dimensions exceed the length of the rope.

PROBLEM 57   (Reproduction Page 167)

The diagram shows the ground plan of a business mall. If the excavation for its foundation is to be 18 feet in depth, how many cubic yards of soil must be removed?

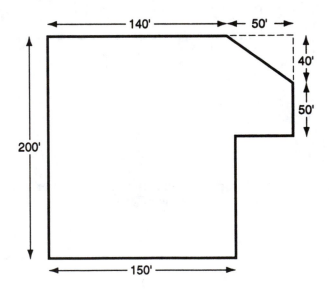

Discussion   Divide and conquer. Find the areas as shown.

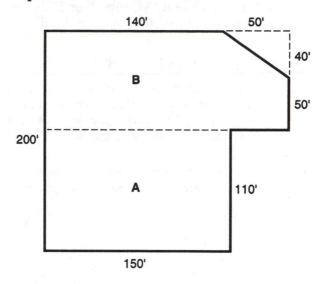

Section A   = 110' × 150' = 16,500 square feet

Section B   = $(90' \times 190') - \frac{1}{2}(40' \times 50')$

               = 17,100 − 1,000 = 16,100 square feet.

Total Area = 16,100 + 16,500 = 32,600 square feet

Volume   = 32,600 × 18' = 586,800 cubic feet

But, since 27 cubic feet = 1 cubic yard,

Volume   = 21,753.53 cubic yards

PROBLEM 58   (Reproduction Page 167)

A multiple-choice test contains 40 items. A correct response earns 5 points, but 2 points are deducted for every incorrect response. Nothing is given nor deducted if the question is unanswered. Michelle scored 96. How might she have done this?

Discussion   Algebra will lead to one equation in 2 variables:

$$5(C) - 2(W) + 0(40 - C - W) = 96$$
$$5C - 2W = 96$$

Now use guess and test with a table.

Correct (× 5)	Incorrect (× –2)	Unanswered
20 (100)	2 (–4)	18
22 (110)	7 (–14)	11
24 (120)	12 (–24)	4

These are the only three possible ways to score 96. Michelle had 20 correct, 2 incorrect, and 18 omitted; or 22 correct, 7 incorrect, and 11 omitted; or 24 correct, 12 incorrect, and 4 omitted.

PROBLEM 59   (Reproduction Page 168)

A municipality is replacing its water supply lines. The current system uses two identical pipes that have circular cross-sections, each with a diameter of one foot. The town decides to use a single replacement pipe with the same capacity. What is the diameter of the new pipe?

Discussion   The cross-sectional area of the new pipe must equal the sum of the cross-sectional areas of the two older pipes.

$$A = \pi(r_1)^2 + \pi(r_2)^2$$
$$= 36\pi + 36\pi$$
$$= 72\pi$$
$$72\pi = \pi R^2$$
$$72 = R^2$$
$$R = \sqrt{72} = 6\sqrt{2}$$

The diameter of the new pipe will be $12\sqrt{2}$, or about 16.97 inches.

PROBLEM 60   (Reproduction Page 168)

David and Mike went fishing. David brought 5 hoagies and Mike brought 3 hoagies. As they were getting ready to eat, their friend, Jerry, joined them. However, Jerry did not bring any hoagies with him. After lunch, during which the three men shared the 8 hoagies equally, Jerry put down 8 coins of equal value to pay for his share of the lunch. How should David and Mike share the 8 coins?

Discussion   To share 8 hoagies among 3 people, divide each hoagie into 3 equal parts, or 24 parts in all. Each of the three men ate $1/3$ of the total, or 8 pieces. David contributed 15 pieces, whereas Mike contributed 9 pieces. Mike gave 1 piece to Jerry, and David gave 7 pieces to Jerry. Therefore, David should take 7 coins and Mike should take 1.

PROBLEM 61   (Reproduction Page 169)

In our school's parking lot one morning, Janice noticed that all but three of the cars parked were made by General Motors, all but three of the cars were made by Chrysler, all but three of them were made by Ford, and all but three of of them were made by Toyota. What is the minimum number of cars parked in the school parking lot?

Discussion   Use logic. There are a minimum of 4 cars in the lot, one by each of the four manufacturers named in the problem.

PROBLEM 62   (Reproduction Page 169)

Imagine a wire band fitted snugly around the earth at the equator. If you cut the band, add a piece exactly 10 feet long, reform the band, and then hold it in a position concentric to the equator, which of the following best describes the space between the earth's surface and the wire band?

    1. You can just crawl under the band.
    2. You can just slide a piece of paper under the band.
    3. You can walk upright under the band.

Discussion   Make a drawing.

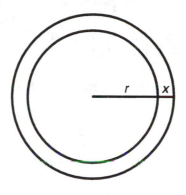

$$C + 10 = 2\pi\,(r + x)$$
$$C + 10 = 2\pi r + 2\pi\,x$$
$$10 = 2\pi\,x$$
$$5/\pi = x$$
$$1.59 = x$$

The answer is item 2: You can just slide a piece of paper under the band.

PROBLEM 63   (Reproduction Page 170)

Two coins, both silver dubloons, are melted down and recast as a single coin of the same thickness. How does the diameter of the new coin compare with the diameter of one of the original coins?

Discussion   The volume of each of the original coins is given by the formula $V = \pi r^2 h$; the volume of the new coin is $V = \pi R^2 h$. Thus, $\pi r^2 h + \pi r^2 h = \pi R^2 h$. Since the thickness is the same in all cases,

$$2r^2 = R^2$$
$$r\,\sqrt{2} = R$$
$$d\,\sqrt{2} = D$$

The diameter of the new coin is $\sqrt{2}$ times that of the original coins.

PROBLEM 64   (Reproduction Page 170)

A group of gymnasts are putting mats on the floor of the gymnasium prior to their exhibition. The room measures 30 feet by 44 feet. They have nine mats that measure 10 feet by 12 feet, and one mat that measures 8 feet by 30 feet. Show how the mats are placed in the room to cover the floor.

Discussion   Make a drawing. Place the 30-foot by 8-foot mat along the 30-foot edge. This leaves 30 feet by 36 feet to cover. The nine mats can be positioned in a 3 × 3 array to fill the room.

PROBLEM 65   (Reproduction Page 171)

A group of people want to rent a house in Aspen, Colorado, to go skiing. For one week, each person will have to chip in $70. If the group can convince three more people to come along, the cost per person will drop by $14. What was the week's rental?

Discussion   Try various multiples of $70. Use guess and test or write an equation.

$$x = \text{the number of original people}$$
$$70 \cdot x = \text{total rental (original)}$$
$$(x + 3)(56) = \text{total rental (new)}$$
$$(x + 3)(56) = 70x$$
$$56x + 168 = 70x$$
$$168 = 14x$$
$$12 = x$$

There were 12 people in the original group, and the weekly rental was $840.

PROBLEM 66   (Reproduction Page 171)

Mrs. Ross has 55 percent of the senior class students in her Advanced Physics class. Mr. Luellan has 35 percent of the senior class in his Calculus class. 10 percent of the senior class is taking both classes. What percent of the senior class is taking neither of these classes?

Discussion   Draw Euler circles as shown here.

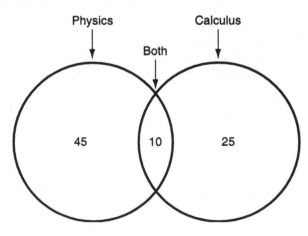

There are 80 percent in one and/or both classes, leaving 20 percent of the senior class who are in neither.

PROBLEM 67 (Reproduction Page 172)

Joe, a professional basketball player, is an 80 percent foul shooter. He is fouled at the final buzzer, and goes to the foul line for two shots. His team is trailing by one point. What is the probability that Joe's team will:

1. Win in regulation time?
2. Lose in regulation time?
3. Go into overtime?

Discussion Set up all three possible situations.

1. Win in regulation time:
    Make – Make = .8 × .8 = .64
2. Lose in regulation time:
    Miss – Miss = .2 × .2 = .04
3. Go into overtime:
    Miss – Make = .2 × .8 = .16
    Make – Miss = .8 × .2 = .16

Those students who are more knowledgable about basketball may consider the situation that occurs in college basketball. That is, the foul situation might be a one-and-one. This means that, in order to be given a second foul shot, Joe must make the first one.

PROBLEM 68 (Reproduction Page 172)

Two parallel sides of a playground are 264 feet apart and are crossed by two other nonparallel sides. The playground is 300 feet long on one side and 250 feet long on the other. If sod costs 32¢ per-square foot, what is the minimum amount of sod to be bought?

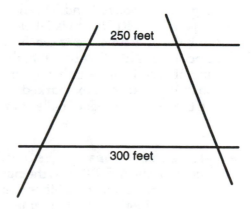

Discussion   Divide the figure up into a rectangle and two right triangles, as shown here.

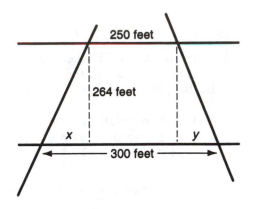

Rectangle = 250 · 264 = 66,000 square feet
Triangle I = $\frac{1}{2}$ (264)(x) = 132x
Triangle II = $\frac{1}{2}$ (264)(y) = 132y
Triangle I + Triangle II = 132 (x + y)
But (x + y) = 300 – 250 = 50

The required area = 66,000 + 132(50)
                  = 66,000 + 6,600
                  = 72,600 square feet of sod
If students know the formula for the area of a trapezoid,

$$A = \frac{1}{2}(h)\,(b + b')$$
$$A = \frac{1}{2}(264)(250 + 300)$$
$$A = 72,600 \text{ square feet}$$

Notice that the price of the sod is extraneous information.

PROBLEM 69   (Reproduction Page 173)

A bag contains 50 red and 50 yellow balls. There are three boxes on a shelf. One is labeled RED; one is labeled YELLOW; and one is labeled MIXED. Two balls at a time are taken from the bag. If both are yellow, they are placed in the YELLOW box; if both are red, they are placed in the RED box. If one of each is picked, they go into the box marked MIXED. What is the probability that the box marked RED and the box marked YELLOW will have the same number of balls after all pairs of balls have been drawn from the bag?

Discussion   Regardless of how many pairs contain one red and one yellow ball, and are therefore in the MIXED box, the number of red balls will equal the number of yellow ones in that box. Since there were an equal number of red and yellow balls to begin with, the remaining number of red balls will equal the remaining number of yellow balls. The probability, therefore, is 1.

Have the students conduct the experiment many times, reducing the number of balls from 50 red and 50 yellow to some smaller number. The experiment will verify that there are always the same number in each of the two boxes.

PROBLEM 70   (Reproduction Page 173)

Newman's Fine Haberdashery store is having its annual spring sale. You can buy suspenders and socks for $18. You can buy socks and a tie for $22. You can buy a tie and cufflinks for $25. You can buy a shirt and a belt for $37. You can buy cufflinks and a shirt for $33. You can buy a belt and socks for $17. How much does each article cost?

Discussion   Algebraically, the problem can be solved with six equations in six variables. However, guess and test with a carefully constructed table is a good alternate approach. The answers are:

1. Belt = $12
2. Cufflinks = $8
3. Shirt = $25
4. Socks = $5
5. Suspenders = $13
6. Tie = $17

PROBLEM 71   (Reproduction Page 174)

Two poles, 60 feet tall and 20 feet tall, stand on opposite sides of a field. The poles are 80 feet apart. Support cables are placed from the top of each pole to the bottom of the opposite pole. How far above the ground is the intersection of the cables? What if the poles were 120 feet apart?

Discussion   A drawing should be made.

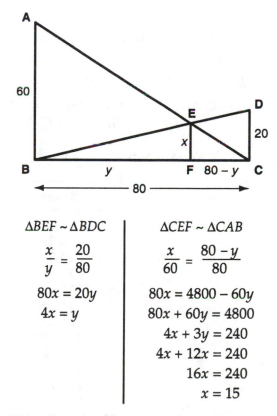

$$\Delta BEF \sim \Delta BDC \qquad\qquad \Delta CEF \sim \Delta CAB$$

$$\frac{x}{y} = \frac{20}{80} \qquad\qquad \frac{x}{60} = \frac{80-y}{80}$$

$$80x = 20y \qquad\qquad 80x = 4800 - 60y$$

$$4x = y \qquad\qquad 80x + 60y = 4800$$

$$4x + 3y = 240$$

$$4x + 12x = 240$$

$$16x = 240$$

$$x = 15$$

The intersection point is 15 feet above the ground. When BC = 120 feet, the height is still 15 feet. In fact, the height is independent of the distance between the poles. We suggest that your more advanced students investigate the proof of this.

It is interesting to note that if a and b represent the heights of the two poles, and x is the height of the intersection point of the cables, then

$$\frac{1}{a} + \frac{1}{b} = \frac{1}{x}$$

PROBLEM 72   (Reproduction Page 174)

In a group of men and women, the average age is 40. The average age of the men is 50 and the average age of the women is 35. What is the ratio of women to men in the group?

Discussion   This problem requires an algebraic solution. Set up an equation as follows:

$$40 = \frac{35w + 50m}{w + m}$$

where w is the number of women and m is the number of men in the group. Now solve for the ratio w/m.

$$40w + 40m = 35w + 50m$$
$$5w = 10m$$
$$\frac{w}{m} = \frac{10}{5}$$

The ratio of women to men is 2:1.

PROBLEM 73   (Reproduction Page 175)

Georgette is writing the page numbers on a handwritten edition of a book that contains 250 pages. How many times will she write the numeral 2?

Discussion   Divide and conquer with a table.

Range	Number of 2s
1–19	2
20–29	11
30–39	7
100–119	2
120–129	11
130–199	7
200–209	11
210–219	11
220–229	21
230–239	11
240–249	11
250	1
	106

There are 106 2s in the book.

PROBLEM 74   (Reproduction Page 175)

On a local TV quiz show, Mr. and Mrs. Halpern are given two red blocks and two blue blocks that they must distribute into two boxes any way they wish. Mrs. Halpern will then be blindfolded and asked to pick one block at random from one of the boxes. If she picks a red block, the Halperns will win $1,000. How should the Halperns distribute the blocks to give Mrs. Halpern the maximum probability of drawing a red block?

Discussion   Examine the three possible situations:

1. If they put two red blocks into one box and two blue blocks into the other, her chances are $\frac{1}{2}$ of drawing the block from the correct box.
2. If they put one red block and one blue block into each box, her chances are $\frac{1}{2}$ regardless of which box she picks.
3. If she puts one red block into box #1 by itself, and puts the other red block and the two blue blocks into box #2, then:

$$P(\text{box \#1} \cdot \text{Red}) + P(\text{box \#2} \cdot \text{Red})$$
$$(\tfrac{1}{2} \times 1) + (\tfrac{1}{2} \times \tfrac{1}{3})$$
$$\tfrac{1}{2} + \tfrac{1}{6} = \tfrac{2}{3}$$

Thus, Mrs. Halgren should put one red block in a box by itself, and the two blue blocks and the remaining red block into the other box.

PROBLEM 75   (Reproduction Page 176)

Mrs. Tanaka makes pins in geometric shapes to give as awards to her students. She takes an 18-inch piece of silver wire, and forms an equilateral triangle as shown in the figure (triangle ABC). Then she takes a piece of gold wire and forms a second equilateral triangle whose vertices are at the trisection points of the sides of the larger triangle (triangle DEF). What is the length of the piece of gold wire?

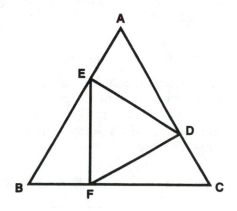

Discussion   The problem can be solved directly by the law of cosines. If you call side EF = x, then

$$x^2 = 4^2 + 2^2 - 2 \cdot 4 \cdot 2 \cos 60°$$
$$x^2 = 16 + 4 - 16 \cdot \tfrac{1}{2}$$
$$x^2 = 20 - 8$$
$$x^2 = 12$$
$$x = \sqrt{12}$$
$$x = 2\sqrt{3}$$

The piece of gold wire is $6\sqrt{3}$ inches long, or approximately 10.4 inches.

Triangle EBF is unique since you were given two sides and the included angle. Thus, triangle EBF is congruent to a 30° – 60° – 90° triangle whose hypotenuse = 4. Thus, you have established that triangle EBF is indeed a 30° – 60° – 90° right triangle; this makes EF = $2\sqrt{3}$.

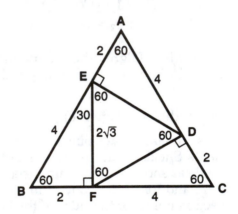

In addition, your students should be able to show that the area of triangle EFD is $\frac{1}{3}$ the area of the original triangle, ABC. This can lead to the same answer.

PROBLEM 76   (Reproduction Page 176)

A sightseeing boat is chartered by a social club at the rate of $10 per person, with a guarantee of 150 people. The boat company agrees to reduce the rate by 5¢ per person for each additional person over the 150 minimum. Find the number of passengers that will yield the boat company the maximum gross income.

Discussion   Use guess and test with a well-organized table.

People	Cost/Person	Total Cost
150	$10.00	$1500.00
170	$ 9.00	$1530.00
173	$ 8.85	$1531.05

(continued)

People	Cost/Person	Total Cost
174	$ 8.80	$1531.20
175	$ 8.75	$1531.25
176	$ 8.70	$1531.20
180	$ 7.50	$1500

At 175 passengers, the boat company will maximize its receipts. More advanced students can develop a function and differentiate for the maximum:

$$I = (150 + n)(10 - .05n)$$

It might be interesting to discuss what would happen if the social club was able to attract 200 additional people.

PROBLEM 77   (Reproduction Page 177)

Bruno and Maria each read ten books over the summer. Beginning in September, Bruno read one new book each month, while Maria read four new books each month. In how many months will Maria have read

1. Twice as many books as Bruno?
2. Three times as many books as Bruno?
3. Four times as many books as Bruno?

Discussion   Make an organized list.

Month	0	1	2	3	4	5	6	7	8	9	10	11	12	...
Bruno	10	11	12	13	14	15	16	17	18	19	20	21	22	...
Maria	10	14	18	22	26	30	34	38	42	46	50	64	58	...

Maria will have read twice as many books at the end of the fifth month; three times as many at the end of the twentieth month. She will *never* have read four times as many books.

As an alternate solution, use an equation.

For part (1): $2(10 + n) = 10 + 4n$
$20 + 2n = 10 + 4n$
$10 = 2n$
$5 = n$

(2): $3(10 + n) = 10 + 4n$
$30 + 3n = 10 + 4n$
$20 = n$

(3): $4(10 + n) = 10 + 4n$
$40 + 4n = 10 + 4n$
$40 = 10$ (never occurs)

PROBLEM 78   (Reproduction Page 177)

A cake in the form of a cube falls into a vat of frosting and comes out frosted on all six faces. The cake is then cut into smaller cubes, each one inch on an edge. The cake is cut so that the number of pieces having frosting on three faces will be one-eighth the number of pieces having no frosting at all. There are to be exactly enough pieces of cake for everyone. How many people will receive a piece of cake with frosting on exactly three faces? On exactly two faces? On exactly one face? On no faces? How large was the original cake?

Discussion   Examine the diagram of the $3 \times 3 \times 3$ cake shown here. You can see that each of the 8 corner pieces will have exactly three faces with frosting. The center piece on each face will have exactly one frosted surface (and there are six of these). The single cube in the exact center of the original cube will have no frosting on any face. There will be exactly 12 small cubes having paint on exactly two faces (the ones numbered 1, 2, 3...) in the figure.

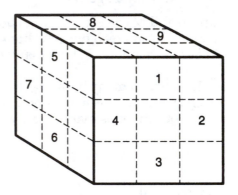

The problem can now be done by reduction and expansion. That is, reduce the size of the cake to a $1 \times 1 \times 1$, then expand it to a $2 \times 2 \times 2$, a $3 \times 3 \times 3$, and so on. This strategy yields the following table:

	Faces with Frosting					
Size	6	3	2	1	0	Total
$1 \times 1 \times 1$	1	0	0	0	0	1
$2 \times 2 \times 2$	0	8	0	0	0	8
$3 \times 3 \times 3$	0	8	12	6	1	27
$4 \times 4 \times 4$	0	8	24	24	8	64
$5 \times 5 \times 5$	0	8	36	54	27	125
$6 \times 6 \times 6$	0	8	48	96	64	216
$n \times n \times n$	0	8	$12(n-2)$	$6(n-2)^2$	$(n-2)^3$	n^3

Thus, there will be 8 pieces with frosting on three faces; 48 pieces with frosting on two faces; 96 pieces with frosting on one face; and 64 pieces with no frosting at all. The original cake was 6" × 6" × 6".

At the bottom of each column is the generalized results for that column. Have your students verify that their sum is, indeed, n^3.

PROBLEM 79   (Reproduction Page 178)

Mrs. Callahan and three of her friends have formed a stock investment club. Each of them picked one favorite stock and invested $3,000 in it. At the end-of-year party and meeting of the club, it turned that three of the four members had made a profit and only one had lost money. From the clues, determine each person's full name, how much each person lost or gained, and the name of the stock each invested in.

    a. Hannah did not invest in General Electric.
    b. Susan, whose last name is neither Robinson nor Drucker, made $100 less than Donna.
    c. Two people made more money than the person who invested in Kodak.
    d. The person who invested in Pfizer was the only one to lose money.
    e. Donna made $500, which was the most profit made by anyone.
    f. Ms. Robinson did not invest in AT&T, but the person who did made the most money.
    g. Mrs. Smith lost $200 and Bobby made $200.

Discussion   Prepare a table with the headings as shown. Then use the clues to complete the table.

First Name	Stock	Profit/Loss	Last Name
Donna	AT&T	+$500	Drucker
Susan	G.E.	+$400	Callahan
Bobby	Kodak	+$200	Robinson
Hannah	Pfizer	–$200	Smith

  1. From clue (e), Donna is #1 with +$500.
  2. From clue (d), Pfizer is #4.
  3. From clue (f), AT&T is #1.
  4. From clue (g), Ms. Smith is #4 and lost $200.
  5. Since Pfizer is #4, clue (c) shows that Kodak is #3.
  6. Clue (b) says that Susan is neither Robinson nor Drucker, and clue (g) states that she is not Smith. Thus, she is Callahan.
  7. Clue (b) says that Susan made $100 less than Donna, or $400.
  8. The only stock left for #2 is General Electric.
  9. Smith is last from clue (g), Robinson is not first from clue (f), and Callahan is second from clues (c) and (g). Thus, Donna is Drucker, leaving Robinson for Bobby.

PROBLEM 80   (Reproduction Page 179)

Keith wants to join an audio cassette club. The Liberty Cassette Club has an offer of a $20 membership initiation fee and only $6.20 per cassette. The Patriot's Cassette Club has no membership initiation fee, but charges $8.10 per cassette. How many cassettes must Keith buy to make joining the Liberty Cassette club the better deal?

Discussion   Use the guess and test strategy, make a table, draw a graph, or solve the inequality $20 + 6.20x \geq 8.10x$.

Number of Cassettes	Liberty Club	Patriot Club
0	$ 20.00	$ 0.00
1	26.20	8.10
2	32.40	16.20
3	38.60	24.30
4	44.80	32.40
5	51.00	40.50
6	57.20	48.60
7	63.40	56.70
8	69.60	64.80
9	75.80	72.90
10	82.00	81.00
11	88.20	89.10

When Keith purchases his eleventh cassette, the Patriot Club will be the better offer.

PROBLEM 81   (Reproduction Page 179)

Pam has decided to open a special money-market account. She noticed a bank advertising a new investment plan. The bank will double the amount of money in an account on the last day of the month. On the first of the next month, however, it will charge a $100 service fee. Pam deposited $100 on the 15th of January. How much money is in her account on January 15th of the following year?

Discussion   Reasoning will show that Pam has exactly $100 at the end of the year.

	January	February	March	...
Balance	$100	$100	$100	...
Double	$200	$200	$200	...
Deduct 100	$100	$100	$100	...

What would happen if Pam had started the account with $50? What would happen if Pam had started the account with $200 ?

PROBLEM 82   (Reproduction Page 180)

A professional basketball team has 12 players on its roster and a player payroll of $20,000,000. Every player earns at least $500,000. Six of the players earn at least $1,500,000 each. One player-earns at least $2,500,000. The star center has demanded at least $3,500,000. His demands must be met. What is the maximum possible salary any one player can earn?

Discussion   Six players earn at least $1,500,000, which totals $9,000,000. One player with at least $2,500,000 and one with at least $3,500,000 constitutes another $6,000,000, for a total of $15,000,000 for eight players. The additional four players must earn at least $2,000,000 ($500,000 each). This totals $17,000,000, leaving $3,000,000. Add this to the highest salary, to get a top possible salary of $6,500,000.

PROBLEM 83   (Reproduction Page 180)

Mrs. Lolla has a semi-circular garden behind her home. The garden has a diameter (COD) of 20 yards. On this diameter, she has built a semi-circular fish pool, as shown in the figure. Parallel to the edge of the garden and tangent to the pool, she has erected a 16-yard long fence (AB) to keep her pet dog, Bandy, away from the pool. She wants to cover the rest of the garden with sod. What is the area of the portion of her garden to be covered with sod?

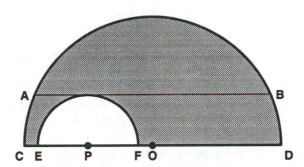

Discussion   The area of the shaded portion is the difference between the areas of the two semi-circles. The larger semi-circle has an area of 50π square yards. The radius of the smaller semi-circle is the distance between the parallel lines AB and CD. Draw this distance, OG, and radius OB to form a right triangle. Since OG bisects chord AB, you can use the Pythagorean Theorem to find OG.

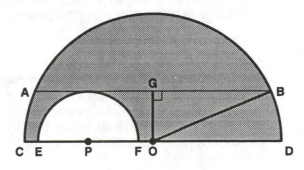

$$100 = \overline{OG}^2 + 64$$
$$36 = \overline{OG}^2$$
$$6 = \overline{OG}$$

The area of the smaller semi-circle is 18π. The portion of the garden to be sodded is 32π, or 100.5 square yards.

PROBLEM 84   (Reproduction Page 181)

Mr. Milou challenged the 15 students in his Statistics class with the following problem. The first two students each chose a number. The third student chooses the arithmetic mean of the first two numbers. Each successive student chooses the arithmetic mean of the numbers selected by all the students who have gone before. What is the number chosen by the 15th student?

Discussion   The 15th student will have as his or her number the arithmetic mean of the numbers selected by the first two students. This is independent of the numbers selected by the first two students, and independent of the number of students in the class. For example, if the first student in the class chose 10, and the second student chose 20, the third student must choose the arithmetic mean of 10 and 20, which is 15. The next student must choose the arithmetic mean of 10, 20, and 15, which is again 15. This will remain a constant choice of 15.

PROBLEM 85   (Reproduction Page 181)

A mathematician on a train traveling from Atlanta to Miami was looking out the window. She noticed a series of 10 telephone poles, which she knows are each 150 yards apart. She looks at her watch and notes that it takes exactly 45 seconds to pass the 10 poles. What is the speed of the train to the nearest mile per hour?

Discussion   Separating the 10 poles will be 9 "spaces." It takes 5 seconds for the train to travel 150 yards. This is 30 yards per second, or 90 feet per second. This is 5,400 feet per minute, or 324,000 feet per hour. Dividing by 5,280 you arrive at 61.36 miles per hour. An alternative is to set up the ratio

$$\frac{1350}{45} = \frac{x}{60}$$

This yields 1,800 yards per minute. Multiplying by 60 gives 108,000 yards per hour. Dividing by 1,760 (yards per mile) gives the same 61.36 miles per hour. The train travels approximately 61 miles per hour.

PROBLEM 86   (Reproduction Page 182)

In Zolt's Hardware Store, you can buy homeowners' tools in saving packs. In the Basic-Pak, you get a hammer, a pair of pliers, and a screw driver for $7.50. In the Starter-Pak, you get two hammers, two pairs of pliers, and four screwdrivers for $18.00. In the Family-Pak, you get five hammers and four pairs of pliers for $28.00. How much do each of the tools cost?

Discussion   This can easily be resolved by setting up three separate equations and solving them simultaneously.

$$H + P + S = 7.50$$
$$2H + 2P + 4S = 18.00$$
$$5H + 4P = 28.00$$

Notice that the first two equations quickly reveal that the cost of a screwdriver is $1.50. Solving the equations gives you the cost of a hammer as $4.00 and the cost of a pair of pliers as $2.00.

PROBLEM 87   (Reproduction Page 182)

There's an antique bike parade in town. Stuart has a bike that his great grandfather had given him in which the radius of the front wheel is 8 times the radius of the rear wheel. When the bike travels 100 feet, the number of rotations made by the smaller wheel is 60 more than the number of rotations made by the larger wheel. Find the diameter of each wheel to the nearest tenth of an inch.

Discussion   The ratio of the circumferences is the same as the ratio of the radii, or 8:1. Thus, their circumferences can be represented by C and $8C$.

$$\frac{100}{8C} = \frac{100}{C} - \frac{60}{1}$$
$$100 = 800 - 480C$$
$$480C = 700$$
$$C = 1.458 \text{ feet}$$
$$8C = 11.667 \text{ feet}$$

$R = 1.85$ feet $= 22.2$ inches $D = 44.4$ inches
$r = .23$ feet $= 2.8$ inches; $D = 5.6$ inches

PROBLEM 88   (Reproduction Page 183)

The Sharks and the Jets, two equally matched teams, are meeting in the preliminary round of the tournament. The first team to win 3 out of 5 games moves on to the next round. The Sharks won Game 1. What is the probability that the Sharks will win the round and move on?

Discussion   Make an organized list of all possible ways the Sharks can win two additional games.

Game #	1	2	3	4	5	Probability
	W	W	W			$\frac{1}{2} \cdot \frac{1}{2} = \frac{1}{4}$
	W	W	L	W		$\frac{1}{2} \cdot \frac{1}{2} \cdot \frac{1}{2} = \frac{1}{8}$
	W	W	L	L	W	$\frac{1}{2} \cdot \frac{1}{2} \cdot \frac{1}{2} \cdot \frac{1}{2} = \frac{1}{16}$
	W	L	W	W		$\frac{1}{2} \cdot \frac{1}{2} \cdot \frac{1}{2} = \frac{1}{8}$
	W	L	W	L	W	$\frac{1}{2} \cdot \frac{1}{2} \cdot \frac{1}{2} \cdot \frac{1}{2} = \frac{1}{16}$
	W	L	L	W	W	$\frac{1}{2} \cdot \frac{1}{2} \cdot \frac{1}{2} \cdot \frac{1}{2} = \frac{1}{16}$

There are six possible ways for the Sharks to win the round after winning Game 1. The total probability is their sum:

$$\frac{1}{4} + \frac{1}{8} + \frac{1}{16} + \frac{1}{8} + \frac{1}{16} + \frac{1}{16} = \frac{11}{16}$$

PROBLEM 89   (Reproduction Page 183)

Mitchell and Jane are going to race their racing cars around an oval track. Mitchell takes 25 minutes to complete a lap and Jane takes 30 minutes to complete a lap. How long will it take Mitchell to lap Jane's car (that is, to overtake her car) if they start together at the same point?

Discussion   Mitchell takes 25 minutes for 1 lap and Jane takes 30 minutes. Thus, Mitchell "saves" 5 minutes per lap. To "make up" 30 minutes will take him 6 laps at 25 minutes per lap, or 150 minutes ($2\frac{1}{2}$ hours).
The problem can also be solved by algebra:

$$\text{Let } Y = \text{the length of one lap}$$

$$\text{Then } \frac{Y}{25} Y = \text{Mitchell's rate, and}$$

$$\frac{Y}{30} Y = \text{Jane's rate.}$$

Let X = the time Mitchell needs to overtake Jane

R	×	T	D
$\frac{Y}{25}$		X	$\frac{XY}{25}$
$\frac{Y}{30}$		X	$\frac{XY}{30}$

$$\frac{XY}{25} = \frac{XY}{30} + Y$$

$$\frac{X}{25} = \frac{X}{30} + 1$$

$$6X = 5X + 150$$

$$X = 150 \text{ minutes, or } 2\frac{1}{2} \text{ hours}$$

Note that algebra is not always the simplest method.

PROBLEM 90

(Reproduction Page 184)

Whenever Morris does his daily walking, he plays a 90-minute tape (45 minutes on each side) in his portable cassette player. He stops walking and notices that the radius of the remaining part of the tape is about $\frac{1}{2}$ of the full tape. How many minutes remain to be played on that side of the tape?

Discussion

Simulate the situation with a drawing:

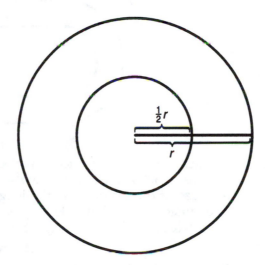

The time-of-play is a function of area. Thus the part remaining is

$$A = \pi(\tfrac{1}{2}r) \text{ or } \frac{\pi r^2}{4}$$

Therefore, $\frac{1}{4}$ of the area remains, and $\frac{1}{4}$ of 45 minutes is approximately 11 minutes.

PROBLEM 91

(Reproduction Page 184)

Carla painted identification numbers on the canoes in her new franchise. Each canoe has three numbers. The first number must be a 1 (her franchise number), and the next two digits must be in ascending order. No zeros were used, and no digits were repeated on any canoe. What is the maximum number of canoes Carla might have had?

Discussion   The first digit is fixed at 1. If 2 is chosen for the second digit, there will be seven choices remaining for the third digit (3–9). If 3 is chosen for the second digit, there will be six choices remaining for the third digit (4–9). If 4 is chosen for the second digit, there will be five choices and so on, until, if 8 is chosen for the second digit, there will only be one choice for the final digit—namely, 9. Thus, the number of possibilities is given by the sum of the series $7 + 6 + 5 + 4 + 3 + 2 + 1 = 28$. Carla has no more than 28 canoes.

PROBLEM 92   (Reproduction Page 185)

The figure shown here shows a running track in the form of a rectangle with a semi-circle on each end and dimensions as shown. The outside lane is three feet from the outer rail while the inside lane is three feet from the inner rail. How many feet do the starting blocks have to be staggered so that both runners run the same distance?

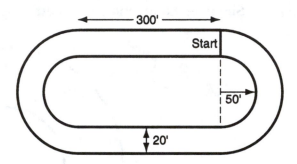

Discussion   In each case, the distance traveled consists of two parts: two straight lengths of 300 feet each and two semi-circles (equivalent to one circle). In the case of the inside lane, the length will be $300 + 300 + 106\pi = 933$ feet. The outside lane will be $300 + 300 + 134\pi = 1{,}021$ feet. The blocks should be placed $1021 – 933 = 88$ feet apart.

PROBLEM 93   (Reproduction Page 185)

Mr. Johannsen and Mr. Yan have decided to separate their property by placing a fence along the property line. They ordered enough fence posts so that the fence would have the posts placed 8 feet apart. However, five of the posts were not usable. They were still able to put the fence up by placing the remaining posts 10 feet apart. How many fence posts did they originally order?

Discussion   Let x represent the number of *intervals* originally planned; the fence will be $8x$ feet long. Since there are 5 fewer posts, there will be 5 fewer intervals. However, the fence-length remains the same.

$$8x = 10(x – 5)$$
$$8x = 10x – 50$$
$$50 = 2x$$
$$25 = x$$

There were 26 posts originally ordered.

PROBLEM 94   (Reproduction Page 186)

Louise and Mable are registered for the Bike-and-Walk-athon for charity. They start together. Louise will bike for half the distance and walk the other half. Mable will bike for half the time and walk the other half. If both of them bike and walk at the same rate, who finishes first?

Discussion   Mable will finish first. Since she will be riding for half the time, she will cover more than half the distance.

PROBLEM 95   (Reproduction Page 186)

The senior class is sponsoring a fair at the school. In the potato race, 10 potatoes" are placed in a straight line, each three feet apart. The first "potato" is three feet from the basket. A contestant runs to the first potato and returns it to the basket. The contestant then runs to the second potato and returns it to the basket. The same thing is done with each potato in succession, until all 10 potatoes are in the basket. How far does a contestant run to complete this race?

Discussion   Make a table as follows:

Potato Number	Total Distance
1	6'
2	12
3	18
4	24
.	.
.	.
.	.
10	60

Thus, you need to find the sum of the first 10 multiples of 6.

$$S = \frac{n}{2}(a + l)$$

$$S = \frac{10}{2}(6 + 60)$$

$$S = 5(66)$$
$$S = 330 \text{ feet}$$

Students who do not know the formula might use a calculator to add the 10 numbers, or might note that there are five pairs of 66s.

PROBLEM 96   (Reproduction Page 187)

There are 125 juniors participating in the Junior-Day Olympics: 59 played football, 49 played baseball, 42 participated in the races, 20 participated in the races and played baseball, 29 participated in the races and played football, 31 played both football and baseball, and 12 entered all three events. Those who did not participate in any of these three events went swimming. How many went swimming?

Discussion   Use a set of three intersecting Euler circles, as shown here. This gives a total of 82 who participated in the three events, leaving 43 who went swimming.

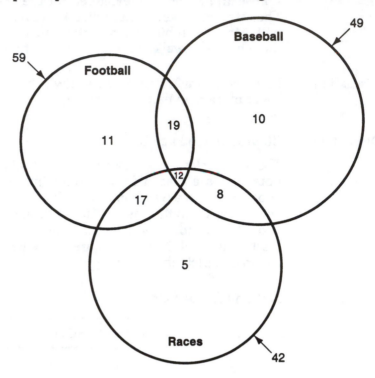

PROBLEM 97   (Reproduction Page 187)

Mr. Fondel is going to build a path from his house to the front walk. The path will be 2 feet wide and 12 feet long. He intends to lay paving blocks along the path. Each paving block is in the shape of a rectangle that is 2 feet by 1 foot. In how many different ways can Mr. Fondel lay the blocks along the path?

Discussion   Use the reduction and expansion strategy and look for a pattern. Because you are working with a Fibonacci sequence, each term is the sum of the previous two terms. Thus, for a 6-foot length, there are 13 ways; for a 7-foot length, there are 21 ways; for 8-foot length, there are 34 ways; for 9-foot length 55 ways, and so on. For the entire 12-foot length, there will be 233 different ways to place the paving blocks.

Length	Number of Ways	Ways
1	1	
2	2	
3	3	
4	5	
5	8	

PROBLEM 98   (Reproduction Page 188)

On a string of 15 opals, the center stone is the largest and the most expensive. Starting from one end, including the center stone, each opal is worth $50 more than the previous one. Starting from the other end and including the center stone, each opal is worth $25 more than the previous one. The total value of the 15 opals is $4,650. What is the value of the center opal?

Discussion   Divide the necklace into two parts. One side includes opals numbered 1 through 8: the other side includes those numbered 8 through 15 (with 8 the center opal).

Opal	Side A	Opal	Side B
1	x	15	y
2	x + 50	14	y + 25
3	x + 100	13	y + 50
4	x + 150	12	y + 75
5	x + 200	11	y+ 100
6	x + 250	10	y + 125
7	x + 300	9	y + 150
8	x + 350	8	y + 175

This yields two equations:

$$x + 350 = y + 175$$
$$8x + 1400 + 7y + 525 = 4650$$
$$8x + 7y = 2725$$
$$x - y = -175$$

From these equations you get $x = 100$ and $y = 275$. The center opal equals $x + 350 = 450$. The center opal equals $y + 275 = 450$.

PROBLEM 99   (Reproduction Page 188)

The local recycling plant has just bought a new metal compactor that produces a smaller cube of scrap iron than does the older machine. Somebody noticed, however, that the combined volumes of one cube from each compactor was numerically the same as the combined lengths of all their edges. What are the dimensions of the cubes, if you consider only integral solutions?

Discussion   Let X and Y represent the edges of the two cubes. Then,

$$X^3 + Y^3 = 12 (X + Y)$$

$$\frac{X^3 + Y^3}{X + Y} = 12$$

$$\frac{(X + Y) (X^2 - XY + Y^2)}{X + Y} = 12$$

$$X^2 - XY + Y^2 = 12$$

Add $-XY$ to both sides of this equation:

$$X^2 - 2XY + Y^2 = 12 - XY$$
$$(X - Y)^2 = 12 - XY$$

Now, since $XY \le 12$ and X and Y are both integers, let us assume that $X < Y$. This makes $X = 1, 2,$ or 3.

If $X = 1$, we substitute:

$$1 - Y + Y^2 = 12$$
$$Y^2 - Y - 11 = 0, \text{ which has no integral solutions}$$

If $X = 2$,

$$4 - 2Y + Y^2 = 12$$
$$Y^2 - 2Y - 8 = 0$$
$$\text{for which } Y = 4$$

If $X = 3$,

$$9 - 3Y + Y^2 = 12$$
$$Y^2 - 3Y - 3 = 0, \text{ which has no integral solutions}$$

Thus, the larger cube has an edge of 4 units and the smaller cube has an edge of 2 units.

PROBLEM 100   (Reproduction Page 189)

Two wheels, each of radius 2 inches, are fastened to a steel shaft with their centers 10 inches apart.

1. What is the length of the belt that goes around both wheels?

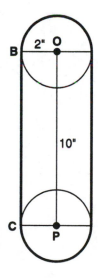

2. What if one of the wheels had a radius of 4 inches, but the wheels still have their centers 10 inches apart? Now how long is the belt?

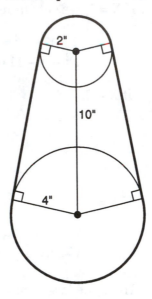

Discussion

1. The belt consists of two lengths of 10 inches each, and 2 semi-circles, each with radius of 2 inches. Thus, the length of the belt is $20 + 8\pi$ inches, or 45.12 inches.
2. Extend PO to A to form similar triangles, as shown in the figure. Triangle ABO is similar to triangle ACP. (We have rotated the drawing into a more standard position in the next figure.)

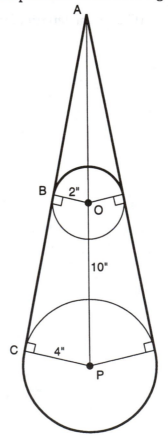

By similarity, AO = 10, and by the Pythagorean Theorem, $t = 9.8$. Then the straight part of the belt equals 19.6 inches.

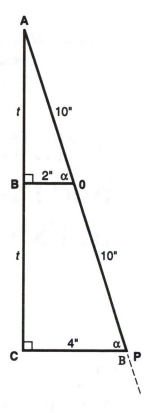

Now you must determine the part of each circumference that is in contact with the wheel. In circle O, $\cos \alpha = .2$ and $\alpha = 78°$. Thus, the central angle contains 156°.

$$\frac{156}{360} \times 4\pi = 5.4"$$

In circle P, $\angle \beta$ is the supplement of $\angle \alpha$. Thus, $2 \cdot P = 204°$.

$$\frac{204}{360} \times 8\pi = 14.2$$

The length of the belt equals 14.2 + 5.4 + 19.6, or 39.2 inches.

CHAPTER EIGHT

A Collection of Open-Ended Problems Requiring an Extended Response

The shift in emphasis from algorithmic processes to reasoning, thinking, and problem solving necessitates that students be confronted by a new type of problem. These new problems are often referred to as *open-ended questions*. However, we prefer to think of them in terms of "What Would You Do?" "Analyzing What Was Done," and "How Would *You* Do It?"

In many of the problems that have appeared throughout this book, as well as in most textbooks, students are required to solve a problem and find THE answer. Rarely do problems with multiple answers confront the students, although multiple solutions do sometimes occur. These new open-ended problems do not always have one unique answer. Rather, the answer is dependent on the students' interpretation, direction, and solution. These problems require students to communicate their thinking in written and/or verbal form, in an extended response. This format enables the teacher to examine the students' thought processes in a way that was not possible in the more traditional settings. These problems lend themselves nicely to consideration by small groups as well as by individual students.

In each of the problems that follow, have the students, either alone or in small groups, solve the problem and support their results with a logical argument and discussion.

PROBLEM 1   (Reproduction Page 190)

Two couples are preparing for a summer trip from their home in Philadelphia to Rome. Their plane leaves from Kennedy Airport in New York at

11:00 P.M., but they must check in approximately three hours prior to departure. Their problem is how to get from their home in Philadelphia to the airport in New York, a distance of about 120 miles. They are considering two options—renting a car or using a limousine service. Here's what they have found out.

Car Rental

Flat rate of $78.00 each way

Insurance (optional): $14.95 each way

Tolls: $8.00 each way

Free unlimited mileage, but gasoline must be replenished.

Limousine Service

Flat rate of $25 per person each way

A gratuity of 15 percent is expected

The limousine schedule:

Leave Philadelphia	Arrive at Kennedy Airport
8:00 A.M.	11:00 A.M.
2:00 P.M.	5:00 P.M.
5:00 P.M.	8:30 P.M.
7:00 P.M.	10:00 P.M.

If you were making the trip, which way would you go? What would you do? Defend your decision.

Discussion   There is probably no "correct" answer to this problem. However, the purpose of the problem is to elicit thinking and decision making based not only on the given facts of the problem but also personal preferences and real-world knowledge, such as traffic patterns, road conditions, time of day, and so forth. Calculations show that the two costs are approximately the same:

Car Rental

Rental	$156.00
Tolls	16.00
Gasoline (based upon 240 miles at approximately 18 miles per gallon and a cost of $1.40 per gallon)	19.00

Thus, the total cost without insurance is approximately $191.00, and with insurance is about $221.00.

Limousine Service

Direct cost	$200.00
Gratuity	30.00

Thus, the total cost, including the gratuity, is $230.00. Many other factors must be considered, however. For example, the limousine schedule versus personal driving time, traffic during the rush hour, driving pressures, door-to-door service by the limousine service versus pick-up time on car rentals, and so on. This is a problem in which approximate calculations are sufficient.

PROBLEM 2   (Reproduction Page 191)

The coach of the Jaguar basketball team has a decision to make! Her team is one point behind and the final buzzer has just sounded. However, just at the buzzer, a bench foul was called on the opponents, the Rockets. The Jaguar's coach has to select one of the five players on the court at that time to shoot the free throw. If the player makes the foul shot, the game goes into overtime; if she misses, the Jaguars lose the game. Here are the foul-shooting statistics for the five players involved:

Name	Free Throws During Season	Free Throws During the Last 2 Minutes
Jody	6 out of 7	1 out of 3
Sara	70 out of 100	18 out of 25
Ellen	85 out of 130	14 out of 17
Becky	10 out of 15	5 out of 5
Rose	100 out of 120	15 out of 25

If you were the coach, which player would you choose? What would you do? Defend your decision.

Discussion   Don't forget the primary purpose of this problem. It is to involve the students in decision making. The foul-shooting percent should be calculated in both cases for each of the five players.

Name	Season	Last 2 Minutes
Jody	86%	33%
Sara	70%	72%
Ellen	65%	82%
Becky	67%	100%
Rose	83%	60%

Students should make a choice and defend it. Students might wish to discuss this problem with the school basketball coach.

PROBLEM 3   (Reproduction Page 192)

For the senior class trip, the faculty sponsor ordered 256 caps, one for each student. The class is divided into four sections, each with the same number of students. When the caps arrived at the school, the sponsor asked each of the four section representatives to pick up $1/4$ of the caps from the supply room and distribute them to the students in their section. Renee arrived first and took one-quarter of the caps. Brad arrived one period later and took one-quarter for his section. Carol arrived an hour later and took one-quarter of the caps for her section. Mitch arrived at the end of the day and took one-quarter of the caps for his section. The following morning, Mrs. Johnson, the sponsor, was surprised to find caps left in the storeroom. In addition, students from three of the sections kept coming in to complain that they did not receive a cap. What was wrong? How many in each group did not get a cap? How would you have avoided the problem? Defend your decision.

Discussion   The error, of course, occurred because each representative took one-fourth of the number of caps that remained after the previous person had taken his or her share. Each representative took the correct fractional part of the wrong "whole" (except the first representative).

Representative	Amount at Start	Amount Taken	Amount Remaining
Renee	256	64	192
Brad	192	48	144
Carol	144	36	108
Mitch	108	27	81

PROBLEM 4   (Reproduction Page 193)

During the morning senior assembly, Mr. Carter, the school principal, announced that he had good news for the group. He told the students that he has just been informed that 50 percent of those who applied for admission into State University have been accepted. Also, 50 percent of those who applied to Temple Tech have also been accepted. Carla turned to her friend Marcie and said, "Great! I've been accepted! I applied to both schools, and 50 percent + 50 percent is 100 percent, so I'm in!" Analyze the action. Is Carla correct? Defend your decision.

Discussion   A Venn diagram clearly reveals Carla's error. Many of the students who were accepted into State University were also accepted into Temple Tech. For illustrative purposes, assume 40 applications were sent to Temple Tech (20 of which were accepted) and 60 applications were sent to State University (30 of which were accepted). The area of intersection shows how 25 could possibly have been accepted by both schools. Carla might have been in the 50 applications that were rejected by both schools.

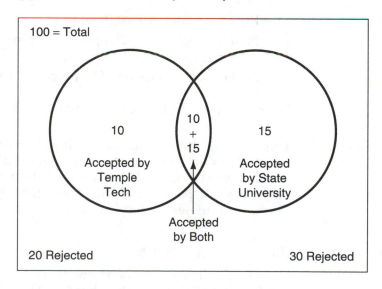

PROBLEM 5   (Reproduction Page 194)

On the boardwalk at the shore, there are three stores within a block of one another. On the first day of the season, each store had a sign advertising a sale on gold chains. Store A offered a 70 percent discount plus an additional 10 percent discount for cash. Store B offered a 60 percent discount plus an additional 20 percent discount for cash. Store C accepted cash only, and offered a $2/3$ discount. Amy wanted to buy a 26-inch gold chain. If you were Amy, from which store would you buy the chain? What would you do? Defend your decision.

Discussion   This is a problem in successive discounts. The students may interpret this as 70 percent followed by 10 percent equals 80 percent, which, of course, is not true. Assume a base price of $100.

Store A

$100 – 70 percent discount = $30
$ 30 – 10 percent discount = $27

Store B

$100 – 60 percent discount = $40
$ 40 – 20 percent discount = $32

Store C

$100 – $2/3$ discount = $33.33

The best buy is from store A.

PROBLEM 6   (Reproduction Page 195)

You have been offered a job. There are three possible salary plans to select from:

Plan A: A salary of $400 per week
Plan B: A salary of $200 per week plus 10 percent commission on all your sales
Plan C: A commission of 25 percent on all your sales.

Which plan would you select? What would you do? Defend your decision.

Discussion   This problem should stimulate active discussion. Its resolution depends on the students' knowledge of the real world. Factors such as the cost of the merchandise being sold (i.e., automobiles vs. stationery), the individual's talent as a salesperson, personal needs for a guaranteed income, and so on. There is no single "correct" answer.

PROBLEM 7   (Reproduction Page 196)

On a local television game show, three contestants enter the final round. Marlene has $8,000, Jonathan has $6,000, and Kim has $4,000. There is one question remaining. Using the money they have, each contestant wagers as much or as little he or she wishes. The winner is the person who has the most money at the end of the game. How much should each of the contestants wager for the final question? What-would you do? Defend your answer.

Discussion   This problem should be done with small groups of students. There is no "correct" answer, but there is lots of room for discussion.

PROBLEM 8   (Reproduction Page 197)

The naturalists at the state park are going to put carp into the pond at the Japanese teahouse. They can put five fish for every 100 square feet of surface area. Marlene was assigned the task of finding the surface area of the pond. Since the shape of the pond was irregular, she walked around it and estimated its perimeter to be 100 yards. She made a rectangle that was 50 feet by 100 feet and found its area to be 5,000 square feet. So, Marlene recommended that the naturalists purchase 250 fish for the pond. Analyze Marlene's action. What would you have done? Defend your decision.

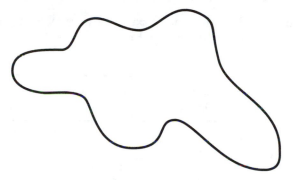

Discussion   Marlene assumed that two figures with equal perimeters would have equal areas. Obviously, this is not true. A more accurate procedure might be to approximate the figure onto a grid and calculate the area.

PROBLEM 9   (Reproduction Page 198)

The school Spirit Club is having a fund-raising drive. You have been appointed chairperson, and have been given the job of preparing tags to sell on Spirit Day to raise the funds. You have a piece of bright green material that is rectangular in shape and measures, 18 inches by 45 inches. Members of your committee have suggested four different shapes for the tags:

1. A circle with a one-inch diameter, to sell for $1.25 each
2. A one-inch square, to sell for $1.25 each
3. An equilateral triangle with a one-inch side, to sell for 75¢ each
4. A one-inch by two-inch rectangle, to sell for $2.50 each

Which shape would you use to earn the most money?
How much would you earn? Defend your decision.

Discussion   Using the one-inch square or the one-inch circle will produce the same number of tags—namely, 18 × 45 or 810. At a sale price of $1.25 each, this would yield $1,012.50. There would be 9 × 45 or 405 of the one-inch by two-inch rectangles, which would also earn $1,012.50. The triangle with the one-inch side yields 35 across, but there are 51 rows, since the height of the triangle is approximately .87. This will yield 1,785 tags, which will earn $1,338.75.

PROBLEM 10   (Reproduction Page 199)

"Hoops" Malone has his contract up for renewal. The team has offered him a choice of three contracts:

1. $700,000 plus $5,000 for every game he plays
2. $600,000 plus $10,000 for every game he plays
3. $1,000,000 with a penalty of $25,000 for every game he misses

The season consists of 32 games. Last season, "Hoops" appeared in only 12 games because of knee surgery. If you were "Hoops" Malone, which contract would you take? What would you do? Defend your decision.

Discussion   The arithmetic part of this problem can be done in several ways: a graph, a table, or by algebra.

Table

Games Played	Games Not Played	Contract #1	Contract #2	Contract #3
0	32	$ 700,000	$ 600,000	$ 200,000
5	27	725,000	650,000	325,000
10	32	750,000	700,000	450,000
15	17	775,000	750,000	575,000
20	12	800,000	800,000	700,000
25	7	825,000	850,000	825,000
26	6	830,000	860,000	850,000
27	5	835,000	870,000	875,000
28	4	840,00	880,000	900,000

Equations

Contract #1	Contract #2	Contract #3
$700 + 5X$	$600 + 10X$	$1000 - 25(32 - X)$

where X represents the number of games "Hoops" plays.
Equating these expressions in pairs,

1. $700 + 5X = 600 + 10X$
$$X = 20$$
2. $600 + 10X = 1000 - 25(32 - X)$
$$X = 26.67$$
3. $700 + 5X = 1000 - 25(32 - X)$
$$X = 25$$

Thus if "Hoops" plays in fewer than 20 games, contract #1 is the best. If he plays in more than 20 games, but fewer than 27, contract #2 is the best. If he plays in 27 or more games, contract #3 is the best.

Drawing a graph of the three contracts on the same set of axes is an interesting activity and reveals these situations quite nicely.

PROBLEM 11   (Reproduction Page 200)

The Lenape Valley High School Math Club was out on its field day. The teacher, Mr. Romeo, assigned Pam and Jason the problem of finding a buried box. He told them that the box was buried at the fourth vertex of the parallelogram having three of its vertices at (–1,4), (1,1), and (3,5), on the Cartesian grid that was laid out on the field. Pam and Jason dug at (1,8), but the box was not there. Why didn't they find the buried box? What would you do? Defend your decision.

Discussion   There are actually three different parallelograms with the given three vertices. By use of the slope or distance formulas, you will discover that the missing vertex not only could have been at (1,8) but also at (-3,0) or at (5,2).

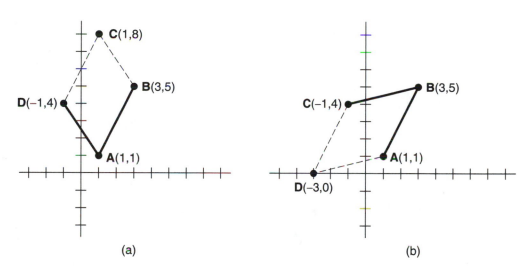

(a)   (b)

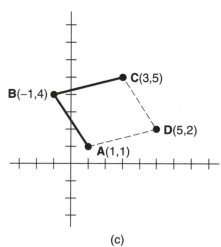

(c)

PROBLEM 12   (Reproduction Page 201)

Ian and Amanda have constructed a robot for a science project. The robot can run at a top speed of 15 miles per hour. They direct the robot's actions from a computer that is 5 miles away. The robot is proceeding from east to west, and is $^3/_8$ of the way across a railroad bridge that spans a canyon. The bridge is 8 miles long. A train, 13 miles east of the bridge, is traveling toward the bridge at a rate of 60 miles per hour. Ian says, "Keep running!" Amanda says, "No! Turn around and run the other way!" Who's right? What would you do? Defend your decision.

Discussion   If the robot reverses direction, it will take 12 minutes to return to the east end of the bridge ($^3/_{15} = ^1/_5 = 12$ minutes). In that time, the train will still be 1 mile away from the bridge, and the robot will be saved. If the robot continues in a westerly direction, it will take 20 minutes to cover the remaining 5 miles of the bridge ($^5/_{15} = ^1/_3 = 20$ minutes). In that 20 minutes, the train will still be 1 mile east of the end of the bridge. Again, the robot will be saved. Both Ian and Amanda were correct. Notice that the 5-mile distance for the computer is extraneous.

SECTION A

Reproduction Pages
for the Heuristics

Name _____ Date _____

MULTIPLE-CHOICE QUESTIONS

1. Jarla is riding her bike from home to the picnic grounds, a distance of 5 miles. She rode for 2 miles and stopped for a 15-minute break to have a cold drink. She then rode an additional 2½ miles, when she stopped to change a flat tire. She rode the remaining distance in 10 minutes. How far did she ride after she changed the flat tire?

   The question being asked in this problem is:

   a. How long does it take Jarla to ride to the picnic grounds?
   b. How far from home was Jarla when she stopped for a cold drink?
   c. How far from the picnic grounds was Jarla when she had the flat tire?
   d. How far are the picnic grounds from Jarla's house?

2. Ariel and Mel went fishing from 8:00 A.M. to 3:00 P.M. Ariel caught 7 flounder, 2 sea bass, and 3 weakfish. Mel caught 3 flounder and 12 weakfish. How many fish did they catch altogether?

   Which of the following answers the question asked in the problem?

   a. They fished for 7 hours.
   b. They caught three different kinds of fish.
   c. They caught 10 flounder.
   d. They caught 27 fish.

3. A team of robots can mount 60 tires on the wheels of cars in one hour. Last week, the team worked for 58 hours. Which of the following is the best estimate of the number of tires the team mounted last week?
   a. 360   b. 3,600   c. 36,000   d. 360,000

4. Luis is permitted to watch 16 hours of television each week. If he watches 8 hours on the weekend, how many hours can he watch television during the week?

   Which of the following statements is true?

   a. The problem deals with the kinds of television programs Luis can watch.
   b. The problem deals with the amount of time that Luis can watch television during the week.
   c. The problem deals with the amount of homework that Luis is required to do before he can watch television.

Name _____ Date _____

5. Mark went to the fruit market and bought some bananas at 59¢ a pound. He also bought five pounds of apples. He gave the clerk a $5 bill. How much change did he receive?

   Which of the following are needed to solve the problem?

   a. The number of pounds of bananas and the number of pounds of apples.
   b. The cost of a pound of bananas and the cost of a pound of apples.
   c. The cost of a pound of bananas and the number of pounds of apples.
   d. The number of pounds of bananas and the cost of a pound of apples.

REPRODUCTION PAGE 2

Name _____ Date _____

MULTIPLE-CHOICE QUESTIONS

1. Mitch Johnson was the high scorer for the Sharks in last night's basketball game. He made 5 out of 8 from the free-throw line, and 8 two-point field goals. The high scorer for the Jets, Bruce Parker, made 3 free throws, 5 two-point field goals, and 2 three-point field goals. Find the number of points separating the two high scorers.

   What is the question being asked?

   a. How many points did Mitch Johnson score?
   b. How many points did Bruce Parker score?
   c. How many more points did Mitch Johnson score than Bruce Parker?
   d. How many points did the two high scorers score altogether?

2. Mr. Patrick has 400 feet of fencing to completely enclose a rectangular field. What is the area of the field?

   What necessary fact is missing from the problem?

   a. The perimeter of the field.
   b. The cost of the fencing.
   c. The length of the field.
   d. The diagonal of the field.

3. On the first five tests of the semester, Joann scored an average of 92. Her scores were 95, 100, 88, 91, and 86.

   What was her median score?

   Which fact is extra?

   a. Her scores were 95, 100, 88, 91, and 86.
   b. Her average was 92.
   c. There were five tests.
   d. She scored 100 on one of the tests.

4. Sandra went to the local convenience store. She bought three pounds of bananas at 59¢ a pound, two boxes of cereal at $3.59 a box, and two loaves of bread at $1.89 each. How much change did Sandra receive?

   What necessary fact is missing from the problem?

   a. The cost of a pound of bananas.
   b. How much money Sandra gave the cashier.
   c. How many boxes of cereal she bought.
   d. The cost of a loaf of bread.

Name _____ Date _____

OPEN-ENDED QUESTIONS

There's a big sale on bananas at the local market. The price per pound is 59¢. However, if one buys 10 pounds, the cost is only $3.50. There are about four bananas in each pound. Mrs. Johnson wants to buy bananas for her family. Discuss what she should do.

Name _____ Date _____

OPEN-ENDED QUESTIONS

At Wilson High School, the counselor reported that 50 percent of the senior class had received acceptance letters from State Tech. She also reported that 50 percent of the senior class had received acceptance letters from out-of-state colleges. William concluded that he did not have to worry—he had been accepted to college!

Discuss William's conclusion.

Name _____ Date _____

OPEN-ENDED QUESTIONS

You have been offered a part-time job selling stereo equipment after school. The job offers four salary plans:

1. Straight salary of $200
2. Salary of $100 + 15 percent commission
3. Salary of $50 + 20 percent commission
4. Straight commission of 30 percent

Which one would you select? What would you do?

Name _____ Date _____

OPEN-ENDED QUESTIONS

The state government is considering increasing the state gasoline tax by 10 cents a gallon. The proceeds will be used to help pay for much-needed road repairs.

1. Estimate the increased cost of gasoline to an average driver over a one-year period.
2. Sketch a graph of the increased cost of gasoline to an average driver over a one-year period for tax increases of 10 cents to 50 cents in increments of 10 cents. Justify or explain your reasoning.

Name _____ Date _____

WHAT'S GOING ON?

Suzy, David, and Barbara are flying their kites on a windy day. Suzy let out 25 yards of string to fly her red kite. David's blue kite has twice as much string. Barbara's yellow kite has 15 yards more that Suzy's. Who let out the most string to fly his or her kite?

Name _____ Date _____

WHAT'S GOING ON?

Ronni, her mother, and her grandmother are all going to the local movie. Children under 12 must pay $1.80. Adult tickets cost $3.50, but senior citizens get a 10 percent discount. If Ronni is 9 years old and her grandmother is a senior citizen, how much do they spend for the three tickets?

Name _____ Date _____

WHAT'S GOING ON?

Air traffic controllers assign cruising altitudes to airplanes in flight. On westbound flights, the planes are assigned cruising altitudes of 31,000 feet, 35,000 feet, 39,000 feet, and so on. On eastbound flights, the planes are assigned cruising altitudes of 33,000 feet, 37,000 feet, 41,000 feet, and so on. What is the closest vertical distance that would separate two airplanes passing over each other?

Name _____ Date _____

RECOGNIZE THE NUMBER

Directions:

1. In the paragraph below, all the numbers have been written in word form. Put a circle around each one you can find. Then make a list of them, and write the numerical form next to each one.
2. Make a list of the numbers in ascending order.

Two high school basketball teams, the Chargers and the Devils, played each other last night. The game started at seven o'clock and ended at ten. The Chargers team only had nine players, since three of them were hurt and couldn't play. The Devils had all twelve players. The star players on both teams wore number fourteen on their uniform shirts. Mitch scored twenty-eight points for the Chargers, while Jeff scored thirty-one for the Devils. One-fourth of Mitch's points were scored on free throws.

Name _____ Date _____

RECOGNIZE THE NUMBER

Directions:

1. In the paragraph below, all the numbers have been written in word form. Put a circle around each one you can find. Make a list of these, and write the numerical form next to each of them. Place them in ascending order.
2. Finish the story. See how many numbers you can put into your ending.

The Lurias are taking a five-day automobile trip. They left their house in Johnson City on Tuesday at eight o'clock in the morning. That day, they drove three hundred fifty miles and stopped in the little town of Williamsport at six o'clock. As they entered the town, they saw a sign that the population of Williamsport was four thousand five hundred sixty. The next morning, Mr. Luria put eighteen gallons of gasoline in their van, for which he spent nineteen dollars and twenty-five cents. The next part of their trip took them to the top of a mountain range, seven thousand two hundred fifty feet high. They spent two-and-one-half hours picnicking and walking along the paths. The three Luria children counted fourteen red-winged blackbirds and eleven sparrows as they walked.

Name _____ Date _____

SELECT THE PROPER NUMBER

Directions:

Read the following paragraph. It is a story about Larry's newspaper route. The numbers have all been taken out and listed below. You are to use each number once and put them in the blanks to make the story true.

Larry has ____ customers on his paper route. He gets ____ cents for each weekday paper he delivers, and ____ cents for each Sunday edition. Last week, he earned $____ and put $____ into his bank account.

10,   25,   60,   78.20,   92

Name ———————————————————— Date ——————————

SELECT THE PROPER NUMBER

Directions:

Read the following paragraph. It is a story about an ecology club. The numbers have all been taken out and listed below. You are to use each number once, and put them in the blanks to make the story true.

Last weekend, ____ members of the Jeffersonville Environmental Club went around town gathering aluminum cans from the streets. On Monday morning, they took the ____ cans they had collected to the recycling plant. They received ____ dollars for their club treasury. In Jeffersonville, the recycling plant pays ____ cents for each can that people bring in to the plant. George, the club president, said, "That amounts to ____ dollars that each of us has contributed to our fund. If we do this each weekend for one year, we would earn ____ dollars. At ____ dollars a tree, we could plant ____ trees along the town's main street and boulevard."

3,   10,   15,   26,   150,   300,   7800

Name _____ Date _____

SELECT THE PROPER NUMBER

Directions:

Read the following paragraph. The numbers have all been taken out and listed below. You are to use each number once, and put them in the blanks to make the story true.

An advertising agency in Hoboken, New Jersey, mailed ____ brochures. Of these, ____ were delivered within the first ____ hours, ____ more were delivered within the next ____ hours, and the remaining brochures took more than ____ hours to arrive. Estimate the probability that a brochure mailed by the ad agency will be received within ____ hours.

24,   24,   48,   72,   345,   800,   1800

REPRODUCTION PAGE 15

Name _____ Date _____

WHAT'S THE WORD?

Directions:

Select the one word from the list that belongs in both sentences of each pair. The word has a mathematical meaning in one sentence and a non-mathematical meaning in the other.

CHORD	ROOT	EVEN	ODD	VOLUME	MEAN
POWER	DIFFERENCE		FACTOR	COUNT	PRIME

Example:

  a. That tree has a very ___ODD___ shape.
  b. The numbers 1, 3, 7, and 17 are all ___ODD___ numbers.

1. (a) Turn up _____ the on your stereo.
   (b) What is the _____ of that glass jar?
2. (a) A radish is the _____ of a plant.
   (b) Find the cube _____ of 27.
3. (a) _____ the number of apples in the box.
   (b) His Royal Highness the _____ of Transylvania.
4. (a) A _____ is a straight line that joins two points on a circle.
   (b) I'll play a 3-note _____ on the piano.
5. (a) The number 2 is the only even _____.
   (b) The television program was scheduled in _____ time.
6. (a) The cruel stepmother was very _____ to the youngest daughter.
   (b) The arithmetic _____ of the numbers 1, 5, 7, and 7 is 5.
7. (a) The numbers 2, 4, 128, and 32 are all _____ numbers.
   (b) _____ the youngest child can play in the pool.
8. (a) Her quick rise to _____ made her one of the most widely admired woman in all of Europe.
   (b) Raise *x* to the fourth _____.
9. (a) The weather is a major _____ in your decision to go to the ballgame or not.
   (b) Seven is a _____ of 28.
10. (a) The _____ between 5 and 9 is 4.
    (b) There is no _____ whether you wear the red one or the blue one.

Name _____ Date _____

WHAT'S THE WORD?

Directions:
Find the word that completes each of the following pairs of sentences. A single word is used in each pair.

1. (a) The window was washed with a _____ of ammonia and water.
   (b) The _____ to the problem was to multiply the number of people attending by $1.50.
2. (a) The seventy-seventh armored _____ was on maneuvers.
   (b) John never learned how to do long _____.
3. (a) Both of the doll's _____ were crushed by the car.
   (b) A right triangle has a hypotenuse and two _____.
4. (a) Please _____ the pump to get it started.
   (b) The numbers 17, 19, and 23 are all _____ numbers.
5. (a) The _____ of sets is all of the elements included in each set.
   (b) The members of the musician's _____ hold a picnic every year.
6. (a) The _____ of 6 and 12 is 72.
   (b) The soap company gave away a coupon to encourage people to try its new _____.
7. (a) In Dickens's novel, *A Christmas Carol*, Scrooge is portrayed as a _____, old miser.
   (b) The _____ score on the final exam was 82.7.
8. (a) Three noncollinear points determine a _____.
   (b) The _____ was three hours late in arriving from Boston.
9. (a) The _____ of the function was the positive integers.
   (b) Ten targets were set up on the firing _____.

Name _____ Date _____

WHAT'S THE QUESTION?

Directions:

For each of the following problems, check the question being asked.

Example:

The local campground has a permanent staff of 24 people. There are twice as many women on the staff as men. Find the number of women who work at the campground.

What's the Question?

_____ How many men work at the campground?

__X__ How many women work at the campground?

_____ How many people are on the permanent staff?

_____ How many people work in the summers only?

1. Mitchell and his family drove 4,500 miles on their five-week vacation last summer. How many miles did they average each week?

   What's the Question?

   _____ How many weeks were they on vacation?

   _____ How many miles did they drive?

   _____ How many miles did they average each day?

   _____ How many miles did they average each week?

2. Lisa has 27 baseball cards. Stacey has three more than Lisa. Jeff has five fewer cards than Lisa. Find the total number of cards they have.

   What's the Question?

   _____ How many cards does Stacey have?

   _____ How many cards does Jeff have?

   _____ How many cards do they have altogether?

   _____ How many more cards does Stacey have than Jeff?

Name _____ Date _____

3. A living room is in the form of a square that is 12 feet on each side. How much of the floor is left uncovered if there is a square carpet on the floor that is 9 feet by 9 feet?

What's the Question?

____ How large is the room?

____ What is the area of the rug?

____ How many square feet are left uncovered?

____ How much does the rug cost?

4. There are 220 children going on a bus trip to the museum. Mark is 53rd in line, and each bus holds 35 children. The buses are numbered from 1 through 7, and the children get on the buses in order. Find Mark's bus number.

What's the Question?

____ How many buses are there?

____ How many children are there?

____ How many children go on each bus?

____ What bus will Mark go on?

5. Jesse and Steve have a lemonade stand at the local golf course. Jesse opened the stand at 9:00 A.M. on Saturday. Steve came to work at 11:00 A.M., and closed the stand at 3:00 P.M. Jesse left at 1:00 P.M. How many hours was the stand open?

What's the Question?

____ How many hours did Jesse work?

____ How many hours did Steve work?

____ At what time did the stand close?

____ How long was the stand open?

Name _____ Date _____

WHAT'S THE QUESTION?

Directions:
For each of the following problems, check the question being asked.

Example:
There were 224 adults and 117 children at the local baseball game. Adult tickets cost $5 each and children's tickets cost $2 each. Find out how much money was paid for all the tickets.

What's the Question?

_____ How many people attended the game?

_____ How many adult tickets were sold?

_____ How much was spent on children's tickets?

__X__ How much money was received for tickets?

1. The Environmental Club collected 300 empty cans on Friday, 350 cans on Saturday, and 400 cans on Sunday. If this pattern continues, how many cans will the club collect on Monday?

   What's the Question?

   _____ How many empty cans do you expect the club to collect on Monday?

   _____ How many cans did the club collect on all three days?

   _____ How many cans did the club collect on Saturday?

   _____ How many more cans did the club collect on Sunday than on Saturday?

2. The Entertainment Committee has $360 to spend. One-half of the money was spent on the dance band, and one-fourth was spent on refreshments. How much money was left to spend on decorations?

   What's the Question?

   _____ How much money was spent on refreshments?

   _____ How much money was spent on the dance band?

   _____ How much money was spent on decorations?

   _____ How much money did the committee spend altogether?

Name _____ Date _____

3. Marcy made a long distance telephone call to her mother. The rates for the call were 90¢ for the first minute and 50¢ for each additional minute. The cost for the call was $2.90. For how many minutes was Marcy on the telephone?

What's the Question?

____ What was the cost of the call?

____ How long was the call?

____ What was the cost for the first minute?

____ Who did Marcy call?

4. George shoveled snow during the last snowstorm. He charged $12 for small sidewalks and $18 for large ones. He shoveled two large walks and three small ones. How much money did he earn?

What's the Question?

____ How much does George charge to shovel a large walk?

____ How much does George charge to shovel a small walk?

____ How many walks did George shovel altogether?

____ How much money did George earn?

5. The 300-mile trip from Philadelphia to Pittsburgh by a commercial jet-liner takes $3/4$ of an hour. On the return trip, it took only $4/5$ of that time due to a tail wind. Find the number of minutes the return trip took.

What's the Question?

____ How many miles is the round trip from Philadelphia to Pittsburg to Philadelphia?

____ How many minutes long is the trip from Pittsburgh to Philadelphia?

____ How many minutes long is the trip from Philadelphia to Pittsburgh?

____ How many miles is the distance from Philadelphia to Pittsburgh?

Name _____ Date _____

6. Steve took 36 pictures at the family picnic. When they were developed, he found that four of them were blurred. What percent of his pictures were good?

What's the question?

_____ What percent of Steve's pictures were bad?

_____ What percent of Steve's pictures were good?

_____ How many pictures did Steve take?

_____ How many of Steve's pictures were good?

7. The area of a rectangular field is 30,000 square feet. The ratio of the length to the width is 3:1. Find the perimeter of the field.

What's the Question?

_____ What is the length of the field?

_____ What is the width of the field?

_____ What is the distance around the field?

_____ What is the area of the field?

Name _____ Date _____

WHAT'S THE QUESTION?

Directions:

In each of the following problems, underline the question that is being asked.

1. A cog railway took 30 people to the top of Pike's Peak. There were three cars with the same number of passengers in each car. How many were in each car?
2. By how many runs did the Cubs defeat the Pirates if the final score was Cubs 11, Pirates 6?
3. Stan has a $5 bill. It will cost him $2.95 to mail a package to his brother. How much change will Stan receive?
4. Jill is having a barbeque and has invited 29 people. Paper plates come in packages of 12. How many packages of paper plates should she buy?
5. Find the amount of fencing needed to enclose a square field that is seven meters on each side.
6. It took Richard 15 minutes to walk to the ballfield. It took him 10 minutes longer to walk back to his home. At what time did he arrive home if he left the ballpark at 5:30 P.M.?
7. Susan bought five books of bridge tickets at $9.00 a book. Find the number of tickets she bought if each book contains 12 tickets.

Name _____ Date _____

WHAT'S THE QUESTION?

Directions:

In each of the following problems, underline the question that is being asked.

1. Find how much Bryan spent for 120 floppy disks for his new computer. Each disk costs 63¢.
2. An ostrich can run at 70 miles an hour, and a cheetah can run at 55 miles per hour. If both run at top speed for two hours, how much farther would the ostrich travel?
3. Jill had $875.90 in her checking account. How much remains after she writes checks in the amount of $37.37, $102.06, and $203.19?
4. After the tennis match, the four players went to an ice cream parlor. Two of them ordered chocolate sundaes and the other two ordered vanilla frappes. The bill of $8.56 was shared equally. How many people paid for the ice cream?
5. Mike left for his summer home on Sunday morning at 9:30 A.M. His sister followed him, but she left at 11:45 A.M. that morning. How fast did his sister travel if they both arrived at the home at 6:15 P.M., and their summer home is 375 miles away?
6. Beth sent a total of 30 postcards and letters to enter a contest. Postcards cost 20¢ each to mail, while letters cost 32¢ each. Find the number of letters she sent if her total bill for the postage was $6.70.
7. Find the mean salary for the five employees at the Ace Bearing Company. Mr. Smith and Mr. Gonzalez each earn $45,000 a year. Ms. Braun and Ms. Jenkins each earn $50,000 a year, and Mr. Connors earns $52,000 a year.

Name ————————————————— Date —————————

WHAT'S THE QUESTION?

Directions:

In each of the following problems, underline the question that is being asked.

1. Derwood is a social worker. Last week, he spent 12½ hours visiting his clients at their homes. He spent 10 hours working in the local youth center, and the rest of his 35-hour work week in his office. How much time did he spend at the office?
2. It costs $12.50 per square yard to tile a recreation room. Find the cost of tiling a rectangular recreation room whose dimensions are 15 feet by 18 feet.
3. There are five islands in Hawaii that tourists usually visit. In how many ways can the Johnson family choose two of these islands to visit?
4. Arlene, Peter, George, and Sally are in line, waiting for the movie-to open. Peter is between George and Sally. Sally is not first, and Arlene is last. List the order in which the four of them are standing in line.
5. What is wrong with the following set of statements: Ron has a large collection of CDs. One-third of them are rap, one-half are classical, and one-fourth are country.
6. A telephone answering machine tape can run for 30 minutes. If no messages can last for more than two minutes, what is the minimum number of messages that can be on the tape if the tape is full?
7. Find the probability of obtaining exactly three "heads" when seven coins are tossed.
8. What score must Jonathan achieve on his next examination if he is to have an average of 82 for the six tests? His other scores are 90, 71, 64, 53, and 48.

Name _____ Date _____

WHAT'S THE QUESTION?

Directions:

For each of the following, make up a question.

1. Jennifer bought a ball for 65¢ and a bat for $2.59.

   What's the Question? _____

   _____

2. Anna caught 62 fish, Jarla caught 53 fish, and Mickey caught 41 fish.

   What's the Question? _____

   _____

3. Ernie has 48 stickers. He puts $\frac{1}{2}$ of them in the red album, $\frac{1}{3}$ of them in the blue album, and $\frac{1}{6}$ of them in the green album.

   What's the Question? _____

   _____

4. Karen was swimming laps in the neighborhood pool. She swam for 20 minutes and covered five laps for a total of 300 feet.

   What's the Question? _____

   _____

5. Len rode his bike 2.5 miles on Tuesday, the first day of his training. He plans to add .5 mile each day for two weeks, so he rode 3.0 miles on Wednesday.

   What's the Question? _____

   _____

6. The four linemen on the Panthers' defensive team weigh 280 pounds, 301 pounds, 292 pounds, and 263 pounds.

   What's the Question? _____

   _____

Name _____ Date _____

WHAT'S THE QUESTION?

Directions:

In each of the following, supply a question to make the situation into a problem.

1. Doreen spent $4.30 to buy lunch for five days. Lunch costs 80¢ without milk and 90¢ with milk.

   What's the Question? _____

   _____

2. Robert can type a paper at the rate of 55 words per minute, whereas a word-processor can produce 250 words per minute. Robert's teacher assigned each student a 5,000-word paper.

   What's the Question? _____

   _____

3. The Perry family took a one-week motor trip for their vacation. They traveled a total of 1,120 miles, and the car averaged 22 miles per gallon of gasoline. Gasoline cost them an average of $1.16 per gallon.

   What's the Question? _____

   _____

4. Mr. Cosby jogs every morning. On Monday, he jogged $2\frac{3}{4}$ miles, on Tuesday $2\frac{1}{2}$ miles, and on Wednesday 3 miles. On Thursday, he jogged $2\frac{3}{4}$ miles and $3\frac{1}{4}$ miles on Friday.

   What's the Question? _____

   _____

5. Jim and Sally have a newspaper route. Each day they deliver 85 papers, and on Sundays they deliver 92 papers. Daily papers cost 35¢, and they keep 5¢ for each paper they deliver. The Sunday paper costs $1.50 and they keep 25¢ for each paper.

   What's the Question? _____

   _____

6. At the Pizza Shop, Tom ordered a 10-inch pizza that costs $6.25. April ordered a 12-inch pizza that costs $8.00.

   What's the Question? _____

   _____

Name _____ Date _____

WHAT'S THE QUESTION?

Directions:

In each of the following, you are presented with a problem situation. Supply the question that makes each situation into a problem.

1. The two leading scorers on the Lions basketball team had a great week last week. In the five games they played, Roger scored 28, 26, 31, 22, and 21 points. Mitchell scored 27, 35, 21, 26, and 29 points.

   What's the Question? _____

   _____

2. Samantha makes bracelets that she sells at the local crafts fair. She spent $22 on materials to make eight bracelets, and she sells them for $7 each.

   What's the Question? _____

   _____

3. The Mellow Tones want to rent a mini-van to carry their equipment to a club gig 64 miles away. Wreck-Renters charges $17 per day plus 35¢ a mile. Rent-a-Cheapy charges $12 a day and 42¢ a mile.

   What's the Question? _____

   _____

4. On five tests, Chelsea scored 87, 89, 92, 85, and 96. In order to get a grade of A, she must average 90 for all seven tests during this marking period.

   What's the Question? _____

   _____

5. A bag contains seven red balls, five white balls, and three blue balls.

   What's the Question? _____

   _____

6. Two bicyclists, Tom and Jerry, leave their homes at 7:00 A.M. and cycle toward each other along a straight road. They meet at 8:00 A.M. The two homes are 20 miles apart, and they meet 5 miles from Jerry's home.

   What's the Question? _____

   _____

Name _____ Date _____

FACTS FROM PICTURES

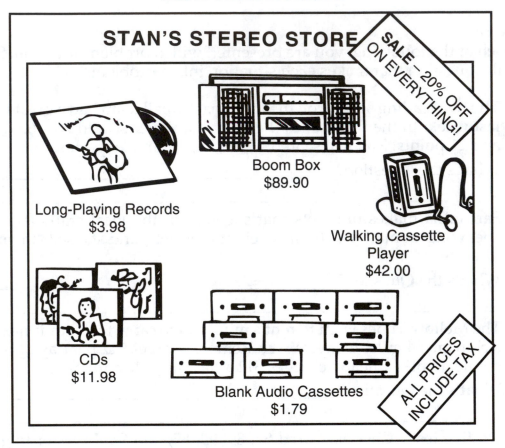

1. How much is the regular price of the Boom Box?
2. What item regularly sold for $3.98 before the sale?
3. What item is the most expensive in the window?
4. Alyssa bought 4 CDs the day before the sale began. How much did she spend?
5. How much would you pay for the Walking Cassette Player during the sale?
6. Carlton bought 4 CDs during the sale. How much did he save?
7. During the sale, Jim bought three CDs and his brother bought eight long-playing records. Who spent more money?

Name _____ Date _____

FACTS FROM PICTURES

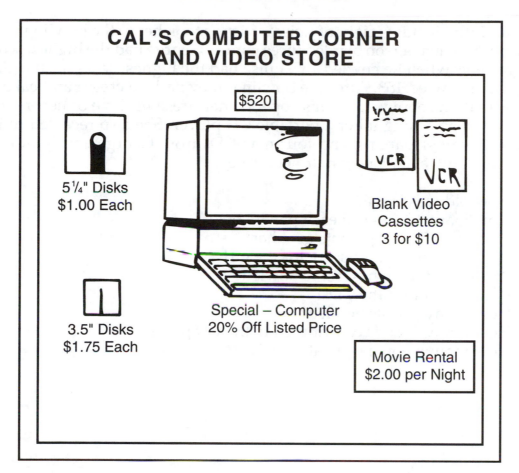

1. Jeff bought three blank video cassettes. How much did he pay?
2. What is the regular listed price of the computer?
3. How much would Eloise pay for the computer if tax is included?
4. Cal charges a 7 percent sales tax on video cassettes. How much would you pay for nine of them?
5. Michael rented four films on Friday evening and returned them on Sunday. How much did he spend?
6. Larry bought the computer and four of the three-inch disks. Tax is included on the computer, but there is a 7 percent tax on the disks. How much did Larry spend?

Name _____ Date _____

FACTS FROM TEXT

For her 15th birthday, eight of Luisa's friends took her to the bowling alley for a party. Each person bowled three games. George had the highest score for the boys when he bowled 165. Luisa had the highest score for the girls when she bowled 153. After the bowling, they had ice cream and cake in the recreation room where Luisa opened her presents. Five of her friends chipped in and bought her a portable CD player. She also received roller blades from her parents, and four new CDs from George and Maureen. One friend gave her a new pair of earrings.

1. How old was Luisa?
2. How many games did each person bowl?
3. What gift did her parents give her?
4. Who had the highest score for the girls?
5. What was the highest score bowled?
6. Who gave Luisa the CDs?
7. How many people bowled?
8. How many friends contributed to the CD player?
9. How many people were at the party?

Name _____ Date _____

FACTS FROM TEXT

In the year 1860, 40-year old William H. Russell began to deliver mail across the United States. This mail system was called the Pony Express. The first riders left St. Joseph, Missouri, on April 10, 1860, and arrived in Sacramento, California, 10 days later.

In the Pony Express, 80 riders were in the saddle at all times, moving the mail. Each would ride for 10 miles between stations and change horses. The Pony Express system lasted until October 24, 1861.

1. What was the name of Russell's mail service?
2. When did the Pony Express service begin?
3. When did the Pony Express service end?
4. How many were riding at all times?
5. How old was William Russell when he began the Pony Express service?
6. What were the terminal points of the Pony Express?
7. How many miles did each horseman ride at a time?

Name _____ Date _____

FACTS FROM TEXT

Last Sunday, Emily and her two older brothers, Charles and Matt, went on a fishing trip. Their mother packed them each two sandwiches. Three of the sandwiches were roast beef and these were on rye bread. The other three were tuna fish and they were on whole wheat bread.

They left their house at 5:00 A.M., and two hours later they began fishing in the lake. After about one hour of fishing, Matt, the oldest brother, said, "I'm hungry! I'm going to eat!", and so he ate a tuna fish sandwich. Emily and Charles decided to join him, but they each ate a roast beef sandwich. About 11:00 o'clock, each of them ate another sandwich, but this time they each ate a sandwich that was different from the one that each had eaten previously. After seven hours at the lake, they went home with their catch of 18 fish. Their mother asked them who had caught the fish. Matt said, "I caught half of them and Emily caught three more than Charles."

1. How many sandwiches did their mother pack?
2. How many tuna fish sandwiches did each of them eat?
3. How many fish did they catch?
4. What time did they leave their house?
5. On what day did they go fishing?
6. What time did they start fishing?
7. At what time did Matt eat a tuna fish sandwich?
8. At what time did the youngest person eat a tuna fish sandwich?
9. By noon, they had caught 10 fish. How many fish did they catch in the afternoon?
10. Who is the middle child in age?
11. How many fish did each person catch?

Name _____ Date _____

FACTS FROM GRAPHS

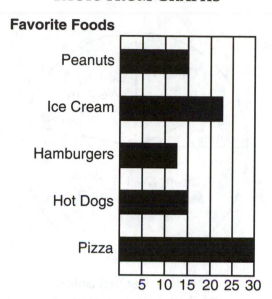

Favorite Foods

1. Which food was selected as favorite by the most students?
2. Which food was selected as the favorite by the fewest students?
3. How many students selected peanuts as their favorite food?
4. How many students selected ice cream as their favorite food?
5. Which two foods were selected as favorites by the same number of students?
6. If you were planning a menu, which two foods would you be sure to choose? Why?

Name _____ Date _____

FACTS FROM GRAPHS

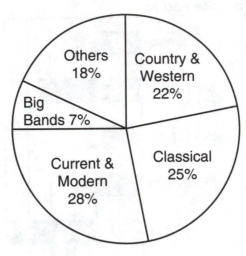

**Monthly Record Sales
at Don's Record Palace**

1. Which kind of recordings sold the most last month?
2. Which kind of recordings sold the fewest last month?
3. How many degrees are there in the angle at the center of the section marked "classical"?
4. Which two sections combined equal 50 percent of the records sold?
5. If Don's Record Palace sold a total of 2,000 records last month, how many of them were Country and Western?

REPRODUCTION PAGE 32

Name _____ Date _____

FACTS FROM GRAPHS

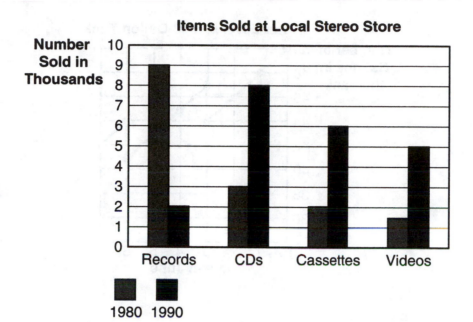

1. Which item sold the most in 1980?
2. Which item sold the most in 1990?
3. Which item sold the fewest in 1990?
4. How many cassettes were sold in 1980?
5. How many videos were sold in 1990?
6. Which item showed a drop in sales from 1980 to 1990?
7. Which item showed the greatest increase in sales from 1980 to 1990?

Name _____ Date _____

FACTS FROM GRAPHS

Water Level in a 50-Gallon Tank

1. How much water was in the tank on June 2?
2. On what date were there 43 gallons in the tank?
3. How much did the water level drop each day?
4. What do you think happened on June 3rd and on June 6th?
5. Do you think the tank will ever be empty? Why?

Name _____ Date _____

FACTS FROM GRAPHS

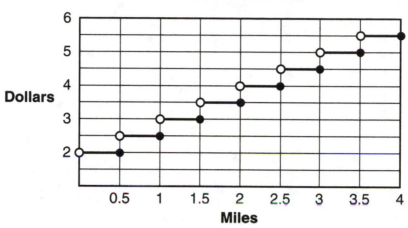

Cost of a Taxi Ride

1. How much does it cost to take a taxi ride for 3 miles?
2. How much does it cost to take a taxi ride for 2½ miles?
3. Juanita spent $4.50 on a taxi ride. How many miles did she ride?
4. John went from the airport to his home. a distance of 10 miles. How much did the ride cost him?
5. What is the difference between a closed dot and an open dot as shown on the graph?
6. Why is this graph not a continuous line?

Name _____ Date _____

FACTS FROM GRAPHS

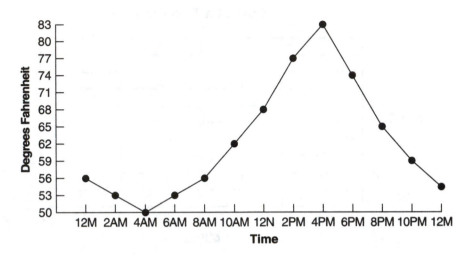

Temperatures on a Spring Day in New York City

1. (a) At what time was the high temperature for the day?
   (b) What was the temperature at that time?
2. (a) At what time was the low temperature for the day?
   (b) What was the temperature at that time?
3. What was the temperature at 12:00 noon?
4. (a) Were there any times during the 24-hour period when the temperatures were the same?
   (b) When?
   (c) What was the temperature at that time?

REPRODUCTION PAGE 36

Name _____ Date _____

FACTS FROM TABLES

	7:00	7:30	8:00	8:30	9:00	9:30	10:00	10:30
2	The World of Disney		Joan and Jake		Sherlock Holmes		News	
5	Animal World		The Way the West Was Won (Film)					
9	Murder, She Wrote		MASH	Sand City	MASH	Perry Mason Mysteries		
12	Together, With Pavarotti		Railroad Journies		Boston Pops Special			
17	Star Trek		Home Alone III (Film)					
20	Sports Talk		Basketball Championship Game					

1. Which channels had a movie during the evening?
2. Which channel had the greatest number of programs during the evening?
3. On which channel would you find the *Perry Mason Mystery*?
4. What was showing on channel 20 at 10:00 ?
5. At what time did the *Boston Pops Special* begin?
6. How long did the *Boston Pops Special* last?
7. Which program was on twice during the evening?
8. Which movie was longer: *The Way the West Was Won* or *Home Alone III*?

REPRODUCTION PAGE 37

Name _____ Date _____

FACTS FROM TABLES

BOX SCORE FOR THE MARLINS

Player's Name and Position	AB	R	H	2B	3B	HR	RBI	PO	A	E
Masters, 2B	5	3	3	1	0	0	0	1	6	0
Johnson, LF	5	1	1	0	0	0	0	4	0	0
Carey, RF	4	0	1	0	0	0	1	0	5	1
Cook, 3B	4	2	3	1	0	1	3	2	4	1
McDougald, 1B	3	0	0	0	0	0	1	10	1	0
Darryl, CF	4	0	0	0	0	0	0	4	0	0
Brooks, C	4	1	1	0	0	1	1	6	1	0
Brentwood, SS	4	0	1	0	0	0	1	0	8	0
Stevens, P	4	0	0	0	0	0	0	0	0	0
TOTALS	37	7	10	2	0	2	7	27	25	2

1. Who was the catcher for the Marlins? Who was their center fielder?
2. Which player had the fewest official at-bats?
3. Which players hit a home run?
4. How many triples were hit?
5. How many hits did the Marlins get in the game?
6. How many runs did Masters score?
7. Who scored the most runs?
8. What was the team batting average for the game?

Name _____ Date _____

FACTS FROM TABLES

FIRES AND FINANCIAL LOSS IN NEW CITY		
Year	Numbers	Amount of Loss
1992	11,204	$20,387,250
1993	13,517	$21,007,200
1994	12,809	$22,073,510
1995	18,726	$29,000,070

1. In what year were the most fires in New City?
2. In what year did the most dollar damage occur?
3. In what year did the number of fires decrease?
4. How much money was lost due to fires from 1992 to 1995?
5. What was the average dollar loss per fire in each year?

Name ————————————————— Date —————

FIND THE HIDDEN QUESTION

Directions:

Some problems have more than one part. You have to find the answer to a "Hidden Question" before you can solve the problem. In each of the following, pick out the hidden question.

1. Last week Amanda sold 18 boxes of Girl Scout cookies. This week she sold 15 boxes. If each box costs $2, how much did she receive for all the boxes of cookies she sold?

    What Is the Hidden Question?

    a. How many boxes of Girl Scout cookies did Amanda sell last week?
    b. How many boxes of Girl Scout cookies did Amanda sell during both weeks?
    c. How much money did Amanda receive for the cookies she sold?

2. Alyce mailed six post cards at 20¢ each and three letters at 32¢ each. How much did she pay in postage?

    What Is the Hidden Question?

    a. How much did she pay in postage?
    b. How much did she pay in postage for the six postcards?
    c. How much did she pay in postage for the three letters?

3. Mary is 7 years old and her brother, Bill, is four years older than Mary. In how many years will Bill be 15 years old?

    What Is the Hidden Question?

    a. In how many years will Bill be 15 years old?
    b. How old is Mary now?
    c. How old is Bill now?

4. The Shoe Shoppe is having a big 20 percent off sale on all athletic shoes. Mr. Klutz bought a pair of running shoes that were originally priced at $45, a pair of basketball shoes that were originally $85, and a pair of golf shoes that were originally $75. How much did he save by buying the shoes on sale?

    What Is the Hidden Question?

    a. How much did he save?
    b. How much did the three pairs of shoes cost originally?
    c. What percent was the sale discount?

Name _____ Date _____

FIND THE HIDDEN QUESTION

Directions:

Some problems have more than one part. You have to find the answer to a "Hidden Question" before you can solve the problem. In each of the following, pick out the hidden question.

1. On his vacation, Jeremy used four rolls of 36-print film. Of these, he discarded 9 prints. How many prints did he keep?

   What Is the Hidden Question?

   a. How many pictures did he discard?
   b. How many pictures did he keep?
   c. How many pictures did he take altogether?

2. The Sharp Image Photography Store charges $9.50 to reprint 24 pictures. Their competitor, The Camera Store, charges $11.50 to reprint 36 pictures. Jeremy wants to reprint 144 pictures. Which store should he use to save the most money?

   What Is the Hidden Question?

   a. How much will it cost Jeremy in each store?
   b. How much did Jeremy spend to have the reprints made?
   c. How many reprints does Jeremy have?

3. One inch of rain is equivalent to 13 inches of snow. Last month, there were 5 snowstorms: 8 inches, 6 inches, 12 inches, 8 inches, and 9 inches. If the snow had been rain, how much rain would have fallen?

   What Is the Hidden Question?

   a. How many inches of rain fell last month?
   b. How many inches of snow fell last month?
   c. How many inches of rain equal 13 inches of snow?

4. Members of the local beauticians' school came to help the senior girls put on their makeup properly. Each beautician helped 5 girls in the morning and 7 girls in the afternoon. If there are 72 girls in the senior class, how many beauticians were helping?

   What Is the Hidden Question?

   a. How many girls did each beautician help?
   b. How many girls did they help in the morning?
   c. How many beauticians were there?

Name _____ Date _____

WRITE THE HIDDEN QUESTION

Directions:
In each of the following, write the hidden question.

1. Ralph and Alice are selling fruit punch at the golf course. They sold $6 worth in the morning and $8 worth in the afternoon. The drinks cost them a total of $5. How much profit did they make?
   Write the hidden question. _____
   _____

2. To win a prize at the county fair, Jeff had to knock all ten bottles off the bottle stand with 3 tosses of the ball. On each of his first two tosses, he knocked off 3 bottles. How many bottles must he knock off with the last toss if Jeff won a prize?
   Write the hidden question. _____
   _____

3. The Crimson Tigers football team scored 14 points in the first half and 12 points in the second half. Their opponents, the Black Sharks, scored 21 points in the first half and only 3 points in the second half. Who won the game and by how many points?
   Write the hidden question. _____
   _____

4. Ed is a baker's helper. This morning he baked 80 muffins. He sold $\frac{1}{4}$ of them while they were still hot. Then he sold $\frac{3}{4}$ of what were left to a local restaurant. How many muffins did Ed sell in all?
   Write the hidden question. _____
   _____

5. John and his friend Charlie went on a bike trip to Lookout Cave last Tuesday. It took them $1\frac{1}{2}$ hours to get to the cave, and twice as long to return. For how many hours did they bike?
   Write the hidden question. _____
   _____

REPRODUCTION PAGE 42

Name _____ Date _____

WRITE THE HIDDEN QUESTION

Directions:
In each of the following, write the hidden question.

1. It takes Suzy about three hours to make 2 bracelets. About how long would it take her to fill an order for 15 bracelets?

   Write the hidden question. _____

   _____

2. There were 250 students from the Blair School going on a picnic. Each of the first six buses took 36 students. How many students were on the seventh bus?

   Write the hidden question. _____

   _____

3. In a restaurant, there were 12 booths that each hold four people, six tables that each hold two people, and two tables that could each seat six people. What is the seating capacity of the restaurant?

   Write the hidden question. _____

   _____

4. Nicholas learned in his geometry class that the sum of the measures of the angles of a triangle is 180°. What is the measure of angle A in triangle ABC, if the measures of angle B = 60° and angle C = 72°?

   Write the hidden question. _____

   _____

5. Mr. Wong wants to buy a camcorder to take pictures of his family. He can buy one for $550 if he pays cash for it. He can also purchase it by making a down payment of $100 and 12 monthly installments of $42 each. How much does he save by paying cash for the camcorder?

   Write the hidden question. _____

   _____

Name _____ Date _____

WRITE THE HIDDEN QUESTION

Directions:
In each of the following, write the hidden question.

1. An automobile insurance policy costs Mr. Afferty $2,850 a year. If he installs an alarm system, he receives a discount of 5 percent per year. The alarm system costs him $325. If he keeps the car for five years, how much does he save?

   Write the hidden question. _____

   _____

2. To get an A in his math course, Larry needs an average of 90 on the four tests. So far, on three tests, he has scored 96, 92, and 74. What must he score on the next test to get the A?

   Write the hidden question. _____

   _____

3. The following figures have the same perimeter. Which has the larger area and by how many square inches?

   Write the hidden question. _____

   _____

4. Mrs. Simpson went from her home to the airport—a distance of 12 miles—in a taxi. If the taxi rates were $1.25 for the first ¹/₂ mile and 50¢ for each additional quarter mile, how much was her cab fare?

   Write the hidden question. _____

   _____

Name _____ Date _____

5. Christopher planned to make a vegetable garden behind his house. To keep out the rabbits, he decided to enclose it with a fence. He has 100 feet of fencing. He decided to make the garden in the shape of a rectangle, but he couldn't decide on the size. He wants to use all of his fencing. If he wanted to make a garden with the largest area, which of the following shapes should he use?

20   30   22   28   25   25

Write the hidden question. _____

_____

6. The selling price of a shirt is $18.00. If the markup was 50 percent, how much did the shopkeeper pay for the shirt?

Write the hidden question. _____

_____

7. A cube has an edge of 20 centimeters. Find its surface area.

Write the hidden question. _____

_____

Name _____ Date _____

WHAT'S EXTRA?

Directions:

Sometimes a problem gives you more information than you need in order to solve it. You must be able to decide which facts are extra. Read each of the problems that follow. Select the fact or facts that are extra.

1. Last Monday 80 books were checked out of the school library. Of these, $\frac{1}{8}$ were mysteries, $\frac{1}{2}$ were science fiction, and $\frac{1}{10}$ were romance novels. The rest were on mixed topics. How many mysteries were checked out?

   What's Extra?

   _____ $\frac{1}{8}$ of the books checked out were mysteries.

   _____ $\frac{1}{10}$ of the books checked out were romance novels.

   _____ $\frac{1}{2}$ of the books checked out were science fiction.

2. On a distant planet, Mrs. Gamma-A runs the local interplanetary zoo. She has twice as many Martian ant-eaters as Saturnian sand-drinkers. She has twice as many moon carnivores as Neptune swimming eels. If she has 400 Neptune swimming eels, how many moon carnivores does she have?

   What's Extra?

   _____ She has twice as many Martian ant-eaters as Saturnian sand-drinkers.

   _____ She has twice as many moon carnivores as Neptune swimmers.

   _____ She has 400 Neptune swimming eels.

3. The local stereo shop is advertising a sale of up to 75 percent off on all LP records, Mike bought a "Show Stoppers" album for $1.95 that originally sold for $8.95. He paid for the album with a $10 bill. How much did he save by buying the record on sale?

Name _____ Date _____

What's Extra?

_____ The savings were up to 75 percent.

_____ The album was called "Show Stoppers."

_____ The original price of the record was $8.95.

_____ The sale price of the record was $1.95.

_____ He paid with a $10 bill.

Directions

Read each of the problems that follow. Put a circle around the facts that you do *not* need to solve the problem.

4. Mr. Johnson inspects kites at the Fly High Kite Factory. One day, of the 150 kites he inspected, 22 did not pass. Eight of the kites failed because the picture was painted on backwards; the other 14 had defective frames. How many kites passed inspection on that day?

5. Find the perimeter of trapezoid ABCD.

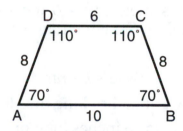

6. During the last softball season, Jane and Marcy had a total of 210 hits. Louise had 20 hits more than Marcy, and Marcy had 20 more hits than Jane. How many hits did Jane have?

7. The bakery sells four different kinds of muffins. They baked 48 muffins on Tuesday. One-fourth of them are oat bran, one-third are raisin bran, one-fourth are blueberry, and the rest are cranberry. How many muffins are bran muffins?

Name _____ Date _____

WHAT'S EXTRA?

Directions:

Sometimes a problem gives you more information than you need in order to solve it. You must be able to decide which facts are extra. Read each of the problems that follow. Select the facts or facts that are extra.

1. In 1989, Mr. Franco bought a new car for $9,800. Three years later, he sold it back to the dealer for $2,400. If he drove the car a total of 51,642 miles during the three years, how much did the car depreciate?

   What's Extra?

   ____ He paid $9,800 for the car when it was new.

   ____ He drove the car 51,642 miles.

   ____ He sold the car for $2,400.

2. Allan and Brittany are competing in a watermelon growing contest. On Monday, Allan's melon was 4 inches long, and each day it grew 2 more inches. Brittany's melon was 6 inches long on Monday, and grew $1\frac{1}{2}$ inches each day. On what day was Allan's melon 18 inches long?

   What's Extra?

   ____ Allan's melon was 4 inches long on Monday.

   ____ Brittany's melon was 6 inches long on Monday.

   ____ Allan's melon grew 2 inches every day.

   ____ Brittany's melon grew $1\frac{1}{2}$ inches every day.

3. The Sharks basketball team won their playoff game by 22 points. The team captain, Elijah Johnson, scored 5 two-point shots and made 16 out of 22 foul shots. Marcus Sawyer scored 7 two-point shots and 11 out of 17 foul shots. "Monster" Arrow scored 3 two-point shots and 5 out of 9 foul shots. Which of the three players had the best foul shooting percent in the game?

Name _____ Date _____

What's Extra?

____ The Sharks won by 22 points.

____ Elijah Johnson scored 5 two-point shots.

____ Elijah Johnson scored 16 foul shots.

____ Elijah Johnson attempted 22 foul shots.

____ Marcus Sawyer scored 7 two-point shots.

____ Marcus Sawyer scored 11 foul shots.

____ Marcus Sawyer attempted 17 foul shots.

____ "Monster" Arrow scored 3 two-point shots.

____ "Monster" Arrow scored 5 foul shots.

____ "Monster" Arrow attempted 9 foul shots.

Directions:

Read each of the problems that follow. Put a circle around the facts that you do *not* need to solve the problem.

4. On Saturday, Janet delivered 68 copies of the *Bulletin*. She delivered twice as many copies on Sunday. The daily paper sells for 40¢ and the Sunday paper sells for $1.35. How much did she collect for Sunday's papers?

5. Tom Ato delivers a pizza every Tuesday to the Browns, who live on the second floor of an apartment building. There are four apartments on the second floor. There are two entrances to the building. There are two stairways and an elevator between the first and second floors. How many different routes can Mr. Ato take to go from the street to the Brown's apartment?

6. Suzie sells seashell necklaces and bracelets at the seashore. Necklaces sell for $5 and the bracelets for $3. Yesterday she sold 26 items and took in $98. She began with 210 items of jewelry and ended the day with 184. How many of each did she sell?

7. Morgan belongs to a video cassette club. During the first year he bought five videos at an average cost of $19.95 per video. He also paid $1.75 for postage and handling of each cassette. How much did he spend for postage and handling for the five cassettes?

Name _____ Date _____

WHAT'S EXTRA?

Directions:

Read each of the problems that follow. Put a circle around the facts that you do *not* need to solve the problem. Then solve each problem.

1. Five people went to lunch last Friday and agreed to divide the cost equally. The bill of $42.00 included 6 percent sales tax. They decided to leave $7.50 as a gratuity. Find each person's share of the total cost.

2. A chart on the back of a box of cereal states that a 1-ounce portion contains .36 milligrams of iron, which is 2 percent of the Minimum Daily Requirement (MDR). It also contains 5 grams of fat, which is 15 percent of the MDR. What is the MDR of iron?

3. A tailor buys $6^1/2$ yards of wool flannel cloth at $12.50 per yard. He needs $2^1/2$ yards to make a jacket and $2^7/8$ yards to make the slacks. What is the cost of the material for the jacket?

4. Each color marker in a game has a different point value: blue is 2 points, red is 5 points, and yellow is 3 points. Mercedes, who has a score of 64 points, has 15 yellows. What is the maximum number of red markers she could have?

5. Find the area of a square whose side is 3 and whose diagonal is $3\sqrt{2}$.

6. The face of a clock on the side of city hall is in the shape of a square. The minute and hour hands on the clock are 18 feet long and 12 feet long, respectively. What is the angle formed by the hands of the clock at 3:00 P.M.?

7. The captain of the hockey team set a goal for his team to win 150 percent of last year's victories this season. The new goal is 27 wins, but they have already lost 7 games. How many games did they win last year?

Name _____ Date _____

WHAT'S MISSING?

Directions:

In each problem, an important fact has been left out. Determine what is missing. Then supply a fact that completes the problem. Now solve the problem.

1. Larry, Moe, and Curly are running a race. Larry finished ahead of Curly. Moe finished ahead of Curly. Who won the race?

   What's Missing? _____

   _____

   The Needed Fact Is: _____

2. At the playoff game, the home team won by five points. What was the final score?

   What's Missing? _____

   _____

   The Needed Fact Is: _____

3. Jerome bought two cassettes and three CD recordings. A CD costs twice as much as a cassette. How much did Jerome spend?

   What's Missing? _____

   _____

   The Needed Fact Is: _____

4. The Chinook salmon is the largest type of salmon. How many more ounces does a 24-pound Chinook salmon weigh than four pink salmon?

   What's Missing? _____

   _____

   The Needed Fact Is: _____

5. Maxine gave $\frac{1}{2}$ of her collection of baseball cards to her brother, Clarence. Then she gave $\frac{1}{4}$ of what was left to her cousin, Peter. She gave the rest to Michael. How many cards did each person receive?

   What's Missing? _____

   _____

   The Needed Fact Is: _____

Name _____ Date _____

6. So far this season, the Bears have won $5/6$ of their games, the Panthers have won $3/4$ of their games, and the Wolves have lost $1/5$ of their games. Who has won the most games so far?

   What's Missing? _____

   _____

   The Needed Fact Is: _____

7. Mrs. Collins wants to tile her recreation room floor. Each tile is a 1-foot square. If the perimeter of the recreation room is 44 feet, how many tiles must she buy?

   What's Missing? _____

   _____

   The Needed Fact Is: _____

Name _____ Date _____

WHAT'S MISSING?

Directions:

In each problem, an important fact has been left out. Determine what is missing. Then supply a fact that completes the problem. Now solve each problem.

1. In Poland, the Carpathian Mountains reach a peak of 8,200 feet. Miguel is climbing to the top of the mountain. How much farther must he climb?

   What's Missing? _____

   _____

   The Needed Fact Is: _____

2. A person burns about 360 calories an hour when walking at about 4 miles per hour. Janet walked around the block three times on Friday. How many calories did she burn?

   What's Missing? _____

   _____

   The Needed Fact Is: _____

3. The annual telethon to raise money for the homeless is scheduled to last 12 hours. Rachel turned on the television set at 8:00 A.M. and watched for 20 minutes. She turned it on again at 11:00 A.M., and watched for another 20 minutes. When will the telethon end?

   What's Missing? _____

   _____

   The Needed Fact Is: _____

4. Before the last test, Gene had an average of 78. In order to get a final grade of B, he must have an average of at least 80. What must he score on the last test to get a B?

   What's Missing? _____

   _____

   The Needed Fact Is: _____

Name ——————————————— Date ——————

WHAT'S MISSING?

Directions:

In each problem, an important fact has been left out. Determine what is missing. Then supply a fact that completes the problem. Now solve the problem.

1. A business earned $1,950 last week and had expenses of $412. How much did each of the partners receive if they divided the profits equally?

   What's Missing? ——————————————————————

   ————————————————————————————————

   The Needed Fact Is: ——————————————————————

2. Mike averaged 21 points per game in 18 regular-season basketball games. He averaged 24 points per game in the postseason tournament. What was Mike's average for all the games played?

   What's Missing? ——————————————————————

   ————————————————————————————————

   The Needed Fact Is: ——————————————————————

3. A driveway is rectangular in shape, 95 feet long and 12 feet wide. It is paved with concrete. If concrete costs $4.00 per cubic foot, how much did it cost to pave the driveway?

   What's Missing? ——————————————————————

   ————————————————————————————————

   The Needed Fact Is: ——————————————————————

4. On the average, Jesse's car uses 10 gallons of gasoline for every 220 miles of travel. Approximately how many miles does his car travel on a full tank of gasoline?

   What's Missing? ——————————————————————

   ————————————————————————————————

   The Needed Fact Is: ——————————————————————

Name _____ Date _____

WHAT'S WRONG?

Directions:
In problems 1 through 6, decide what is wrong.

1. (a) Judy is three years older than her sister, Barbara.
   (b) In four years, Judy will be seven years older than Barbara.
   What's Wrong? _____
   _____

2. (a) Renee bowled 3 games.
   (b) Her average for the 3 games was 150.
   (c) She scored 120, 132, and 144.
   What's Wrong? _____
   _____

3. The Chew family took a drive last Sunday. Yuen Ling checked the odometer and it read 26,431 miles. For the first hour, they averaged 45 miles per hour. For the second hour, they averaged 55 miles per hour. At the end of the two hours, the odometer read 26,541 miles.
   What's Wrong? _____
   _____

4. The Elm Street bus started its run with 5 passengers aboard. At the first stop, 2 people got off and 7 got on. At the next stop, 5 people got off and 5 people got on. One block later, the bus got a flat tire and all 11 passengers had to get off to wait for the next bus.
   What's Wrong? _____
   _____

5. The Panthers basketball team scored 15 points in the first quarter, 21 points in the second quarter, and only 37 points in the entire second half. The Screamin' Eagles scored 39 points in the first half, then outscored the Panthers by 3 points in the second half. The Panthers won the game by only 6 points.
   What's Wrong? _____
   _____

Name _____ Date _____

WHAT'S WRONG?

Directions:
In problems 1 through 6, decide what is wrong.

1. (a) The temperature outside my house has been in the low 80s for more than a week.
   (b) My father's car got stuck in the snow outside of our garage today.
   What's Wrong? _____
   _____

2. (a) $x > 0 \quad y > 0$
   (b) $x \cdot y = -27$
   What's Wrong? _____
   _____

3. (a) On Malcolm's flight from New York City to Los Angeles, the flying time was exactly five hours.
   (b) When he left New York, the clock in the terminal read 9:00 A.M., and when he arrived in Los Angeles, that airport clock read 2:00 P.M.
   What's Wrong? _____
   _____

4. (a) The perimeter of equilateral triangle ABC is 15 feet.
   (b) The measure of angle B equals the sum of the measures of the other two angles.
   What's Wrong? _____
   _____

5. Lisa and her brother, Marty, went fishing with their father. They left the house at 7:00 A.M. It took one hour to get to the lake. They began fishing at 7:30 and by 9:15 Lisa had caught five fish and Marty had caught four fish.
   What's Wrong? _____
   _____

6. Michelle jogs every morning to prepare for the coming marathon. Tuesday, she left her house, jogged 6 miles due east, then 8 miles due north, and returned to her home by jogging 10 miles due west.
   What's Wrong? _____
   _____

Name _____ Date _____

WHAT'S WRONG?

Directions:

In each of the following problems, the statements given are true. Determine whether the conclusion correctly follows from the given statements.

1. (a) All cats have four legs.
   (b) All dogs have four legs.
   Conclusion: All cats are dogs.

2. (a) Anthony is older than Steve.
   (b) Anthony is older than Megan.
   Conclusion: Steve is older than Megan.

3. (a) Stan, Stu, and Selma are in a three-person race.
   (b) Stan passed Stu just before the finish line.
   (c) Selma finished 10 seconds ahead of Stu.
   Conclusion: Stu finished third in the race.

4. (a) Last week, the grass was 10 inches high.
   (b) This week, the grass is 14 inches high.
   Conclusion: The grass is 24 inches high.

5. (a) The Panthers outscored the Bears by 7 points in the first half of the game.
   (b) The Bears outscored the Panthers by 22–12 in the second half of the game.
   Conclusion: The Bears won the game by 4 points.

6. (a) Fifty percent of the graduating seniors in Maywood High School were accepted to UCLA.
   (b) Fifty percent of the graduating seniors in Maywood High School were accepted to Harvard.
   Conclusion: All the seniors in Maywood High School were accepted to college.

7. (a) The probability of rain on Saturday is $1/2$.
   (b) The probability of rain on Sunday is $1/2$.
   Conclusion: The probability of rain on both days is $3/4$.

8. (a) Mary bought 6-inch, round pizza for lunch.
   (b) Janet bought a 12-inch, round pizza for lunch.
   Conclusion: Janet has twice as much pizza as Mary.

Name _____ Date _____

MAKE UP THE PROBLEM

Directions:

Most of the time in school, the teacher or the textbook gives you the problem and you are expected to supply the solution. Let's turn things around! Here are the answers. For each of these answers, you make up the problem.

1. The answer is 24.   *Problem:* _____

_____

_____ .

2. The answer is 15 feet.   *Problem:* _____

_____

_____ .

3. The answer is 75 percent.   *Problem:* _____

_____

_____ .

4. The train arrived at 7:30 P.M.   *Problem:* _____

_____

_____ .

5. Janet used six gallons of paint.   *Problem:* _____

_____

_____ .

6. The perimeter is 57 meters.   *Problem:* _____

_____

_____ .

7. The mountain is 12,000 feet high at its peak.   *Problem:* _____

_____

_____ .

8. The answer is 37 inches, and it was arrived at by subtraction.   *Problem:* _____

_____

_____ .

Name _____ Date _____

MAKE UP THE PROBLEM

Directions:

Most of the time in school, the teacher or the textbook gives you the problem, and you are expected to supply the solution. Let's change things around. Here are the answers. For each of these answers, you make up the problem.

1. The answer is 120 square feet.   *Problem:* _____

    _____

    _____.

2. The probability is $^{1}/_{4}$.   *Problem:* _____

    _____

    _____.

3. The mean weight is 248 pounds.   *Problem:* _____

    _____

    _____.

4. The vertex angle contains 40°.   *Problem:* _____

    _____

    _____.

5. Marci received $4.62 in change.   *Problem:* _____

    _____

    _____.

6. The answer is 2π.   *Problem:* _____

    _____

    _____.

7. John raised his average by 5 points.   *Problem:* _____

    _____

    _____.

8. She had 12 different outfits consisting of a skirt and a blouse.   *Problem:* _____

    _____

    _____.

Name _____ Date _____

MAKE UP THE PROBLEM

Directions:
Make up a problem using some or all of the given facts. You may wish to add some facts of your own.

1.

Acceleration Time for Selected Automobile	
Car	*Seconds to Reach 60 MPH*
A	15
B	12
C	18
D	19
E	14

2. *Movie Tickets*

Monday–Thursday

　Before 6:00 P.M. $3.50

　After 6:00 P.M. $6.00

Friday–Sunday

　Before 7:00 P.M. $4.00

　After 7:00 P.M. $6.50

Senior Citizens .... $3.00 at all times

3.

Mathematics Test Grades		
Interval	*Number of Students*	*Frequency*
Below 59	̶H̶H̶ //	7
60–69	///	3
70–79	̶H̶H̶ ///	8
80–89	̶H̶H̶ /	6
90–99	///	3

4. Lenny has eight red socks, six blue socks, and four white socks in his bottom drawer.

5. A bicycle wheel is 26 inches in diameter. The circular track has an outside diameter of 15 yards, and is 6 yards wide.

Name _____ Date _____

MAKE UP THE PROBLEM

Directions:

Make up a problem using some or all of the given facts. You may wish to add some facts of your own.

1. Mr. Richards buys a *Golf Magazine* every month for $2.75. A one-year subscription to the magazine costs $17.50.
2. Georgia's test scores for the semester prior to the final examination were 89, 78, 53, 96, 64, and 71.
3. The township is planting a new grove of trees. The grove is 100 feet by 250 feet, rectangular in shape. Each tree will need 25 square feet of room to grow.
4. Melanie put 12 gallons of gasoline in her car before she started on her trip. Her car averages 28 miles per gallon. On the map, her trip is $4\frac{1}{2}$ inches. (Map Scale: 1" = 60 miles.)

Name _____ Date _____

MAKE UP THE PROBLEM

Directions:
Make up a problem from the data supplied by the graph.

1.

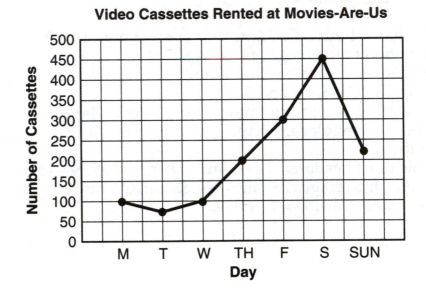

Video Cassettes Rented at Movies-Are-Us

2.

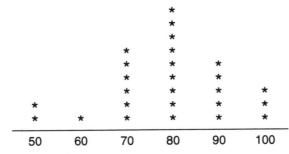

Student Grades on a Mathematics Test

Name _____ Date _____

3.

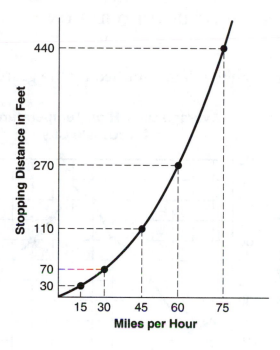

Name _____ Date _____

MAKE UP THE QUESTION

Directions:
Make up a problem from the data supplied by the graph.

1.

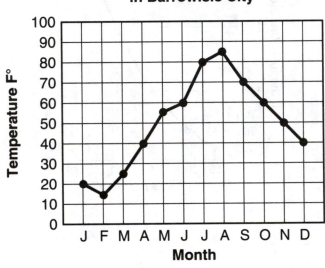

**Average Daily High Temperatures
in Barrowisle City**

2.

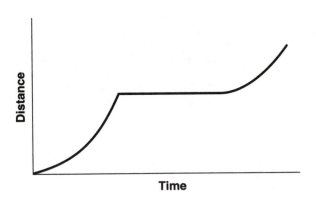

Name _____ Date _____

3.

Number of Students in Each Grade

Name _____ Date _____

PATTERNS

Directions:

For each of the following, tell in your own words what the pattern rule is. Then write another element.

1. carrots, beets, stringbeans, peas, _____

   Pattern Rule: _____.

2. baseball, football, soccer, tennis, _____

   Pattern Rule: _____.

3. dogs, cats, gerbils, canaries, _____

   Pattern Rule: _____.

4. Minneapolis, New York, Seattle, Chicago, _____

   Pattern Rule: _____.

5. cat, bag, lap, man, _____

   Pattern Rule: _____.

6. Carol, Susan, Janet, Karen, _____

   Pattern Rule: _____.

7. apple, street, butter, cook, _____

   Pattern Rule: _____.

8. bib, mom, Otto, toot, _____

   Pattern Rule: _____.

9. 27, 7, 37, 177, _____

   Pattern Rule: _____.

10. 2, 16, 148, 36, _____

    Pattern Rule: _____.

11. 15, 10, 25, 35, _____

    Pattern Rule: _____.

12. $1/2$, $3/4$, $5/7$, $2/3$, _____

    Pattern Rule: _____.

Name _____ Date _____

PATTERNS

Directions:

For each of the following, tell in your own words what the pattern rule is. Then write another element.

1. bicycle, car, airplane, roller skates, _____
   Pattern Rule: _____.

2. team, orchestra, class, troop, _____
   Pattern Rule: _____.

3. diamonds, emeralds, rubies, garnets, _____
   Pattern Rule: _____.

4. shirts, ties, socks, jackets, _____
   Pattern Rule: _____.

5. battle, cook, zipper, stall, _____
   Pattern Rule: _____.

6. pressure, potato, stop, nap, _____
   Pattern Rule: _____.

7. river, paper, mother, strainer, _____
   Pattern Rule: _____.

8. blink, apple, grass, train, _____
   Pattern Rule: _____.

9. 3443, 1221, 7227, 4004, _____
   Pattern Rule: _____.

10. 31, 17, 2, 29, _____
    Pattern Rule: _____.

11. 6, 180, 42, 120, _____
    Pattern Rule: _____.

12. $\tan 45°$, $\sin^2 70° + \cos^2 70°$, $\cos 0°$, $\sin 90°$, _____
    Pattern Rule: _____.

Name _____ Date _____

PATTERNS

Directions:
For each of the following, tell in your own words what the pattern rule is. Then write another element.

1. dollar, lire, franc, shekel, _____

   Pattern Rule: _____ .

2. court, field, diamond, pool, _____

   Pattern Rule: _____ .

3. radishes, potatoes, carrots, beets, _____

   Pattern Rule: _____ .

4. Mars, Jupiter, Saturn, Uranus, _____

   Pattern Rule: _____ .

5. jar, jaguar, jacket, jump, _____

   Pattern Rule: _____ .

6. camel, lemon, comet, tumor, _____

   Pattern Rule: _____ .

7. rumor, ticket, window, Alabama, _____

   Pattern Rule: _____ .

8. able, deaf, store, note, _____

   Pattern Rule: _____ .

9. 1991, 57275, 868, 14041, _____

   Pattern Rule: _____ .

10. 61, 17, 29, 23, _____

    Pattern Rule: _____ .

11. 27, 729, 243, 81, _____

    Pattern Rule: _____ .

12. 502, 98, 202, 398, _____

    Pattern Rule: _____ .

Name _____ Date _____

WHAT'S NEXT?

Directions:
In each of the following, tell in your own words what the pattern rule is.
Then write the next term in the sequence.

1. 1, 3, 5, 7, _____
   Pattern Rule: _____.

2. 12, 23, 34, 45, _____
   Pattern Rule: _____.

3. ½, ¾, 1, ⁵/₄, _____
   Pattern Rule: _____.

4. 1, 2, 3, 5, _____
   Pattern Rule: _____.

5. a, ab, abc, abcd, _____
   Pattern Rule: _____.

6. ab, bc, cd, de, _____
   Pattern Rule: _____.

7. I, no, yes, girl, _____
   Pattern Rule: _____.

8. Frank, Grace, Henry, Irene, _____
   Pattern Rule: _____.

9. △, □, ⬠, _____
   Pattern Rule: _____.

10. □, ■, □□, ■■, □□□, _____
    Pattern Rule: _____.

Name _____ Date _____

WHAT'S NEXT?

Directions:

In each of the following, tell in your own words what the pattern rule is. Then write the next term in the sequence.

1. 80, 40, 20, 10, _____

   Pattern Rule: _____.

2. 1, 2, 4, 7, 11, _____

   Pattern Rule: _____.

3. 3, 4, 7, 14, _____

   Pattern Rule: _____.

4. 12, 34, 56, _____

   Pattern Rule: _____.

5. 1z, 3y, 5x, 7w, _____

   Pattern Rule: _____.

6. run, four, alive, jacket, _____

   Pattern Rule: _____.

7. □, △, □ □, △ △, _____

   Pattern Rule: _____.

8. ▦, ▦, ▦, _____

   Pattern Rule: _____.

9. △, ▲, ○, ●, _____

   Pattern Rule: _____.

10. x^3, x^2, x, 1, _____

   Pattern Rule: _____.

Name _____ Date _____

WHAT'S NEXT?

Directions:

In each of the following, tell in your own words what the pattern rule is. Then write the next two terms in the sequence.

1. 16, 37, 58, _____ , _____

   Pattern Rule: _____.

2. 2, 3, 5, 8, _____ , _____

   Pattern Rule: _____.

3. 5–7, 11–13, 17–19, 29–31, _____ , _____

   Pattern Rule: _____.

4. 1, 3, 6, 10, _____ , _____

   Pattern Rule: _____.

5. 36, 18, 9, 4½, _____ , _____

   Pattern Rule: _____.

6. Ann, Brad, Carol, Daniel, _____ , _____

   Pattern Rule: _____.

7. O, T, T, F, _____ , _____

   Pattern Rule: _____.

8. tr, qu, pe, he, _____ , _____

   Pattern Rule: _____.

9. _____ , _____

   Pattern Rule: _____.

10. _____ , _____

   Pattern Rule: _____.

Name _____ Date _____

WHICH IS DIFFERENT?

Directions:

In each of the following sets, one element does not belong. Place a ring around the one that is different and tell why it does not belong.

1. 2, 14, 6, 13, 18 _____

2. $\frac{1}{8}$, $\frac{2}{3}$, $\frac{3}{8}$, $\frac{5}{8}$ _____

3. 15, 13, 19, 22, 17 _____

4. 3, 6, 9, 11, 15 _____

5. blue, black, orange, brown, beige _____

6. peas, beans, salmon, carrots, beets _____

7. Washington, Eisenhower, Franklin, Truman, Roosevelt _____

8. mom, noon, dad, dog, level _____

9. 4, 64, 81, 8, 4096 _____

10. sin 270°, cos 180°, i^2, tan 225°, cot 135° _____

Name ⎯⎯⎯⎯⎯⎯⎯⎯⎯⎯⎯⎯⎯⎯⎯ Date ⎯⎯⎯⎯⎯⎯⎯

WHICH IS DIFFERENT?

Directions:

In each of the following sets, one element does not belong. Place a ring around the one that is different and tell why it does not belong.

1. 64, 81, 4, 9, 17   ⎯⎯⎯⎯⎯⎯⎯⎯⎯⎯
2. 23, 56, 41, 78, 34   ⎯⎯⎯⎯⎯⎯⎯⎯⎯⎯
3. 19, 56, 28, 37   ⎯⎯⎯⎯⎯⎯⎯⎯⎯⎯
4. 9, 33, 25, 18, 21   ⎯⎯⎯⎯⎯⎯⎯⎯⎯⎯
5. baseball, football, basketball, bowling ball   ⎯⎯⎯⎯⎯⎯⎯⎯⎯⎯
6. duck, chicken, turkey, pig   ⎯⎯⎯⎯⎯⎯⎯⎯⎯⎯
7. submarine, helicopter, dirigible, airplane   ⎯⎯⎯⎯⎯⎯⎯⎯⎯⎯
8. New Years, July 4th, Thanksgiving,
   Halloween, Christmas   ⎯⎯⎯⎯⎯⎯⎯⎯⎯⎯
9. (2, 1), (14, 8), (6, 3), (12, 6), (20, 10)   ⎯⎯⎯⎯⎯⎯⎯⎯⎯⎯
10. $x^2 - 1$, $x^2 + 2x + 1$, $x^2 + 2x - 3$, $x^2 + 1$,
    $x^2 - 5x + 6$ ⎯⎯⎯⎯⎯⎯⎯⎯⎯⎯

Name _____ Date _____

WHICH IS DIFFERENT?

Directions:

In each of the following sets, one element does not belong. Place a ring around the one that is different and tell why it does not belong.

1. 17, 81, 19, 29, 61   _____
2. 7, 41, 2, 17, 39   _____
3. 3–4–5, 5–12–13, 8–15–17, 7–9–11   _____
4. 84, 57, 47, 147, 39   _____
5. Dodgers, Yankees, Packers, Royals, Braves   _____
6. oak, maple, sycamore, pine   _____
7. Maine, New Hampshire, Texas, Vermont,   _____
   Massachusetts
8. Lincoln, Nixon, Eisenhower, Jefferson,   _____
   Roosevelt
9. $(x^2)^0$, $(x^0)^3$, (i^4), (tan 45°), (cos 180°)   _____
10. adjacent angles, vertical angles,   _____
    complementary angles, alternate
    interior angles

Name _____ Date _____

Problem:

How many beads are on the chain shown?

Name _____ Date _____

Problem:

How many beads are on the chain shown?

Name _____ Date _____

Problem:

Jose is arranging grapefruits in the produce department of the supermarket, in the form of a triangle. When he has finished, the first (or top) row had 1 grapefruit, the second row had 3 grapefruits, the third row had 6 grapefruits, the fourth row had 10 grapefruits, and so on for a total of 7 rows. How many grapefruits did Jose use in the display?

Name _____ Date _____

Problem:

The local Public Broadcasting System is having a five-day fundraiser. On the first day, Monday, the host called 3 people. He asked each of them to call 3 of their friends on Tuesday and to ask each of them to call 3 friends on Wednesday. Everyone who is called will call 3 different friends on the next day. After the Friday calls had been made, how many people will have been called?

Name ——————————————————— Date ——————

Problem:

A mooring rope that is 1 inch thick and 63 feet long is being coiled on the dock. The first coil took 12 inches of rope, the second coil took 24 inches, the third took 48 inches, and so on. How many coils are needed for the entire rope? What is the diameter of the circle formed by the coiled rope?

Name _____ Date _____

Problem:

The seventh grade is going on a field trip to the local aquarium. The teacher told the children to remember which of the three buses they had been assigned to—Bus Two, Bus Three, or Bus Eight. She assigned Amy, Nancy, and David to Bus Two. She put Jeff, Danny, Charlotte, and Clarissa on Bus Three. Mabel, Justin, Nora, Lars, and Denise were assigned to Bus Eight. To which bus did the teacher assign each of these children: Booker, Steve, Barbara, Michael, Susanne, Claire, Alex, Helen, Amanda, Matthew, Stanley, Murray, Jimmy, and Hope? To which bus should she assign Dennis? Why?

Name _____ Date _____

Problem:
For Gilda's party, the Hoagie House prepared a huge sub sandwich on a 7-foot long hoagie roll. Gilda wants to feed 16 people. How many cuts must she make?

Name _____ Date _____

Problem:

Eric is arranging the dining room in his restaurant to accommodate a party of 34 people. He is taking small, square tables that seat one person on each side, and is placing them end-to-end to make one long table. How many tables will Eric need?

Name ———————————————— Date ——————————

Problem:

Joanne and her friends are seated around a large, circular table at a banquet. Twenty-five dishes are passed around the table, with each person taking one dish in turn, until there are no dishes left. Joanne takes the first dish and also gets the last one. She may have more than just the first and last dishes, however. How many people are at the banquet?

Name ——————————————— Date ——————

Problem:

Laura is training her pet white rabbit, Ghost, to climb up a flight of 10 steps. Ghost can only hop up 1 or 2 steps each time he hops. He never hops down, only up. How many different ways can Ghost hop up the flight of 10 steps?

Name _____ Date _____

Problem:

The circus is setting up its tent. There are 12 poles holding the tent upright. Between every two poles, there will be a rope full of banners. How many ropes will there be?

Name _____ Date _____

Problem:

Mr. Rafaelo runs a bicycle store. He sells a bike for $165, including the tax. To determine his selling price, he added $10 to the cost of the bike for a child's seat on the back. Then he doubled the total for his own markup. Last, he added $15 for sales tax. How much did the bike cost Mr. Rafaelo?

Name _____ Date _____

Problem:

The local library fine schedule for overdue books is as follows:

    25¢ per day for each of the first three days

    10¢ per day thereafter

Sandra paid a fine of $1.35. How many days overdue was her book?

Name _____ Date _____

Problem:

Mr. Davis wants to encourage his son Jimmy to save money. Each time Jimmy puts $3 into a savings account (once a month), Mr. Davis doubles the amount of money in the account. Jimmy now has exactly $90 in the account. How many months ago did he start?

Name _____ Date _____

Problem:

Loretta owns a pet shop that specializes in exotic tropical fish. In April, Loretta doubled the number of fish she had on hand, and then sold 30 of them. In May, she tripled the number of fish she had on hand, and then sold 54 of them. In June, she quadrupled the number of fish she had, and then sold 72 of them. She now had 48 fish left. How many fish did she start with?

Name _____ Date _____

Problem:

Place 20 pennies on the table in a row. Now replace every fourth coin with a nickel. Now replace every third coin with a dime. Now replace every sixth coin with a quarter. What is the value of the 20 coins now on the table?

Name _____ Date _____

Problem:

There are four boys and five girls standing outside the new record shop. The sign in the window offers a prize to every couple (one boy and one girl) that enters the store. How many prizes can the nine people get?

Name ———————————————————— Date ——————

Problem:

The Art Club at the Carroll School decided to exchange gifts at the end-of-school party. Each of the eight members brought a gift for each of the other members. How many gifts were exchanged?

Name _____ Date _____

Problem:

The new school has exactly 1,000 lockers and exactly 1,000 students. On the first day of school, the students meet outside the building and agree on the following plan: The first student will enter the school and open all the lockers. The second student will then enter the school and close every locker with an even number (2, 4, 6, 8,...). The third student will then "reverse" every third locker (3, 6, 9, 12,...). That is, if the locker is closed, the student will open it; if the locker is open, he or she will close it. The fourth student will then reverse every fourth locker, and so on until all 1,000 students in turn have entered the building and reversed the proper lockers. Which lockers finally remain open?

Name ＿＿＿＿＿＿＿＿＿＿＿＿＿＿＿＿＿ Date ＿＿＿＿＿＿

Problem:

The Continental Hockey League consists of two conferences, each with six teams. Every team plays the teams within its own conference twice and plays each team in the other conference once. How many games are played during the season?

Name _____ Date _____

Problem:

Matt is selling baseball cards at a local flea market. Rookie cards sell for $5 each, Champion cards sell for $6 each, Old-Timer cards sell for $7 each, and Hall-of-Famer cards sell for $9 each. Renee bought 3 cards and spent $18. What cards did she buy?

Name ———————————————————— Date ——————————

Problem:

Nancy sells rings and bracelets at the local crafts fair. She receives $6 for a bracelet and $4 for a ring. She started the day with the same number of bracelets as rings, and, at the end of the day, she found that she had twice as many rings left as bracelets. She had taken in $96 altogether. How many of each did she sell?

Name _____ Date _____

Problem:

In a game at the County Fair, each color marker has a different point value: black = 2, green = 3, and red = 5. Howard has a score of 55 points. He has 12 green markers. How many red markers does he have?

Name _____ Date _____

Problem:

Ruth took a multiple-choice test with 20 questions. The test is scored +5 for each correct answer, –2 for each incorrect one, and 0 if the question is not answered. She scored 48 on the test. How did she do this?

Name _____ Date _____

SYLLOGISMS

Directions:

For each pair of statements there is a conclusion listed. Tell whether the conclusion is true, false, or cannot be determined.

1. Roy drank orange juice or grapefruit juice for breakfast.
   He did not drink orange juice.
   Conclusion: Roy drank grapefruit juice for breakfast.   _____

2. Janet's birthday is today or tomorrow.
   Her birthday is not tomorrow.
   Conclusion: Her birthday is next week.   _____

3. Mark is in history class, math class, or art class.
   He is not in art class.
   Conclusion: Mark is in math class.   _____

4. All canaries are yellow.
   Maria owns a canary.
   Conclusion: Maria's canary is yellow.   _____

5. All squares are rectangles.
   ABCD is a rectangle.
   Conclusion: ABCD is a square.   _____

6. Some styx live in Nyx.
   Paul is a styx.
   Conclusion: Paul lives in Nyx.   _____

7. Some cats are white.
   Anna has a cat.
   Conclusion: Anna's cat is white.   _____

8. All barbers are named Robin.
   John is a barber.
   Conclusion: John is named Robin.   _____

Name ————————————————————— Date ——————————

SYLLOGISMS

Directions:

For each pair of statements there is a conclusion listed. Tell whether the conclusion is true, false, or cannot be determined.

1. All triangles have three angles.
   LMN is a triangle.
   Conclusion: LMN has three angles. ——————

2. All parallelograms are quadrilaterals.
   ABCD is a quadrilateral.
   Conclusion: ABCD is a parallelogram. ——————

3. Bonnie Clyde owns a Dodge or a Jeep.
   She does not own a Dodge.
   Conclusion: Bonnie Clyde owns a Jeep. ——————

4. Some books are paperbacks.
   Beauty and the Beast is a book.
   Conclusion: *Beauty and the Beast* is a hardback. ——————

5. If it is raining, then the street is wet.
   It is raining.
   Conclusion: The street is wet. ——————

6. If it is raining, then the street is wet.
   The street is wet.
   Conclusion: It is raining. ——————

7. All lupus are drus.
   Ray is a drus.
   Conclusion: Ray is a lupus. ——————

8. All prime numbers are odd numbers.
   Two is a prime number.
   Conclusion: Two is an odd number. ——————

Name _____ Date _____

REASONING

Directions:

Below are two sets of conditions, each with four conclusions. Decide which of these are true, which are false, and which cannot be determined. Circle your choice for each.

1. All schoolteachers are college graduates. Ms. Jones is a mathematics teacher. Mrs. Williams is a college graduate. Mr. Carlin is a biology teacher.

   a. Ms. Jones is a college graduate.   T   F   Unable to tell

   b. Mrs. Williams is a teacher.   T   F   Unable to tell

   c. Mr. Carlin is not a college graduate.   T   F   Unable to tell

   d. Ms. Jones and Mr. Carlin teach at the   T   F   Unable to tell
   same school.

2. All professional football tackles weigh over 250 pounds. John Werner weighs 275 pounds. Mitch Larkin is a professional football tackle. So is Nigel White.

   a. Mitch Larkin weighs 280 pounds.   T   F   Unable to tell

   b. Nigel White weighs 217 pounds.   T   F   Unable to tell

   c. John Werner is a professional football   T   F   Unable to tell
   tackle.

   d. Mitch Larkin and John Werner together T   F   Unable to tell
   weigh over 500 pounds.

Name _____ Date _____

REASONING

Directions:

Below are two sets of problems, each with four conclusions. Decide which of these are true, which are false, and which cannot be determined. Circle your choice for each.

1. Fast Food Freddy sells burgers for 95¢ each, pizza for $1.25 a slice, and soft drinks for 65¢ (small) and 85¢ (large). All prices include tax.

   a. Jill bought 2 slices of pizza and a large   T   F   Unable to tell
   soft drink, and received $1.75 change
   from a $5 bill.

   b. Arlene bought a burger and received   T   F   Unable to tell
   50¢ change.

   c. Martha bought a burger and a small   T   F   Unable to tell
   soft drink and spent $1.60.

   d. Michelle bought a burger and an order   T   F   Unable to tell
   of fries. She spent $3.00.

2. The Jets played the Colts in basketball last night. The final score was Jets 83, Colts 82. The high scorer for the Colts scored 31 points.

   a. The Colts lost by 1 point.   T   F   Unable to tell

   b. At the end of the half, the score was tied.   T   F   Unable to tell

   c. There were 165 points scored in the   T   F   Unable to tell
   entire game.

   d. The high scorer in the game scored 31   T   F   Unable to tell
   points.

   e. There were 35 foul shots made.   T   F   Unable to tell

Name _____ Date _____

DRAWING CONCLUSIONS

Arlene, Brad, and Carl each have a hat. One hat is red, one hat is green, one hat is blue.

1. Arlene does not have a blue hat.
2. Carl's hat is green.

1. What conclusion(s) can you draw from statement 1?
   a. Arlene's hat is red or green.
   b. Carl's hat is not red.
2. What conclusion(s) can you draw from statement 2?
   a. Brad's hat is red.
   b. Carl's hat is not red.
3. What conclusions can you draw from statements 1 and 2?
   a. Arlene's hat is red.
   b. Carl's hat is blue.
4. What color is each person's hat?

Name _____ Date _____

DRAWING CONCLUSIONS

Luisa, Marty, Nora, and Paul own four pets: a dog, a cat, a parakeet, and a goldfish.

1. Luisa's pet does not have four legs.
2. Nora owns the goldfish.
3. Marty went to the pet show with the cat's owner.

1. What conclusions can you draw from statement 1?
   a. Luisa owns the parakeet or the dog.
   b. Luisa owns the parakeet or the goldfish.
   c. Luisa owns the goldfish.
2. What conclusions can you draw from statements 1 and 2?
   a. Luisa owns the goldfish.
   b. Luisa and Marty came to the pet show in the same car.
   c. Luisa owns the goldfish.
3. What conclusions can you draw from statements 1 and 3?
   a. Nora and Paul are brother and sister.
   b. Marty does not own the cat.
   c. Luisa owns the parakeet.
4. What conclusions can you draw from statements 1, 2, and 3?
   a. Paul owns the goldfish.
   b. Marty owns the dog.
   c. Luisa owns the parakeet.
   d. Luisa owns the cat.
5. Tell who owns each pet.

Name _____ Date _____

DRAWING CONCLUSIONS

Alex, Helen, Mandy, and Penny each went to a different movie last night. They saw *Star Trek 22*, *Creature from Planet X*, *The Marshal Returns*, and *Dancing in the Snow*.

1. Penny saw Helen coming out of the theater showing *Star Trek 22*.
2. Alex did not want to see *Creature from Planet X*.
3. Alex and Mandy had already seen *The Marshal Returns* last week.

1. What conclusion(s) can you draw from statement 1?
   a. Alex saw *Star Trek 22*.
   b. Penny saw *Star Trek 22*.
   c. Helen saw *Star Trek 22*.
2. What conclusions can you draw from statements 1 and 2?
   a. Alex saw *Dancing in the Snow*.
   b. Alex saw *Star Trek 22*.
   c. Alex saw either *Dancing in the Snow* or *The Marshal Returns*.
3. What conclusions can you draw from statements 1 and 3?
   a. Penny saw *The Marshal Returns*.
   b. Alex saw *Dancing in the Snow* or *Creature From Planet X*.
   c. Mandy saw *Dancing in the Snow*.
4. What conclusions can you draw from statements 1, 2, and 3 ?
   a. Alex saw *Dancing in the Snow*.
   b. Helen and Alex are sisters.
   c. Penny saw *The Marshal Returns*.
5. Which movie did each girl see?

Name _____ Date _____

Problem:

There were three prizes given at the Arithmetic Contest: a calculator, a book, and a ruler. The winners were Roger, Sally, and Tom.

1. Tom did not win the calculator.
2. Sally won the book.

Who won each prize?

Name _____ Date _____

Problem:

The electrician, plumber, and grocer in a small town are Ruiz, Johnson, and Lee. Lee lives next door to the plumber. The electrician is Lee's daughter. Ruiz and the plumber were on the school debating team back in high school. Which job does each person have?

Name _____ Date _____

Problem:

Today is really your busiest day! You have to meet Mark for lunch at the neighborhood deli, visit the Art Museum, and go to the dentist. In addition, you promised to visit your sick buddy. The deli is closed on Monday, and the Art Museum is open only on Monday, Wednesday, and Friday. Your dentist has office hours on Thursday, Friday, and Saturday. Your sick buddy can have visitors only on Friday and Saturday. What is your busiest day?

Name _____ Date _____

Marv, Stan, Ralph, and Anita (in that order) came to pick up the last four uniforms at the athletic office. There was one of each shirt left on the shelf: a baseball sweatshirt, a football Jersey, a basketball shirt, and a hockey jersey. These were orange, green, black, and yellow, but not in that order. Use the following clues to match the person with the sport and color shirt:

1. Anita did not want the football jersey, but she was required to take it.
2. After Marv picked up his shirt, he wished he had gotten the green one or the baseball sweatshirt.
3. When Stan left, the basketball shirt was still on the shelf.
4. Stan received either the black shirt or the football jersey.
5. Ralph received the yellow shirt.

Name _____ Date _____

Problem:

The following figure shows one side of a diving submarine that takes people down under the water to look at a coral reef. Everyone wears a colored-hat. A green hat is just below a yellow hat. A yellow hat is just above a red hat. A blue hat is in front of two yellow hats. Which seat is empty?

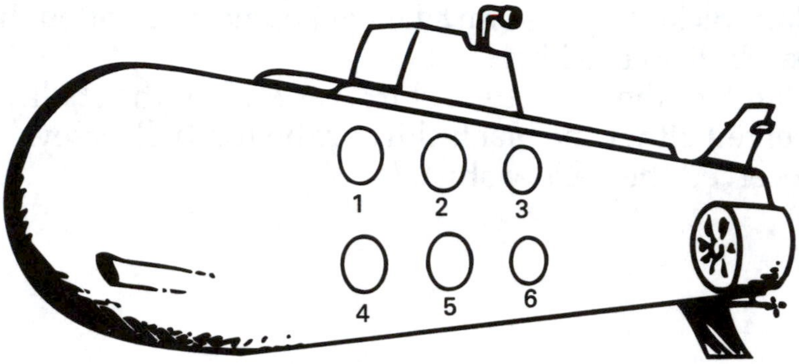

Name ———————————————————————— Date ————————

Problem:

Laurie, Allan, Scott, and Adam all entered their pet frogs in a distance-jumping contest. Laurie's frog finished ahead of Allan's, but was not first. Scott's frog finished behind Laurie's, but was not last. In what order did the frogs finish?

Name _____ Date _____

Problem:

The main event at the auto races had seven entries. In what order did the cars finish?

1. The driver of car #1 was the only one wearing green.
2. Car #6 blew a tire and finished last.
3. Car #2 and car #3 crossed the finish line together.
4. Car #4 beat car #7 by two lengths.
5. Only one car finished ahead of car #5.
6. The winning car had an even number.
7. The driver of car #2 saw green on the driver of the car ahead of him.
8. Car #7 finished two lengths ahead of car #1.

Name ——————————————————— Date ——————————

Problem:

Four married couples went to the theater last week. The wives' names were Carol, Sue, Jeanette, and Arlene. The husbands' names were Dan, Bob, Gary, and Frank. Bob and Jeanette are brother and sister. Jeanette and Frank were once engaged, but they broke up when Jeanette met her husband. Arlene has a brother and a sister, but her husband is an only child. Carol is married to Gary. Who is married to whom?

Name _____ Date _____

Problem:

The citizens of Surreytown have decided to put a license plate on every bicycle. Each license plate will consist of a letter followed by a numeral. The possible letters are the vowels, A, E, I, O, and U. The possible numerals are 1, 2, 3, 4, 5, and 6. How many different license plates are possible?

Name _____ Date _____

Problem:

In an elevator bank of two elevators, the following schedule is installed: Elevator #1 takes two minutes between floors, whereas Elevator #2 takes only one minute between floors. The elevator that arrives at a given floor first must wait three minutes before leaving. No waiting time is required of the elevator that arrives second at a given floor. Both elevators leave the sixth floor on a downward trip at exactly 1:00. Which elevator arrives at the ground floor first, and at what time?

Name _____ Date _____

Problem:

Mr. Homeowner wants to put fresh grass seed down on his front lawn. Grass seed is available in three-pound boxes and in five-pound boxes. A three-pound box costs $4.50, and a five-pound box costs $6.58. Mr. Homeowner needs 17 pounds of the grass seed. How many of each size box should he purchase to get the best buy?

Name _____ Date _____

Problem:

During the recent census, a man told the census taker that he had three children. When asked their ages, the man replied, "The product of their ages is 72. The sum of their ages is the same as my house number." The census taker ran to the door and looked at the house number. "I still can't tell," she complained. The man replied, "Oh, that's right. I forgot to tell you that the oldest one likes chocolate pudding." The census taker promptly wrote down the ages of the three children. How old are they? (Consider only integral ages).

Name _____ Date _____

Problem:

There is a game at the County Fair in which five balls are placed into a basket. Each ball has a number printed on it: 0, 2, 4, 6, 7. A person picks three of the balls from the basket at one time and adds the numbers.

1. How many different sums are possible?
2. What is the probability of scoring higher than 12?

Name ——————————————————— Date ——————————

Problem:

Billy and Maria ordered flyers to advertise the school dance. Flyers cost $8.75 for the first 50, and $1.50 for each additional 10. The bill was $19.25. How many flyers did they order?

Name _____ Date _____

Problem:

This chart shows the cost of birthday cards in Mrs. Henry's Card Shop:

Number of cards	1–3	4–6	7–9	10–12	13 or more
Cost per card	$2.50	$2.25	$2.00	$1.65	$1.50

Mrs. Ross went into the store in the morning and bought 5 cards. That same afternoon, Mr. Ross bought 8 cards. How much could Mr. and Mrs. Ross have saved if they had made their purchase together?

Name ———————————————————— Date ——————————

Problem:

Andy went to the local supermarket to shop for his family. He bought 3 loaves of bread at $1.59 a loaf, 5 pounds of bananas at 59 a pound, and 2 boxes of cereal at $2.59 a box. He had a 45¢ coupon for 1 box of the cereal, which the store doubled. How much change did he receive from a $20 bill?

Name _____ Date _____

Problem:

Mr. Ryan's total income was $53,750. His deductions were as follows:

Contributions	$ 856
Mortgage Interest	$1250
Deductible Taxes	$2630
Casualty Losses	$1550

Mr. Ryan can either take the standard deduction of 10 percent, or he can itemize his deductions. Which method gives the larger deduction and by how much?

Name _____ Date _____

Problem:

A firefighter is standing on the middle rung of a ladder. She moved up 9 rungs. The smoke got worse, so she moved back down 13 rungs. When the smoke cleared, she went up 19 rungs to the top. How many rungs does the ladder have?

Name _____ Date _____

Problem:

Renee collects baseball cards. She has 240 cards in her collection. For every outfielder card, she has 5 cards of players from other positions. How many cards with outfielders does she have?

Name —————————————————————— Date ——————————

Problem:

Mike puts 104 feet of plastic edging around the perimeter of Mrs. Flores's garden in order to make it easy to trim. If her garden is in the shape of a rectangle with a length of 25 feet, how wide is it?

Name _____ Date _____

Problem:

The new movie, *Return to Monkey Island*, opened on Monday, March 1st. On the first day, 50 people attended the show. On the second day, there were 78 people in attendance. On the third day, 106 people were there. If the pattern continues, what is the first day on which there will be at least 200 people in the audience?

Name _____ Date _____

Problem:

At the zoo, Michelle paid $7.00 for two sandwiches and a container of milk. Her brother, Ralph, paid $5.00 for one sandwich and two containers of milk. How much would one sandwich and one container of milk cost?

Name _____ Date _____

ESTIMATING ANSWERS

Directions:

Use estimation to locate the decimal point on the right-hand side of each equation.

1. $4.87 \times 17 = 8\ 2\ 7\ 9$
2. $31.5 \times 2.2 = 6\ 9\ 3$
3. $85.28 \div .96 = 8\ 8\ 8\ 3\ 3\ 3\ 3\ 3$
4. $52{,}520 \div 103.62 = 5\ 0\ 6\ 8\ 5\ 1\ 9\ 6$
5. $48.32 \div 17.5 + 9.64 = 1\ 2\ 4\ 0\ 1\ 1\ 4\ 2$

Directions:

The following computational exercises have been performed with the use of a calculator. In each case, two answers are given—one is correct and the other is not. Use your estimation skills to find the correct answer.

6.	$25.6 + 6.3 + .023 =$	31.923	3.1923
7.	$695 \times .96 =$	572.12	667.2
8.	$95{,}243 \times 1.12 =$	10,667.216	106,672.16
9.	$47{,}236 \times 2.2 =$	103,919.2	21,470.909
10.	$54{,}291 \div 641 =$	84.697348	846.97348

Name _____ Date _____

SUPERMARKET SHOPPING

Directions:

Estimate how much each of the following shopping lists would cost on a trip to the local supermarket. Then compute the actual costs and compare.

	Your Estimate	*Actual Cost*
I.		
2 jars of peanut butter at 97¢ each	_____	_____
3 cans of string beans at 37¢ each	_____	_____
2 bottles of soda at two for 69¢	_____	_____
Total	_____	_____
II.		
2 packages of gelatin at 21¢ each	_____	_____
2 cans of fruit cocktail at 43¢ each	_____	_____
1 can of spaghetti sauce at $1.12	_____	_____
2 boxes of spaghetti at 63¢ each	_____	_____
1 package of ground cheese at 79¢	_____	_____
Total	_____	_____
III.		
1 box of dishwashing detergent at $1.49	_____	_____
3 cakes of soap at 67¢ each	_____	_____
2 cans of tuna fish at $1.19 each	_____	_____
4 cans of soda at two for 49¢	_____	_____
3 gallons of ice cream at $2.79 each	_____	_____
Total	_____	_____

Name _____ Date _____

IV.
7 grapefruits at 19¢ each   _____ _____
3 pounds of apples at 37¢ a pound   _____ _____
3 cans of sardines at 63¢ each   _____ _____
2 packages of pretzels at 92¢ each   _____ _____
5 pounds of sugar at 43¢ a pound   _____ _____
2 bags of potato chips at 49¢ each   _____ _____

                                 Total   _____ _____

V.
2 quarts of milk at $1.59 each   _____ _____
1 pint of sour cream at 52¢   _____ _____
2 packages of cream cheese at 49¢ each   _____ _____
1 loaf of bread at $1.12   _____ _____
2 cans of shaving cream at $1.29 each   _____ _____
2 packs of razor blades at $2.95 each   _____ _____

                                 Total   _____ _____

VI.
3 pounds of salami at $1.59 a pound   _____ _____
2 pounds of roast turkey at $3.95 a pound   _____ _____
2 pounds of potato salad at 72¢ a pound   _____ _____
2 pounds of tomatoes at 99¢ a pound   _____ _____
2 heads of lettuce at 87¢ each   _____ _____
1 bag of pretzels at 99¢   _____ _____

Name _____ Date _____

ESTIMATING ANSWERS

Directions:

Read each of the problems on the sheet. First estimate the answer. Then solve the problem and compare the actual answer with your original estimate.

1. The Dunbar School is taking the entire band to the football game next Saturday. The band has 265 members and each bus will hold 37 people. How many buses do we need to transport the band?
2. A taxi ride from Janet's house to her school costs $8.75 and she gives the driver a $1.50 tip. How much change should she receive from a $20 bill?
3. Stan bought two CDs that cost $9.95 each and three tapes that cost $4.95 each. How much change will he receive from a $50 bill?
4. Next week, the junior high school is going to give the standardized test. The school needs to order pencils. It needs 29 pencils for each class, and there are 32 classes in the school. How many boxes of pencils should the school order if pencils come a dozen in a box?
5. The distance that the Canadian goose flies from Canada to its winter retreat in Texas is about 2,870 miles. If the Canadian goose can cover about 190 miles a day, how many days will it take to reach Texas from Canada?
6. The local movie theater charges $1.95 for children and $4.95 for adults. Last night there were 48 children and 17 adults at the show. How much money was collected?
7. Before leaving on a camping trip, the Jonas family wishes to buy some new camping supplies. They need three sleeping bags that sell for $34.98 each, two cooking kits that sell for $19.98 each, and a pup tent that sells for $47.75. How much money will these supplies cost?
8. A computer programmer usually earns $14.95 an hour and loses approximately $\frac{1}{3}$ in deductions. If Annie works a 39-hour week, how much money will she take home?

Name _____ Date _____

ESTIMATING ANSWERS

Directions:

Read each of the problems on the sheet. First estimate the answer. Then solve the problem and compare the actual answer with your original estimate.

1. Michelle was selling tickets to the Drama Club's spring show. One week she had sales of $15.75, $11.25, $6.75, $3.25, and $12.75. How much were her total sales for the week?

2. The Statue of Liberty stands on a pedestal in New York Harbor. The figure is 151 feet tall, the pedestal is 89 feet tall, and the base is 65 feet tall. How tall is the Statue of Liberty?

3. Janet wants to buy 15 gallons of gasoline that costs $1.30 a gallon. Will $20 be enough to fill the tank? Would she have 50¢ left for an ice cream cone?

4. John's dad wants to buy a computer that costs $1,699, a printer that costs $875, a dust cover that costs $11, and a software package that costs $61. How much money does he need to pay for his purchases?

5. Randy owns 73 jazz tapes, 189 classical tapes, 157 country and western tapes, and 207 rock tapes. His mom bought him a tape cabinet for his birthday that holds 600 tapes. Can he put his entire collection in the cabinet?

6. There is a Chagall exhibit at the Art Museum. It's a sell-out! For each of the five weekdays, 1,485 tickets are sold. On each of the two weekend days, the extended hours permitted the sale of 2,155 tickets. How many people bought tickets for the Chagall exhibit that week?

7. Marcy and Mike are buying ground beef for a barbeque. They need 5 pounds. When they arrive at the market, there are only three packages left. They weigh 2.1 pounds, 1.6 pounds, and 1.3 pounds. Will they have enough meat?

8. Leslie wants to tile the floor in her recreation room. She will use tiles that are 1 foot by 1 foot square and come 48 in a box. If her recreation room is 27 feet by 12 feet, how many boxes of tiles will Leslie order to do the job?

Name _____ Date _____

FIND THE ERROR

Directions:

Below are eight problems that appeared on a mathematics test. Each is followed by an answer that was given by a student. The answer is wrong! Tell where the student made the error and give the correct answer.

1. On a trip up Mt. Polk, the Hiking Club climbed to a marker that reads 3,090 feet above sea level. They began their climb from a point 857 feet above sea level. How many feet did they climb?

   Student's Answer: 3,947 feet   *Error*: The student added instead of subtracting. The correct answer is 2,233 feet.

2. The school was renting buses to take students to the state competition. It can put 35 students on each bus. There are 500 students waiting to go. How many buses should the school rent?

   Student's Answer: 14   *Error*: _____

3. The grades for Jessie's math tests were 75, 84, 65, and 72. What was Jessie's average for the four tests?

   Student's Answer: 69   *Error*: _____

4. Tulip bulbs come in packages of five. Each package costs $2.00. Lisa bought 45 tulip bulbs. How much did she spend?

   Student's Answer: $14.00   *Error*: _____

5. In the storeroom at the local ice cream parlor, there are seven boxes of ice cream cones. Each box contains 12 cones. There are also 9 cones on the counter. How many cones are there altogether?

   Student's Answer: 756   *Error*: _____

Name _____ Date _____

6. Rhona used 3⅓ cups of mandarin oranges and 2½ cups of strawberries to make a fruit cup. How many cups of fruit did she use altogether?

   Student's Answer: 5²⁄₅   *Error*: _____

   _____

7. At a banquet, 72 desserts were served: 30 desserts were apple pie, half of the desserts were ice cream, and the rest were fruit cups. How many fruit cups were served?

   Student's Answer: 21   *Error*: _____

   _____

8. The gardener is putting fencing around a rectangular garden whose dimensions are 20 feet by 30 feet. Fencing comes in 12-foot lengths. How many lengths must he buy?

   Student's Answer: 8⅓   *Error*: _____

   _____

Name _____ Date _____

CHECK THE ANSWER

Directions:

Below are seven problems that appeared on a mathematics test. Each is followed by an answer that was given by a student. The answer *may* or *may not* be correct. You must decide if the answer given is right or wrong. if it is wrong, you should find the correct answer.

1. The 25 members of the graduating class of Ferris High are donating an auditorium clock to the school. The clock costs $250. The class treasury already has $50. How much will each member have to contribute if they share the cost equally?

   Student's Answer: $10   *Error:* _____

   _____

2. A snowstorm caused the cancellation of basketball game last night. The coach called three players to tell them. They each called three players, who, in turn, each called three players. How many players were called about the game?

   Student's Answer: 27   *Error:* _____

   _____

3. A farmer paid $7,440 in land-use taxes last year. This year, the cost was increased to $12,136. What was the percent of increase?

   Student's Answer: 38.6%   *Error:* _____

   _____

4. Reggie is sharing his comic book collection. He gave 10 comic books to his younger sister and shared the remainder equally with three of his friends. He took home 15 comic books. How many comic books did he have in the original collection?

   Student's Answer: 55   *Error:* _____

   _____

5. On the first three tests, Mark had an average grade of 85. On his next two tests, he had an average grade of 95. What was Mark's average for the five tests?

   Student's Answer: 90   *Error:* _____

   _____

Name _____ Date _____

6. A father divided $63 among his five children. He gave $1 more to each of the three oldest than he gave to each of the two youngest. How much did he give to each child?

Student's Answer: Oldest get $13;   *Error*: _____
youngest get $12   _____

The length of a rectangle is twice its width. If each dimension is

7. The length of a rectangle is twice its width. If each dimension is increased by 5 feet, the perimeter becomes 80 feet. Find the perimeter of the original rectangle.

Student's Answer: 20' × 10'   *Error*: _____

_____

Name _____ Date _____

CHECK THE ANSWER

Directions:

Below are seven problems that appeared on a mathematics test. Each is followed by an answer that was given by a student. The answer *may* or *may not* be correct. You must decide if the answer is right or wrong. If it is wrong, you should find the correct answer.

1. The cost of a long-distance telephone call is 25¢ for each of the first three minutes, and 15¢ for each additional minute. Lauren's telephone call cost her $2.80. How long was her call?

   Student's Answer: 18 minutes   *Error:* _____

   _____

2. Mrs. Roper bought a car that lists for $14,500 on an installment plan for four years. Her monthly payment was $450. How much extra did she pay in order to spread her payments over the four years?

   Student's Answer: $7,100   *Error:* _____

   _____

3. George just filled his prescription and received 30 tablets. The doctor told him to take 6 the first day and 3 each day after that. For how many days will George take the medicine?

   Student's Answer: 13 days   *Error:* _____

   _____

4. Mr. Agin had a bad week on Wall Street last week. On Monday, he lost half of his money. On Tuesday, he lost half of his remaining money. On Wednesday, he lost $300. On Thursday, he lost half of his remaining money. Finally, on Friday, there was a market rally and his stocks gained $350. He now had $1,350 left. How much did he start the week with?

   Student's Answer: $9,200   *Error:* _____

   _____

Name _____ Date _____

5. The Cumberland Hoopsters offered their star forward, Jim Nikuls, a new contract for the upcoming season. They offered him a base salary of $600,000 plus an additional $5,000 for every game in which he appears. Jim wants an $800,000 base salary, and $1,500 for every game in which he appears. How many games must Jim appear in, in order to come out ahead if he accepts the team's offer?

Student's Answer: <u>57</u>   *Error*: _____

_____

6. Play number 47 in the team's playbook is the "Down-and-Out Pass." The tight end starts right on the 30-yard line and runs straight down the field to the 45-yard marker. He then cuts directly to the sideline for 8 yards, at which point he catches the pass. How far is he from his original starting position?

Student's Answer: <u>23 yards</u>   *Error*: _____

_____

7. The new brand of sneakers were put on the shelves at 50 percent above cost. When they didn't sell, the manager ran a sale, and told the stockboy to mark everything half price. All of the sneakers were sold at the new price. Did the store make money, lose money, or break even?

Student's Answer: <u>Broke even</u>   *Error*: _____

_____

Name _____ Date _____

WHICH MAKES THE MOST SENSE?

Directions:

Each of the questions below is followed by several choices. Circle the choice that makes the most sense.

1. Mr. Adams drives to and from work every day. The average time for his one-way trip is 45 minutes. About how far is his place of business from his home?
   (a) 2 miles   (b) 22 miles   (c) 222 miles

2. On Pizza Special Night at the Pizza Haven, 12-inch pizzas are on sale. How much did Michael pay for three 12-inch pizzas?
   (a) $10   (b) $20   (c) $40

3. There are four sizes of popcorn at the local movie: small, medium, large, and giant. How much does the giant size weigh?
   (a) .05 ounce   (b) .5 ounce   (c) 5 ounces

4. The Stage Club wants to sell buttons to help raise the $200 they need for costumes in their next production. The buttons cost the club 25¢ each. About how many buttons must they sell?
   (a) 30   (b) 300   (c) 1,000

5. The state is installing overhead lights on both sides of a one-mile stretch of the highway. On each side of the road the workers will place the lights 100 feet apart. Approximately how many lights will they need?
   (a) 100   (b) 500   (c) 1,000

6. In New City, the Parks Department collects old Christmas trees and chops them up for mulch. Each day the townspeople take away $1/10$ of the remaining mulch About how many days will it take to remove the pile?
   (a) 10   (b) 20   (c) never

7. Tina has a photograph of her sister that is in the shape of a rectangle that is 3" × 4". She orders an enlargement with each dimension three times the original. What is the area of the new photograph in square inches?
   (a) 36   (b) 42   (c) 108

Name _____ Date _____

WHICH MAKES THE MOST SENSE?

Directions:

Each of the questions below is followed by several choices. Circle the choice that makes the most sense.

1. Helen bought herself a new tapedeck with an AM/FM radio for her 17th birthday. How much did she spend?
   (a) $10   (b) $100   (c) $1,000
2. Louis went swimming in the ocean last July 4th off the California coast. What was the water temperature?
   (a) 30°F   (b) 90°F   (c) 70°F
3. Miss Brower's statistics class calculated the average height of the players on the high school boys' varsity basketball team. What was the average height?
   (a) 66 inches   (b) 72 inches   (c) 78 inches
4. The Johnsons started their trip with 15 gallons of gasoline in the tank. Approximately how far can they drive before the tank is empty?
   (a) 100 miles   (b) 200 miles   (c) 400 miles
5. What is the probability of drawing a red or a black card in one draw from a standard deck of 52 playing cards?
   (a) 0   (b) 1   (c) 100
6. A small gymnasium measures 50' × 100'. The school decides to shellac the floor with polyurethane that costs 20¢ per square foot. How much will it cost to do the job?
   (a) $100   (b) $500   (c) $1,000
7. Janet solved the equation $x^2 + 6x + 5 = 0$ on her homework. What was one of her answers?
   (a) –1   (b) 0   (c) 17

Name _____ Date _____

HAS THE QUESTION BEEN ANSWERED CORRECTLY?

Directions:
Below are nine questions that appeared on a math test. Each one is followed by an answer that was given by one of the students. Determine whether the answer given is correct. If it is not correct, tell what was wrong and give the correct answer.

1. Mr. Adams's car can drive 28 miles to the gallon of gas. His tank holds 16 gallons. Gasoline costs $1.30 a gallon. How far can he drive on a tankful of gas?

   Student's Answer: $20.80

2. Sales tax in New Jersey is 6 percent. Luana bought a new car for $10,200. How much was the sales tax?

   Student's Answer: $612

3. Four men had dinner at a local restaurant. The bill was $42 and they left an $8 tip. If they agreed to divide the cost of the dinner equally, how much was the total cost of the dinner and the tip?

   Student's Answer: $12.50

4. The dorsal fin of a shark is shaped like a triangle. The fin was measured at 7 inches at its base and 8 inches high. What is the approximate surface area of the shark's dorsal fin?

   Student's Answer: 60 square inches

5. A hotel has 100 rooms. On any given night, it makes a profit of $40 for every room that is occupied, and it loses $10 for every room that is vacant. Last Thursday, the hotel was 70 percent occupied. How much profit or loss did the hotel have last Thursday?

   Student's Answer: $2,500

6. The local radio station is having a telephone poll on whether to build a new trash-to-steam plant. For every 25 calls saying "Yes," there were 45 calls saying "No." If the station received 180 calls saying "No," how many calls did it get that said "Yes"?

   Student's Answer: 250

Name _____ Date _____

7. On a field trip to the aquarium, 100 percent of the boys and 40 percent of the girls saw the porpoise show. What percent of the students saw the porpoise show?

   Student's Answer: <u>110%</u>

8. Mrs. Owens is a calligrapher. She gets paid 20¢ for each digit she writes. How much does she earn for numbering the pages of a 250-page manuscript?

   Student's Answer: <u>642 digits</u>

9. The batter hits a line drive directly to the third baseman who is standing right on third base. He quickly throws the ball to the first baseman for a double play. How far did the ball travel?

   Student's Answer: <u>180 feet</u>

Name _____ Date _____

Problem:

A landscape architectural firm is constructing a fence by cementing granite blocks together in a row. Each block is a cube, four feet on each edge, and having a sculptured design on each face. If 10 blocks are used in constructing the fence, how many sculptured designs are visible?

Name _____ Date _____

Problem:

A bicycle dealer just put together a shipment of two-wheel bicycles and three-wheel tricycles. He used 50 seats and 130 wheels. How many bikes and how many trikes did he put together?

Name _____ Date _____

Problem:

Find the dimensions of all rectangles such that their perimeter and area are numerically equal. (Consider only integral answers.)

Name ——————————————————— Date ——————

Problem:

Jan hit the dart board shown with four darts. They landed on 17, 3, 10, and 31. What was her score?

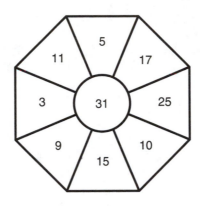

WHAT IF?

What if Jan hit the dart board with four darts? What if she scored 61? How might she have done this?

What if the 10 is removed from the board? Now, how might Jan have scored 61 with exactly four darts?

Name _____ Date _____

Problem:

A gardener has 36 poinsettia plants to ship to local florists. He ships them in boxes that hold 4 plants. How many boxes does he need?

WHAT IF?

What if the gardener has boxes that hold 3 plants and boxes that hold 4 plants? How might he ship 36 plants if all boxes shipped must be full?

What if the gardener has boxes that hold 3 plants and boxes that hold 4 plants? What number of plants can he *not* ship if each box must be full?

Name _____ Date _____

Problem:

Edward had grades of 68, 70, 78, 76, and 88 on five mathematics tests. What was his average?

WHAT IF?

What if Edward needs an 80 average to receive a grade of B and qualify for the honor roll? What must he score on the next test?

Edward has grades of 68, 70, 78, 76, and 88 on five math tests. There is one more exam—the final, which will count as two tests. What must he score to have an average of 90?

Name _____ Date _____

Problem:

In the state aquarium, there is a reserve tank that is used to store and age water. Through leakage and evaporation, the tank loses two gallons each day. At the end of every fourth day, an automatic timer opens a valve and allows five gallons of water to flow into the tank. If the tank contained 1,000 gallons at the start, how many gallons are in the tank at the end of the 21st day?

How many gallons of water are in the tank at the end of the 42nd day?

How many gallons of water are in the tank at the end of the *n*th day?

On what day will the tank become empty, in order to move it?

WHAT IF?

What if the timer releases only four gallons of water? How does this affect your answers?

Name —————————————————————— Date ——————————

Problem:

At the end of the eighth inning of the baseball game, the score was tied at 8–8. How many different scores were possible at the end of the seventh inning?

WHAT IF?

What if the score had been b–b?

What if the score had been b–c?

SECTION B

Masters for Selected Problems
(Problem Cards)

Georgette earned $500 a week for the first 20 weeks of the year. She then received a 10 percent raise. How much did she earn for the entire year?

Here are the current rates for the Metro Taxi Company:

Taxi Rates

$2.00 for the first half-mile

45¢ for each additional quarter-mile

25¢ for each minute of waiting time

$1.00 additional after 6:00 P.M.

$1.00 for each additional passenger

Mr. Robbins took a taxi from the airport to his downtown hotel at 8:00 P.M. An accident blocked the highway for 10 minutes, but otherwise the trip went smoothly. Mr. Robbins gave the driver $23.50, which included a $3.60 tip. How far was the hotel from the airport?

Miguel and Charles started their new jobs on the same day. Miguel's schedule provides for 3 workdays, followed by 1 day off. Charles's schedule provides for 7 workdays followed by 3 days off. On how many of their first 500 days will they both have a day off on the same day?

Raymond and Boris went to the ball game last evening. They spent exactly $20.00 on hot dogs and soft drinks. They bought at least 5 hot dogs at $2.00 each and at least 5 soft drinks at $1.00 each. What exactly did they buy?

There is a big special at the local pizza shop! You can buy either a square pizza, 12 inches on a side, or a round pizza with a 12-inch diameter for the same price. Which is the better buy? Explain your answer.

Farmer McDonald rotates his herd of cattle weekly, by allowing them to graze in each of three pastures, as shown in the diagram. In order to be most economical, he uses his knowledge of mathematics to design three gates, such that when two of them are swung together, they completely close the entrance to one of the pastures with no overlap. How long is each gate if Farmer McDonald used whole number lengths?

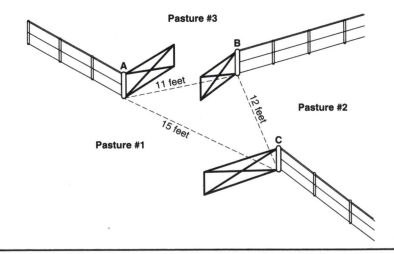

Richard Rodgers and Oscar Hammerstein wrote four smash musical hits in a short period of time. The four musicals were *Carousel, The King and I, Oklahoma,* and *South Pacific.* They wrote the first one in 1943. *Carousel* was written 2 years after *Oklahoma. South Pacific* was written 2 years before *The King and I. The King and I* was written last, 8 years after *Oklahoma.* Which of the musicals was written in the year 1949?

Ruth and Jeanette are taking Gladys to lunch for her birthday. At the last minute, Harriett decides to come along. Ruth and Jeanette are paying Gladys's share of the bill, but Harriett is paying only for her own share. If the total bill came to $72, how much does each girl pay?

A couple wanted to buy a piece of land on which to build their home. They saw an ad in a local newspaper offering a plot of land with an excellent location. The asking price was $50 per square foot. The couple requested a drawing of the plot of land and were given the following sketch:

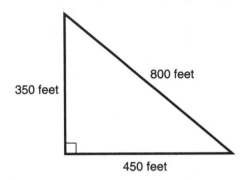

How much should they pay for the land?

A square mile of land (1 × 1) has become contaminated. The Environmental Protection Agency has regulated that no one can live within one mile of any point in the contaminated area. Find the area of the uninhabitable land.

The students in the Douglass School have left for their annual school trip. One-third of the students went to Washington, D.C. One-third of them went to Annapolis. One-fourth of them went to Williamsburg, and the remaining 100 students went to Monticello. How many students are in the class? How many went to each place?

On the quiz show "How Much Do You Really Know?" each question is worth four times as much as the previous question. The fourth question is worth $1,600. How much was the first question worth?

Lucille makes copper bracelets to sell at the local crafts show. Each bracelet requires a rectangular strip of hammered copper that is 5" × 7". She buys the copper in rectangular sheets that measure 21" × 24". What is the maximum number of bracelets she can get from a single sheet of copper?

Maxine paid her restaurant check of $3.00 by using the same number of half-dollars and quarters. How many of each did she use?

Jenny has a nickel-box with 40 nickels in it, and a penny-box with 50 pennies in it. Her younger brother took 10 coins from the nickel-box, put them into the penny-box, and mixed them all up. Then he took 10 coins from the penny-box, put them into the nickel-box, and mixed them all up. Are there more pennies in the nickel-box, or more nickels in the penny-box?

Laura and Bernadette each bought the same number of computer disks at a closeout sale. The drawing shown below shows how many each bought. Each box contains the same number of disks. How many disks are in each box?

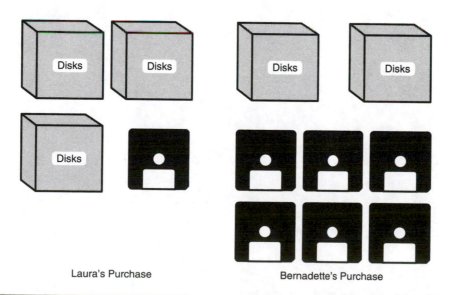

Laura's Purchase   Bernadette's Purchase

There are 23 students in the school orchestra. There are 25 students in the school band. Seven of these students are in both. How many students are there altogether?

Jaime opened his mathematics textbook and multiplied the two page numbers that were facing him. Their product was 1806. To what pages was the book opened?

The arithmetic mean of George's 10 tests was 87. His teacher decided to discard the best and worst grades, a 95 and a 55. What was George's new arithmetic mean?

A dartboard has sections labeled 2, 3, 5, 11, and 13. Patti scored exactly 150. What is the minimum number of darts she might have thrown?

Jones High School is constructing a circular ice-skating rink. It wants to design the rink so that 15 trips around the outside rail will equal 1 mile. To the nearest foot, what should be the radius of the rink?

An automobile driveway is 54 feet long by 8 feet wide. It is to be covered with blacktop. If 3 loads of blacktop are available for the job, how deep a layer of blacktop is possible? (One load = 2 cubic yards.)

A man spent ⅓ of his money and then lost ⅔ of the remainder. He was left with $12.00. How much did he start with?

Kevin can mow a square lawn that is 30 yards on each side in 45 minutes. At the same rate, how long will it take him to mow a square lawn that is 60 yards on a side?

Find all triangles with integral lengths for sides whose perimeter is 12 inches.

About how many feet of audiotape are there in a 90-minute cassette, if the tape moves at a rate of $1\frac{7}{8}$ inches per second?

The floor of a storage shed is a rectangle with an area of 99 square feet. The volume of the shed is advertised as 627 cubic feet. Lawrence is six feet, three inches tall. Can Lawrence stand upright in the storage shed?

The new playing field behind the school is in the shape of a rectangle that is 80 yards long and 50 yards wide. On each of the shorter sides, there is a semi-circle whose diameter is the shorter side. Approximately how much will it cost to sod the new field if sod costs $1 per square yard?

Janice has an average of 74 on the first three tests in her algebra class. On the final four tests, she scored 92, 90, 94, and 76. What was her average for the entire year?

A bowling ball and a bag together cost $88. The ball costs three times as much as the bag. How much does each cost?

A manufacturer of novelty buttons uses square sheets of metal that are 24 inches on each side. The press punches out 144 circular buttons, each with a diameter of 2 inches, from a sheet. How much metal is wasted from each sheet?

In the old west, Eric and his gang stole a wagon full of gunpowder from Fort Laramie at 9:00 P.M. one night. They drove off at the rate of 16 miles per hour, across the plains, and stopped after 2 hours to rest the horses. Unfortunately for them, one of the powder kegs had a hole and left a trail of gunpowder all the way back to the fort along their path. An hour after they stole the wagon, a soldier discovered the trail and set it on fire. If the fire travels at the same rate of 16 miles per hour, at what time was Eric jolted?

A recycling plant was packaging aluminum cans in containers. They packed five containers and weighed them in pairs. The weights were 110, 112, 113, 114, 115, 116, 117, 118, 120, and 121 pounds. What were the weights of the individual containers?

After the first 57 games of the basketball season, the Supersonics have a winning percent of .561 and the Jazz have a winning percent of .491. How many games behind the Supersonics are the Jazz?

Ann is the weakest foul shooter on the girls' basketball team. Out of her first 30 foul shots, she made only 50 percent. Her coach had her go through several practice sessions. She raised her season's percent to 60 percent after 20 more foul shots in the next three games. How many of these 20 shots did she make?

Bikeport uses license plates for its motorcycles. Each license plate consists of one vowel followed by one digit. There are 5 possible vowels and 10 possible digits. Since the zero and capital O look the same, they cannot be used together. How many different license plates are possible?

Michelle has 72 baseball cards. She gave 2-for-1 in five trades, and received 3-for-1 in three trades. How many cards does she now have?

The Stewarts are buying cups and plates for the annual family picnic. Cups come in packages of 54, whereas plates come in packages of 42. How many packages of each must the Stewarts buy to have the same number of cups and plates?

In order to win a prize in the state lottery, a person must select the correct three-digit number. Jane chose 345. What is the probability that she will win? Someone told her to "box" the number to have a better chance of winning. ("Box" the number means the digits can occur in any order, such as 354, 534, 453, etc.) What would be the probability of Jane winning if she did "box" her numbers?

The players on the Hawks hockey team wear the numbers from 1 through 18 on the backs of their jerseys. On opening night, as the players were being introduced, Maura noticed that the players were standing in nine pairs. She also noticed that the sum of the numbers on the jerseys of each pair was a perfect square. The goalie wore number 1. With what numbered player was he paired?

The coach of the tennis team was having problems selecting his team. He had to choose four players, two men and two women, from the six who had tried out. Personal feelings were making it difficult for him.

1. Paul said, "I'll play only if Sarah plays."
2. Sarah said, "I won't play if Eric is on the team."
3. Eric said, "I won't play if David or Linda is chosen."
4. David said, "I'll play only if Amy plays."
5. Amy had no likes nor dislikes.

Who will the coach select?

In the Appalachian Hockey League, a team gets 2 points for a win, 1 point for a tie, and 0 points for a loss. In the five-team Northern Division, each team played each of the other teams twice. The computer failed to print part of the league standings. Complete the table.

Teams	Games				Points			Standings
	Played	*Won*	*Lost*	*Tied*	*Win*	*Tie*	*Total*	
Suns	8	4	3	1	8	1	9	
Devils	8		2	1				
Mountaineers	8	4			8			
Sharks	8	2						
Panthers	8	2						

There are 55 containers of milk in the school refrigerator. Some are chocolate milk and some are white milk. If you select any 2 containers without looking at them, at least 1 of them will be chocolate milk. How many of each kind of milk are there in the refrigerator?

The Acme Tinplate Corporation has been asked to manufacture one million cans for a new product about to go to market. Each can is to be cylindrical, with a radius of 3 inches and a height of 6 inches. How many square feet of tinplate are used in making the cans?

The bow and arrow target shown here has a 4-foot diameter. Each ring is 6 inches wide, and the bull's eye is 1 foot across. Johanna fired an arrow that stuck in the target. What is the probability that it landed in the "200" region?

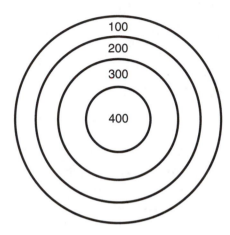

Mike, Ray, and Lucy went into the record store for the big "Dollars Only Sale." Mike bought 2 CDs and 1 cassette for $16. Ray bought 1 CD and 2 cassettes for $11. Lucy bought 1 CD and 1 cassette. How much did she pay?

The school board has commissioned a local artist to create the five-circle sculpture shown in the figure. The centers of the five circles are all collinear. The diameter of the larger circle is 12 feet, and the diameters of each of the four smaller circles are equal. Tubing is sold by the foot. What is the minimum number of feet of tubing required to make the sculpture?

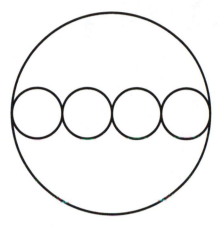

Jennifer's mother is in Paris; Jennifer lives in Los Angeles. When it is 11:00 A.M. in New York, it is 5:00 P.M. in Paris. Jennifer wants to call her mother from Los Angeles at 1:00 P.M., Paris time. At what time in Los Angeles should she place her call?

The distance between Exit 1 and Exit 20 on the turnpike is 130 miles. If any two exits must be at least 6 miles apart, what is the largest number of miles between any two consecutive exits?

Sarah, Amanda, and Ian took a true-false test last week. The test had three questions. Only one of their test papers had all three questions answered correctly; the other two papers each had two correct answers and one incorrect answer. Who had all three questions answered correctly?

Sarah	Amanda	Ian
1. True	1. False	1. False
2. True	2. False	2. True
3. False	3. False	3. False

The Great Western Limited express train is exactly one kilometer long and is traveling at 80 kilometers per hour. It passes through a tunnel that is 7 kilometers long. How long will it take the train to pass completely through the tunnel?

A garden is laid out in the shape as shown in the drawing here. Only the shaded isosceles, right triangles are to be used for planting vegetables. The unshaded portion is to be filled in with stones to make paths. What is the total area that is to be used for planting? What is the total area of the paths?

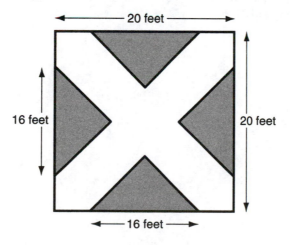

A new airline is beginning flights next week. In the preliminary instructions, all flight attendants are told that they must wear a different outfit every day. Maria is one of the new flight attendants. She has three times as many blouses as pairs of slacks, and twice as many colorful scarves as blouses. How many blouses, scarves, and pairs of slacks must Maria own in order to be able to wear a different outfit every day for at least three years?

Amy and Nancy bought three sets of golf clubs at the Golfland going-out-of-business sale. All three sets of clubs are of equal value. They paid $1,680 in all. Nancy paid $900 and Amy paid $780. They took the clubs to an auction for resale. One set was sold for $1,680. At the end of the auction, Amy decided to take the remaining two sets for herself. How should they divide the cash equitably?

Two people were sitting on a blanket on the beach. One of the two is male. What is the probability that they are both male?

A rectangular barn measures 50 feet by 100 feet. At one corner, a horse is tethered with a 28-foot rope, as shown in the figure. On how many square feet of grass is the horse able to graze? What if the dimensions of the barn were 60 feet by 150 feet?

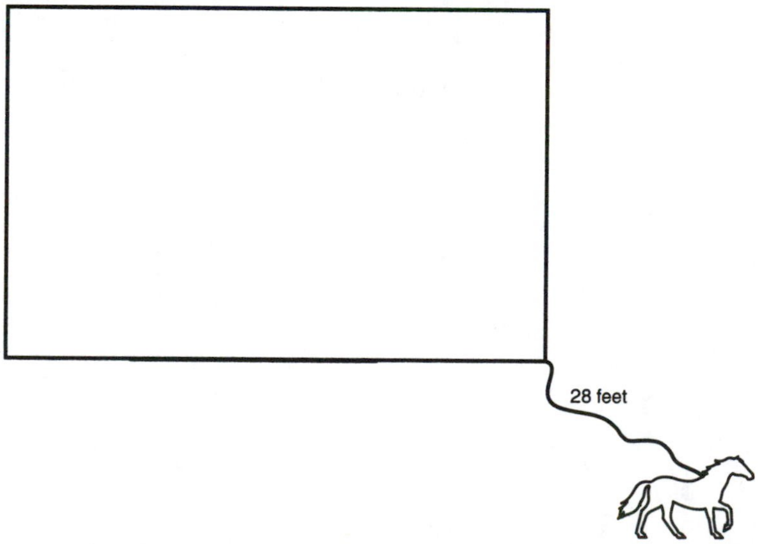

28 feet

The diagram shows the ground plan of a business mall. If the excavation for its foundation is to be 18 feet in depth, how many cubic yards of soil must be removed?

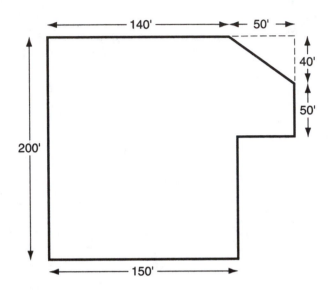

A multiple-choice test contains 40 items. A correct response earns 5 points, but 2 points are deducted for every incorrect response. Nothing is given nor deducted if the question is unanswered. Michelle scored 96. How might she have done this?

REPRODUCTION PAGE 168

A municipality is replacing its water supply lines. The current system uses two identical pipes that have circular cross-sections, each with a diameter of one foot. The town decides to use a single replacement pipe with the same capacity. What is the diameter of the new pipe?

David and Mike went fishing. David brought 5 hoagies and Mike brought 3 hoagies. As they were getting ready to eat, their friend, Jerry, joined them. However, Jerry did not bring any hoagies with him. After lunch, during which the three men shared the 8 hoagies equally, Jerry put down 8 coins of equal value to pay for his share of the lunch. How should David and Mike share the 8 coins?

In our school's parking lot one morning, Janice noticed that all but three of the cars parked were made by General Motors, all but three of the cars were made by Chrysler, all but three of them were made by Ford, and all but three of them were made by Toyota. What is the minimum number of cars parked in the school parking lot?

Imagine a wire band fitted snugly around the earth at the equator. If you cut the band, add a piece exactly 10 feet long, reform the band, and then hold it in a position concentric to the equator, which of the following best describes the space between the earth's surface and the wire band?

1. You can just crawl under the band.
2. You can just slide a piece of paper under the band.
3. You can walk upright under the band.

Two coins, both silver dubloons, are melted down and recast as a single coin of the same thickness. How does the diameter of the new coin compare with the diameter of one of the original coins?

A group of gymnasts are putting mats on the floor of the gymnasium prior to their exhibition. The room measures 30 feet by 44 feet. They have nine mats that measure 10 feet by 12 feet, and one mat that measures 8 feet by 30 feet. Show how the mats are placed in the room to cover the floor.

A group of people want to rent a house in Aspen, Colorado, to go skiing. For one week, each person will have to chip in $70. If the group can convince three more people to come along, the cost per person will drop by $14. What was the week's rental?

Mrs. Ross has 55 percent of the senior class students in her Advanced Physics class. Mr. Luellan has 35 percent of the senior class in his Calculus class. 10 percent of the senior class is taking both classes. What percent of the senior class is taking neither of these classes?

Joe, a professional basketball player, is an 80 percent foul shooter. He is fouled at the final buzzer, and goes to the foul line for two shots. His team is trailing by one point. What is the probability that Joe's team will:

1. Win in regulation time?
2. Lose in regulation time?
3. Go into overtime?

Two parallel sides of a playground are 264 feet apart and are crossed by two other nonparallel sides. The playground is 300 feet long on one side and 250 feet long on the other. If sod costs 32¢ per square foot, what is the minimum amount of sod to be bought?

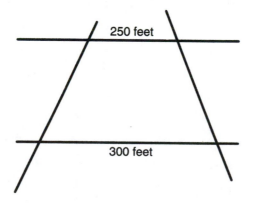

A bag contains 50 red and 50 yellow balls. There are three boxes on a shelf. One is labeled RED; one is labeled YELLOW; and one is labeled MIXED. Two balls at a time are taken from the bag. If both are yellow, they are placed in the YELLOW box; if both are red, they are placed in the RED box. If one of each is picked, both go into the box marked MIXED. What is the probability that the box marked RED and the box marked YELLOW will have the same number of balls after all pairs of balls have been drawn from the bag?

Newman's Fine Haberdashery store is having its annual spring sale You can buy suspenders and socks for $18. You can buy socks and a tie for $22. You can buy a tie and cufflinks for $25. You can buy a shirt and a belt for $37. You can buy cufflinks and a shirt for $33. You can buy a belt and socks for $17. How much does each article cost?

Two poles, 60 feet tall and 20 feet tall, stand on opposite sides of a field. The poles are 80 feet apart. Support cables are placed from the top of one pole to the bottom of the opposite pole. How far above the ground is the intersection of the cables? What if the poles were 120 feet apart?

In a group of men and women, the average age is 40. The average age of the men is 50 and the average age of the women is 35. What is the ratio of women to men in the group?

Georgette is writing the page numbers on a handwritten edition of a book that contains 250 pages. How many times will she write the numeral 2?

On a local TV quiz show, Mr. and Mrs. Halpern are given two red blocks and two blue blocks that they must distribute into two boxes any way they wish. Mrs. Halpern will then be blindfolded and asked to pick one block at random from one of the boxes. If she picks a red block, the Halperns will win $1,000. How should the Halperns distribute the blocks to give Mrs. Halpern the maximum probability of drawing a red block?

Mrs. Tanaka makes pins in geometric shapes to give as awards to her students. She takes an 18-inch piece of silver wire, and forms an equilateral triangle as shown in the figure (triangle ABC). Then she takes a piece of gold wire and forms a second equilateral triangle whose vertices are at the trisection points of the sides of the larger triangle (triangle DEF). What is the length of the piece of gold wire?

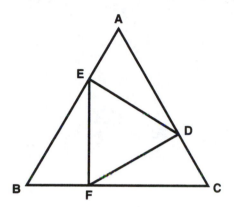

A sightseeing boat is chartered by a social club at the rate of $10 per person, with a guarantee of 150 people. The boat company agrees to reduce the rate by 5¢ per person for each additional person over the 150 minimum. Find the number of passengers that will yield the boat company the maximum gross income.

Bruno and Maria each read ten books over the summer. Beginning in September, Bruno read one new book each month, while Maria read four new books each month. In how many months will Maria have read

1. Twice as many books as Bruno?
2. Three times as many books as Bruno?
3. Four times as many books as Bruno?

A cake in the form of a cube falls into a vat of frosting and comes out frosted on all six faces. The cake is then cut into smaller cubes, each one inch on an edge. The cake is cut so that the number of pieces having frosting on three faces will be one-eighth the number of pieces having no frosting at all. There are to be exactly enough pieces of cake for everyone. How many people will receive a piece of cake with frosting on exactly three faces? On exactly two faces? on exactly one face? On no faces? How large was the original cake?

Mrs. Callahan and three of her friends have formed an investment club. Each of them picked one favorite stock and invested $3,000 in it. At the end-of-year party and meeting of the club, it turned out that three of the four members had made a profit and only one had lost money. From the clues, determine each person's full name, how much each person lost or gained, and the name of the stock each invested in.

a. Hannah did not invest in General Electric.

b. Susan, whose last name is neither Robinson nor Drucker, made $100 less than Donna.

c. Two people made more money than the person who invested in Kodak.

d. The person who invested in Pfizer was the only one to lose money.

e. Donna made $500, which was the most profit made by anyone.

f. Ms. Robinson did not invest in AT&T but the person who did made the most money.

g. Mrs. Smith lost $200 and Bobby made $200.

Keith wants to join an audio cassette club. The Liberty Cassette Club has an offer of a $20 membership initiation fee and only $6.20 per cassette. The Patriot's Cassette Club has no membership initiation fee, but charges $8.10 per cassette. How many cassettes must Keith buy to make joining the Liberty Cassette Club the better deal?

Pam has decided to open a special money-market account. She noticed a bank advertising a new investment plan. The bank will double the amount of money in an account on the last day of the month. On the first of the next month, however, it will charge a $100 service fee. Pam deposited $100 on the 15th of January. How much money is in her account on January 15th of the following year?

A professional basketball team has 12 players on its roster and a player payroll of $20,000,000. Every player earns at least $500,000. Six of the players earn at least $1,500,000 each. One player earns at least $2,500,000. The star center has demanded at least $3,500,000. His demands must be met. What is the maximum possible salary any one player can earn?

Mrs. Lolla has a semi-circular garden behind her home. The garden has a diameter (COD) of 20 yards. On this diameter, she has built a semi-circular fish pool, as shown in the figure. Parallel to the edge of the garden and tangent to the pool, she has erected a 16-yard long fence (AB) to keep her pet dog, Bandy, away from the pool. She wants to cover the rest of her garden with sod. What is the area of the portion of her garden to be covered with sod?

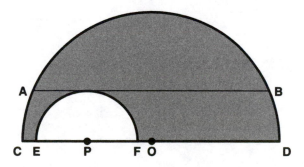

Mr. Milou challenged the 15 students in his Statistics class with the following problem. The first two students each choose a number. The third student chooses the arithmetic mean of the first two numbers. Each successive student chooses the arithmetic mean of the numbers selected by all the students who have gone before. What is the number chosen by the 15th student?

A mathematician on a train traveling from Atlanta to Miami was looking out the window. She noticed a series of 10 telephone poles, which she knows are each 150 yards apart. She looks at her watch and notes that it takes exactly 45 seconds to pass the 10 poles. What is the speed of the train to the nearest mile per hour?

In Zolt's Hardware Store, you can buy homeowners' tools in savings packs. In the Basic-Pak, you get a hammer, a pair of pliers, and a screwdriver for $7.50. In the Starter-Pak, you get two hammers, two pairs of pliers, and four screwdrivers for $18.00. In the Family-Pak, you get five hammers and four pairs of pliers for $28.00. How much do each of the tools cost?

There's an antique bike parade in town. Stuart has a bike that his great grandfather had given him in which the radius of the front wheel is 8 times the radius of the rear wheel. When the bike travels 100 feet, the number of rotations made by the smaller wheel is 60 more than the number of rotations made by the larger wheel. Find the diameter of each wheel to the nearest tenth of an inch.

The Sharks and the Jets, two equally matched teams, are meeting in the preliminary round of the tournament. The first team to win 3 out of 5 games moves on to the next round. The Sharks won Game 1. What is the probability that the Sharks will win the round and move on?

Mitchell and Jane are going to race their racing cars around an oval track. Mitchell takes 25 minutes to complete a lap and Jane takes 30 minutes to complete a lap. How long will it take Mitchell to lap Jane's car (that is, to overtake her car) if they start together at the same point?

Whenever Morris does his daily walking, he plays a 90-minute tape (45 minutes on each side) in his portable cassette player. He stops walking and notices that the radius of the remaining part of the tape is about 1/2 of the full tape. How many minutes remain to be played on that side of the tape?

Carla painted identification numbers on the canoes in her new franchise. Each canoe has three numbers. The first number must be a 1 (her franchise number), and the next two digits must be in ascending order. No zeros were used, and no digits were repeated on any canoe. What is the maximum number of canoes Carla might have had?

The figure shown here shows a running track in the form of a rectangle with a semicircle on each end and dimensions as shown. The outside lane is three feet from the outer rail and the inside lane is three feet from the inner rail. How many feet do the starting blocks have to be staggered so that both runners run the same distance?

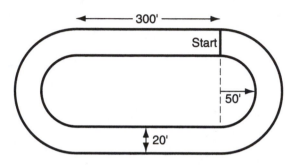

Mr. Johannsen and Mr. Yan have decided to separate their property by placing a fence along the property line. They ordered enough fence posts so that the fence would have posts placed 8 feet apart. However, five of the posts were not usable. They were still able to put the fence up by placing the remaining posts 10 feet apart. How many fence posts did they originally order?

Louise and Mable are registered for the Bike-and-Walk-athon for charity. They start together. Louise will bike for half the distance and walk the other half. Mable will bike for half the time and walk the other half. If both of them bike and walk at the same rate, who finishes first?

The senior class is sponsoring a fair at the school. In the potato race, 10 "potatoes" are placed in a straight line, each three feet apart. The first "potato" is three feet from the basket. A contestant runs to the first potato and returns it to the basket. The contestant then runs to the second potato and returns it to the basket. The same thing is done with each potato in succession, until all 10 potatoes are in the basket. How far does a contestant run to complete this race?

There are 125 juniors participating in the Junior-Day Olympics: 59 played football, 49 played baseball, 42 participated in the races, 20 participated in the races and played baseball, 29 participated in the races and played football, 31 played both football and baseball, and 12 entered all three events. Those who did not participate in any of these three events went swimming. How many went swimming?

Mr. Fondel is going to build a path from his house to the front walk. The path will be 2 feet wide and 12 feet long. He intends to lay paving blocks along the path. Each paving block is in the shape of a rectangle that is 2 feet by 1 foot. In how many different ways can Mr. Fondel lay the blocks along the path?

On a string of 15 opals, the center stone is the largest and the most expensive. Starting from one end, including the center stone, each opal is worth $50 more than the previous one. Starting from the other end and including the center stone, each opal is worth $25 more than the previous one. The total value of the 15 opals is $4,650. What is the value of the center opal?

The local recycling plant has just bought a new metal compactor that produces a smaller cube of scrap iron than does the older machine. Somebody noticed, however, that the combined volumes of one cube from each compactor was numerically the same as the combined lengths of all their edges. What are the dimensions of the cubes, if you consider only integral solutions?

Two wheels, each of radius 2 inches, are fastened to a steel shaft with their centers 10 inches apart. What is the length of the belt that goes around both wheels?

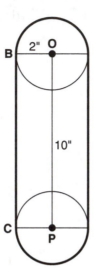

Two wheels, one with a radius 2 inches and one with a radius of 4 inches, are fastened to a steel shaft with their centers 10 inches apart. What is the length of the belt that goes around both wheels?

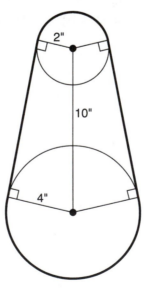

SECTION C

Masters for
Open-Ended Problems

Name _____ Date _____

Two couples are preparing for a summer trip from their home in Philadel-phia to Rome. Their plane leaves from Kennedy Airport in New York at 11:00 P.M., but they must check in approximately three hours prior to departure. Their problem is how to get from their home in Philadelphia to the airport in New York, a distance of about 120 miles. They are consider-ing two options—renting a car or using a limousine service. Here's what they have found out:

Car Rental

Flat rate of $78.00 each way

Insurance (optional): $14.95 each way

Tolls: $8.00 each way

Free unlimited mileage, but gasoline must be replenished

Limousine Service

Flat rate of $25 per person each way

A gratuity of 15% is expected

The Limousine Schedule:

Leave Philadelphia	Arrive at Kennedy Airport
8:00 A.M.	11:00 A.M.
2:00 P.M.	5:00 P.M.
5:00 P.M.	8:30 P.M.
7:00 P.M.	10:00 P.M.

If you were making the trip, which way would you go? What would you do? Defend your decision.

Name _____ Date _____

The coach of the Jaguars' basketball team has a decision to make! Her team is one point behind and the final buzzer has just sounded. However, just at the buzzer, a bench foul was called on the opponents, the Rockets. The Jaguars' coach has to select one of the five players on the court at that time to shoot the free throw. If the player makes the foul shot, the game goes into overtime; if she misses, the Jaguars lose the game. Here are the foul-shooting statistics for the five players involved:

Name	Free Throws During the Season	Free Throws During the Last 2 Minutes
Jody	6 out of 7	1 out of 3
Sara	70 out of 100	18 out of 25
Ellen	85 out of 130	14 out of 17
Becky	10 out of 15	5 out of 5
Rose	100 out of 120	15 out of 25

If you were the coach, which player would you choose? What would you do? Defend your decision.

Name _____ Date _____

For the senior class trip, the faculty sponsor ordered 256 caps, one for each student. The class is divided into four sections, each with the same number of students. When the caps arrived at the school, the sponsor asked each of the four section representatives to pick up $\frac{1}{4}$ of the caps from the supply room and distribute them to the students in their section. Renee arrived first and took one-quarter of the caps. Brad arrived one period later and took one-quarter for his section. Carol arrived an hour later and took one-quarter of the caps for her section. Mitch arrived at the end of the day and took one-quarter of the caps for his section. The following morning, Mrs. Johnson, the sponsor, was surprised to find caps left in the storeroom. In addition, students from three of the sections kept coming in to complain that they did not receive a cap. What was wrong? How many in each group did not get a cap? How would you have avoided the problem? Defend your decision.

Name ————————————————————— Date —————————

During the morning senior assembly, Mr. Carter, the school principal, announced that he had good news for the group. He told the students that he has just been informed that 50 percent of those who applied for admission into State University have been accepted. Also, 50 percent of those who applied to Temple Tech have also been accepted. Carla turned to her friend Marcie and said, "Great! I've been accepted I applied to both schools, and 50 percent + 50 percent is 100 percent, so I'm in!" Analyze the action. Is Carla correct? Defend your decision.

Name _____ Date _____

On the boardwalk at the shore, there are three stores within a block of one another. On the first day of the season, each store had a sign advertising a sale on gold chains. Store A offered a 70 percent discount plus an additional 10 percent discount for cash. Store B offered a 60 percent discount plus an additional 20 percent discount for cash. Store C accepted cash only, and offered a ⅔ discount. Amy wanted to buy a 26-inch gold chain. If you were Amy, from which store would you buy the chain? What would you do? Defend your decision.

Name _____ Date _____

You have been offered a job. There are three possible salary plans to select from:

Plan A: A salary of $400 per week

Plan B: A salary of $200 per week plus 10 percent commission on all your sales

Plan C: A commission of 25 percent on all your sales

Which plan would you select? What would you do? Defend your decision.

Name ——————————————————— Date ——————————

On a local television game show, three contestants enter the final round. Marlene has $8,000, Jonathan has $6,000, and Kim has $4,000. There is one question remaining. Using the money they have, each contestant wagers as much or as little as he or she wishes. The winner is the person who has the most money at the end of the game. How much should each of the contestants wager for the final question? What would you do? Defend your answer.

Name _____ Date _____

The naturalists at the state park are going to put carp into the pond at the Japanese teahouse. They can put five fish for every 100 square feet of surface area. Marlene was assigned the task of finding the surface area of the pond. Since the shape of the pond was irregular, she walked around it and estimated its perimeter to be 100 yards. She made a rectangle that was 50 feet by 100 feet and found its area to be 5,000 square feet. So, Marlene recommended that the naturalists purchase 250 fish for the pond. Analyze Marlene's action. What would you have done? Defend your decision.

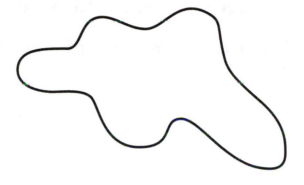

Name ⎯⎯⎯⎯⎯⎯⎯⎯⎯⎯⎯⎯⎯⎯⎯⎯ Date ⎯⎯⎯⎯⎯⎯⎯⎯⎯

The school Spirit Club is having a fund-raising drive. You have been appointed chairperson, and have been given the job of preparing tags to sell on Spirit Day to raise fund. You have a piece of bright green material that is rectangular in shape and measures 18 inches by 45 inches. Members of your committee have suggested four different shapes for the tags:

1. A circle with a one-inch diameter, to sell for $1.25 each
2. A one-inch square, to sell for $1.25 each
3. An equilateral triangle with a one-inch side, to sell for 75¢ each
4. A one-inch by two-inch rectangle, to sell for $2.50 each

Which shape would you use to earn the most money? How much would you earn? Defend your decision.

Name _____ Date _____

"Hoops" Malone has his contract up for renewal. The team has offered him a choice of three contracts:

1. $700,000 plus $5,000 for every game he plays
2. $600,000 plus $10,000 for every game he plays
3. $1,000,000 with a penalty of $25,000 for every game he misses

The season consists of 32 games. Last season, "Hoops" only appeared in only 12 games because of knee surgery. If you were "Hoops" Malone, which contract would you take? What would you do? Defend your decision.

Name _____ Date _____

The Lenape Valley High School Math Club was out on its field day. The teacher, Mr. Romeo, assigned Pam and Jason the problem of finding a buried box. He told them that the box was buried at the fourth vertex of the parallelogram having three of its vertices at (–1,4), (1,1), and (3,5) on the Cartesian grid that was laid out on the field. Pam and Jason dug at (1,8), but the box was not there. Why didn't they find the buried box? What would you do? Defend your decision.

Name _____ Date _____

Ian and Amanda have constructed a robot for a science project. The robot can run at a top speed of 15 miles per hour. They direct the robot's actions from a computer that is 5 miles away. The robot is proceeding from east to west, and is $\frac{3}{8}$ of the way across a railroad bridge that spans a canyon. The bridge is 8 miles long. A train, 13 miles east of the bridge, is traveling toward the bridge at a rate of 60 miles per hour. Ian says, "Keep running!" Amanda says, "No! Turn and run the other way." Who's right? What would you do? Defend your decision.

NOW...SAVE 20% ON THESE GREAT BOOKS!

The New Sourcebook For Teaching Reasoning And Problem Solving In <u>Elementary</u> Schools
Stephen Krulik and Jesse A. Rudnick both of Temple University

For Grades K-6

Each Volume Offers...

✔ Over 100 tested, realistic, classroom-ready activities for teaching problem solving and reasoning skills.

✔ Over 200 Blackline Masters and Reproducibles teachers can use to assemble their own "Problem Decks."

✔ Broad arrays of problems and open-ended questions that can be used with students at various skill levels.

✔ Includes solutions to all questions, plus strategies for assessing responses to open-ended questions.

✔ Introductory materials and instructional suggestions to help teachers effectively introduce problem solving and reasoning challenges in the classroom.

✔ Shows teachers how to evaluate problem solving and reasoning activities.

The New Sourcebook For Teaching Reasoning And Problem Solving In <u>Secondary</u> Schools
Stephen Krulik and Jesse A. Rudnick both of Temple University

For Grades 7-12

About the Authors...

Dr. Stephen Krulik's professional background includes 15 years of classroom teaching as well as more than 25 years as a professor of Mathematics Education at Temple University. He has authored more than a dozen professional books for teachers, as well as numerous articles in major journals on problem solving and reasoning. He was editor of the NCTM's 1980 yearbook, *Problem Solving in School Mathematics* as well as a member of the team that wrote the *Professional Standards for Teaching Mathematics*. He has spoken at literally hundreds of conferences, and has conducted numerous workshops for school districts across the country.

Dr. Jesse A. Rudnick has spent over 25 years as a professor of Mathematics Education at Temple University, preceded by a 15 year tenure as a teacher in the Philadelphia public schools. With Stephen Krulik he has authored more than a dozen professional books for students, including the best-selling *Problem Solving...* series with Allyn & Bacon. Dr. Rudnick was past director of the NCTM, a regional director of NCSM, and president of the Association of Teachers of Mathematics of Philadelphia and Vicinity. He has spoken at hundreds of conferences and has conducted numerous workshops for school districts across the country.

Drs. Krulik and Rudnick are the Senior Problem Solving Authors for the Silver Burdett Ginn K-8 Basal Mathematics Series.

✂ —

20% DISCOUNT ORDER FORM

Code	Title	Single Copy Price	20% Discount (1 of each, or 2 or more total copies)	Quantity	Total
H48267	The New Sourcebook For Teaching Reasoning And Problem Solving In **Elementary** Schools	$38.95	**Only $31.16**		
H65204	The New Sourcebook For Teaching Reasoning And Problem Solving In **Secondary** Schools	$38.95	**Only $31.16**		

Ship To:

Name_____

School/Company_____

Address_____

_____

City_____

State_____ZIP_____

*Tax exempt institutions must provide a copy of Tax Exempt Certificate.
**Shipping & Handling is FREE with credit card and pre-paid orders. Direct-bill and P.O. buyers can call TOLL-FREE for Shipping & Handling cost.

Subtotal	
State & Local Sales Tax*	
Shipping & Handling**	
Total	

KRSESBI-3
MPG002

Payment Method:

❏ Check enclosed, payable to Allyn & Bacon

❏ Bill me directly

❏ Invoice against P.O. # _____

Charge My: ❏VISA ❏ MasterCard ❏ AMEX

Signature_____

Card #_____

Exp. Date_____

100% Satisfaction Guaranteed or your money back! You must be satisfied. It's our policy!

For Fastest Service Call TOLL-FREE

1·800 - 278 - 3525

24 hours a day, 7 days a week

Send completed form to:
**Longwood Division
Allyn & Bacon**
P.O. Box 10695
Des Moines, IA 50336-0695